Call of Duty

MY LIFE BEFORE, DURING, AND AFTER THE BAND OF BROTHERS

Lt. Lynn "Buck" Compton
with MARCUS BROTHERTON

BERKLEY CALIBER, NEW YORK

THE BERKLEY PUBLISHING GROUP
Published by the Penguin Group
Penguin Group (USA) Inc.
375 Hudson Street, New York, New York 10014, USA
Penguin Group (Canada), 90 Eglinton Avenue East, Suite 700, Toronto, Ontario M4P 2Y3, Canada
(a division of Pearson Penguin Canada Inc.)
Penguin Books Ltd., 80 Strand, London WC2R 0RL, England
Penguin Group Ireland, 25 St. Stephen's Green, Dublin 2, Ireland (a division of Penguin Books Ltd.)
Penguin Group (Australia), 250 Camberwell Road, Camberwell, Victoria 3124, Australia
(a division of Pearson Australia Group Pty. Ltd.)
Penguin Books India Pvt. Ltd., 11 Community Centre, Panchsheel Park, New Delhi—110 017, India
Penguin Group (NZ), 67 Apollo Drive, Rosedale, North Shore 0632, New Zealand
(a division of Pearson New Zealand Ltd.)
Penguin Books (South Africa) (Pty.) Ltd., 24 Sturdee Avenue, Rosebank, Johannesburg 2196,
South Africa

Penguin Books Ltd., Registered Offices: 80 Strand, London WC2R 0RL, England

This book is an original publication of The Berkley Publishing Group.

The publisher does not have any control over and does not assume any responsibility for author or third-party websites or their content.

This work is a memoir. It reflects the author's present recollections of his experiences over a period of years. Names, dates, and actions are intended to be accurate as presented. Some dialogue has been re-created to facilitate flow.

PRINTING HISTORY
Berkley Caliber hardcover edition / May 2008
Berkley Caliber trade paperback edition / May 2009

ISBN: 978-0-425-22787-9

The Library of Congress has catalogued the Berkley Caliber hardcover edition as follows:

Compton, Lynn D., 1921–
    Call of duty : my life before, during, and after the Band of Brothers / Lynn "Buck" Compton, with Marcus Brotherton. — 1st ed.
        p.   cm.
    Includes index.
    ISBN 978-0-425-21970-6
    1. Compton, Lynn D., 1921–   2. World War, 1939–1945—Personal narratives, American.
3. World War, 1939–1945—Campaigns—Western Front.   4. United States. Army. Parachute Infantry Regiment, 506th. Company E—History.   5. United States. Army—Parachute troops—Biography.   6. Soldiers—United States—Biography.   7. College athletes—California—Biography 8. Public prosecutors—California—Biography.   9. Kennedy, Robert F., 1925–1968—Assassination. 10. Sirhan, Sirhan Bishara, 1944—Trials, litigation, etc.   I. Brotherton, Marcus.   II. Title.

    CT275.C744A3 2008
    940.54'21421092—dc22

To the memory of my wife, Donna Compton,
the most loving and unselfish person I've ever met.
She had a keen sense of character and discernment.
Full of wisdom and honor, Donna was a totally devoted mother and wife.

To my daughters, Tracy and Syndee.
You are the two greatest things that have ever happened to Donna and me.
We are so very blessed to have had you.

And to my grandchildren,
Samantha, Lyndsie, Shannon, and Hayley.
Today, with my daughters,
you are my whole life.

CONTENTS

FOREWORD

by John McCain

The *Band of Brothers* story took America by storm. In telling of that remarkable generation of men who risked everything—everything—to defeat the evils of fascism, the tale of Easy Company's bravery and valor has inspired its own, new generation of Americans.

As rightly it should. America has relied throughout its history on the courage and honor of extraordinary citizens who, though they may come from the most ordinary of situations, stand up when duty calls them to act. The "Band of Brothers," that company of citizen-soldiers who helped our country wage and win World War II, represented that timeless virtue, the unselfish determination to serve a cause greater than self-interest. In choosing this course, no matter its cost, an entire generation of men and women helped save the world from the evils of Nazism. We today, and all who follow, are in their debt.

Men and women, no matter how meager their origins or difficult their circumstances, possess within them the potential to alter the course of history. Buck Compton knew this, and this understanding shaped his life and destiny. He knew that there is no greatness without courage, no faith in country without devotion to fellows, no commitment to duty without service to others. Through his life and his words, we can find much to admire in men like him.

Second Lieutenant Compton commanded the second platoon of Easy Company in the 506th Parachute Infantry Regiment, part of the famed 101st Airborne Division about which so many tales are told. In an episode familiar to any viewer of the *Band of Brothers* series, in 1944 Buck Compton and others assaulted a German battery operating four 105mm howitzers directed at Utah Beach, disabling the guns and routing the enemy. Buck was awarded the Silver Star for that action. Later, after being wounded in an operation aimed at seizing bridges in the Netherlands, Buck returned to his unit in time for the monthlong siege that would in time become known as the Battle of the Bulge.

During the course of my military service, I learned what it's like to fight on foreign soil. When bullets begin flying and fighting grows thick, the ability of any individual to make correct decisions is sorely tested. Indecisiveness can be costly; poor judgment deadly. As this memoir so ably details, Buck Compton's performance in battle demonstrates that firmness and strategic thinking can save lives. In critical moments on the World War II battlefront, Buck Compton was there: fighting, persevering, and never relenting.

Yet Buck's story doesn't end there. He returned from war to a life of public service, measuring success not only by victories on the battlefield but also through his conduct during seasons of peace. Turning down an offer to play minor league baseball, he focused on a career in law, became a detective with the Los Angeles Police Department and, ultimately, an Associate Justice on the California Courts of Appeal. In reaching a level of success in civilian life commensurate with his victories in battle, Buck Compton showed us the many ways in which Americans fight for justice.

This memoir does his story the service it deserves. This book is the next best thing to having this courageous, thoughtful, and exceedingly modest hero relate in person the adventures and exploits of Easy Company, the prosecution of Sirhan Sirhan, and other tales from the life of an extraordinary American called to duty in an extraordinary time. In understanding the life of honor and service Buck Compton has bestowed upon his country, we glimpse anew the greatness that is America.

—United States Senator John McCain
Phoenix, Arizona
January 2008

PREAMBLE

In 1970, I was fortunate enough to be appointed to the position of Associate Justice of the California Courts of Appeal. My friends and associates in the Office of the District Attorney for Los Angeles County, where I had been serving up to the time of the appointment, staged a great going-away party for me. It was attended by several hundred people from various sectors of the legal community and local and state government. The Honorable J. Steve Williams, judge of the Superior Court of San Bernardino County, was selected to serve as emcee.

Steve was an old high school classmate of mine. He was a great judge, a staunch patriot, and devout in his religious faith. Steve came from an unpromising background similar to mine and appreciated the opportunities we both had been afforded in life. During his remarks he referred to my appointment by saying, "This could only happen in America."

That statement has really struck home with me over the years.

It's true. The life I've led has been made possible only because I'm an American. The astounding people I've met along the way, the astonishing experiences I've had, and the amazing opportunities I've been given have far exceeded anything I could ever have hoped for or expected.

The only real personal asset that I feel I've brought to this adventure is that I was a "fair to middlin' " baseball player, a factor that did not provide the career in the pros that every college ballplayer hopes for, but which, as you will see, had an uncanny way of influencing my life and career in more ways than one.

—*Buck Compton*
Burlington, Washington
October 2007

· 1 ·

First Training Jump

IN THOSE FIRST FEW SPLIT SECONDS AFTER JUMPING OUT OF the Douglas C-47 Skytrain military transport, nothing existed. No feeling of falling. No rush. No markers or indicators of orientation. Just floating.

I don't recall fear. And though it was my first official jump from an airplane, everything appeared to be going smoothly. I didn't know it yet, but something was horribly wrong.

In my mind raced a thousand thoughts. And no thoughts. By the time you get to your first official jump, you know it by the numbers. It's reflex. The drop zone nears. You stand up, hook up, check the equipment of the guy ahead of you, count off—*Ten okay! Nine okay! Eight okay! Seven okay!*—you shuffle to the door, the jumpmaster taps your calf, when the guy ahead of you clears, you jump. It's all so routine by then, you do it without thinking. The training that leads up to the time when you make your first exit from a plane is so intense that you step forward without hesitation.

Accelerating downward, I knew I'd soon feel the static line jerk my chute from its pack. I'd soon float gracefully the rest of the way down to the drop zone at Fort Benning, Georgia, where the paratrooper school was situated. No more than a few yards long, the static line connected the deployment bag of my parachute to the aircraft. Once the line caught, it would separate from the parachute and remain in tow behind the aircraft, later to be pulled in and stowed by the crew chief. Nobody told us why we jumped with static lines. I assumed it was for safety and uniformity. If you had a bunch of soldiers freefalling, they'd all pull their chutes whenever they saw fit—and that would never do in the military. You'd have increased casualties and a very erratic pattern of landing.

We absolutely couldn't be scattered when we hit the ground. Our whole point was to jump as a unit, ready to fight. We were soldiers first, before we were parachutists. The tactical advantage we offered was our ability to be slotted from the sky into virtually any battlefield. We could parachute into areas not accessible by land and attack enemy fortifications normally considered untouchable because of geography. On paper, it was a crack idea. But America was still working out the bugs.

Military parachuting, in theory, was nothing new. The idea of soldiers falling from the sky had been around since the days of Benjamin Franklin. America had sketched out some plans for it as early as 1918. Toward the end of World War I, Brigadier General Billy Mitchell suggested dropping a few troops from the United States 1st Infantry Division behind German lines near Metz. The war ended before such an attack could be seriously planned, which was probably a good thing, given the state of development of both the parachute and aircraft at the time.

But now it was 1943, and technology had advanced. Strong military planes were commonplace. Strapped to my back and chest as I plummeted downward were two large, round jellyfish chutes made from silk. Suspension lines were made from nylon. Parachuting had come a long way, but it wasn't without danger. The chutes were pure drag devices, steerable to some extent, but mostly designed to get you to the ground in one piece. If you didn't do things right, a broken ankle wasn't unusual. Worst case scenario was to be in an upward swing on your approach. If your feet missed the ground you could land on your back. That could mean a broken neck.

We knew the Germans had perfected the practice of military parachuting. Already they had successfully dropped troops by parachute in Norway, Denmark, and France. In Belgium, a small group of German gliderborne troops had landed on top of the Belgian fortress of Eban Emael on the morning of May 10, 1940. It was captured in a matter of hours, which opened up Belgium to attack by the Nazis. Small packets of enemy paratroopers had also seized the crucial bridges that led directly across the Netherlands, opening the way for the 10th Panzer Division. Within a day after the jump, the Dutch position was hopeless.

America, it seemed, was having more problems.

Our country's first major paratroop drop occurred late in 1942 during Operation Torch in North Africa. Navigation and communications problems scattered the forces from Gibraltar to Tunisia. That drop was considered a fiasco.

Similar difficulties occurred a few months later as part of Operation Husky, the Allied invasion of Sicily. Strong winds blew the dropping aircraft off course and scattered troops widely. Half the U.S. paratroops failed to make it to their rallying points. British glider troops involved in the same operation fared little better—only 12 of 144 gliders landed on target. Many landed in the sea. When some reserve 82d Division paratroopers were dropped later during the campaign, U.S. Navy landing craft mistakenly shot down twenty-three of the transports as they flew over the beachhead, resulting in heavy friendly-fire casualties.

Prior to volunteering, I didn't know much about being a paratrooper, or even what kinds of successes or problems they were having so far in the war. I knew that military jumpers existed—that was about it. A guy I knew at UCLA—he was older than I was by about a year—had graduated, joined the paratroopers, then came back to school one day with his uniform on. He looked pretty glamorous in his boots. He was the only paratrooper I had ever known. My primary motivation for joining the paratroopers was to not miss the war. And, strangely, that meant I somehow needed to get myself out of playing baseball.

When the Japanese attacked Pearl Harbor on December 7, 1941, the United States went on a war footing almost immediately. After war broke out, a young man would be embarrassed to be on the streets without having a uniform on of some kind. The country was unified, and we never questioned the fact that we were going to serve. If we weren't going to defend our country, who would?

Like all UCLA men in the early 1940s, as well as every male student in a state university, I was required to take two years of the Reserve Officers' Training Corps (ROTC) system. Those who chose to could opt for two more years and get a commission, which is what I did. One requirement for completing the ROTC program and receiving a commission as an officer in the Army Reserve was to finish three months of active duty at a regular army base. Because the regular armed forces began to prepare immediately for combat, all military bases were soon devoted entirely to that preparation. It was determined that when ROTC students finished classroom training, we would be enrolled in a regular Officer Candidate School at Fort Benning, Georgia.

At UCLA, I was a two-sport athlete—football and baseball. Jackie Robinson was a teammate in both sports. When I arrived at Fort Benning and completed my basic training, most of my classmates were posted to various infantry replacement centers around the country. My assignment, for some reason, was the 176th Infantry Regiment, a Virginia National Guard outfit, the unit that provided the demonstration troops for the school. We were housed in brick buildings on the main post at Benning. To my surprise, I learned that my sole purpose for being in the regiment, according to my superiors, was to be a member of their baseball team.

On base was a first-class ballpark with a good-sized grandstand, well lighted for night games. A number of professional ballplayers were in this league, including Ewell "The Whip" Blackwell, the Reds' starting left-handed pitcher, and Bob Ramazzotti, the Cubs' star infielder. We played day games on weekends and night ball during the week. For my part, the only military duty I was required to perform was a one-hour class each morning in aircraft identification. This consisted of me holding up various model airplanes and telling the assembled soldiers what they were.

The rest of the day was free time until it was time to report to the ballpark. I used some of that time to write home and warn my mother not to tell anybody what I was doing. There was a war on, and I was embarrassed that my only contribution was exhibiting model airplanes and playing baseball. Having a winning regimental baseball team was considered a prime commodity for any commanding officer. It was well known that COs would routinely block any application for transfer made by a ballplayer. The only two exceptions (where a commander was powerless to stop a transfer) were for flight training or parachute training. Flight training took about a year. If I chose flight training, I was afraid the war would end before a year passed and I would miss it. Jump training took only one month.

I joined the paratroopers. That decision proved to be one of the most fateful of my life. The parachute school was located right there on the grounds at Benning. Fort Benning had four of the 249-foot drop towers used for training paratroopers. Called "control descent towers," they were familiar Fort Benning landmarks. I made countless practice jumps in the month required for jump training—one week was devoted entirely to physical training, a second week to jumping out of a mock fuselage into a sawdust pit, a third week to being dropped from a tower with my chute already deployed. It was all so repetitive. The motions quickly became as familiar as brushing

my teeth. The first three stages were uneventful except for the August
heat and humidity in Georgia. At six feet tall and about 215 pounds,
I was fortunate to be in pretty good shape from a recent season of
college football. Everything seemed smooth.

The final training stage involved making five live jumps from a
C-47. This qualified you as a parachutist and entitled you to wear the
wings. Falling, falling, split seconds ticking by—everything about this
first jump out of a real airplane felt textbook so far: I had exited the
plane by leading out with my right leg, then turned to the left to face
the tail of the plane with my body in the pike position—bent slightly
forward at the waist with my feet and knees together, knees locked to
the rear. My eyes were open, my chin was on my chest, my elbows
were tight into my sides, and my hands were over the ends of the reserve parachute with fingers spread.

So far, so good. All I had to do was wait. The chute would soon
open automatically over my head. After the jolt of the chute opening,
the next step was to look up to see that the canopy was fully opened.
Then it was an easy glide down to the drop zone. All felt good. All
looked good. Pure text book. Everything seemed perfect.

So why were there . . . *could that actually be what I think it
is?* . . . shroud lines around the bottoms of my feet? About as thick as
a pencil, the small nylon shroud lines connected the harness to the rim
of the chute. The lines shouldn't have been around my feet. They
should be feeding out from my pack over my head and stretching up
to my unfurling chute. Hurtling through the air in those first few seconds after jumping from the plane, the sudden realization slammed
me that something had gone terribly wrong. When I stepped out of
the plane, I must have tumbled without realizing it. In all my practice
jumps, I had never before experienced anything like this. I knew that
what I saw was the unopened parachute feeding out below my feet.

And I was racing to the ground now—

Headfirst.

· 2 ·

From Benning to Normandy

IN A FLASH, THINGS WENT FROM BAD TO WORSE.

As the shroud lines fluttered, five or six of them threw half hitches around my left ankle. My leg was now tangled in the lines. When my chute caught enough air to open, the shock spun me right side up. My leg jerked up high over my head and tethered more tightly in the lines. All I could think was, *Undo it! Undo it!* There was no time to panic. No thought of the future. I couldn't pull my reserve chute—it would have fouled the main chute by winding around it. I could land like this—but there'd be a hell of a good chance I'd break my leg. At least my main had opened fully.

As my chute caught more air and settled, I began to drift. At least I wasn't plummeting anymore. From the door of the airplane, the ground had looked just like the aerial photographs I had seen before—small buildings, fences, trucks and cars. Now I was moments away from impact and the ground was coming up fast. Our drop zone was a field somewhere right there on the base. I had no idea where that was just then.

But I knew what I needed to do.

I reached over my head and pulled down the riser. The chute spilled air. The engineers who designed our chutes couldn't care less if we could steer—they just wanted to get us down in one piece. But by nature of how they were made, our chutes were crafted so you could spill some air and nudge it in whatever direction you wanted to go. I didn't want to go any direction except down. I just had to pull on the riser to get my leg out. I could just about reach my leg. I leaned into the pull more. I was spilling a lot of air now. The nylon lines dug into my fingers. As quickly as possible I released the tension from the lines. One wrap. Drifting. Drifting. Another wrap. Drifting. Drifting. Another wrap. Drifting. Drifting.

And my foot came free.

The rest of the way down—about thirty seconds' worth—was actually quite pleasant. It was a warm summer day with little wind. Updrafts were minimal near the ground. As I landed, both feet hit the ground at the same time—an ideal landing considering what I had just been through. I tumbled, just as I had been taught, stood up, brushed myself off, and looked around. Only then did I realize what all the tugging at my chute had produced.

I was completely alone.

At least fifteen soldiers had made the practice jump with me. I knew I was still on the base somewhere, but it comprised hundreds of square miles. I had drifted so far off course, I had no idea where I had landed. I shrugged, packed up my chute, made a guess as to where the drop zone might be, and began the long hike back to where I hoped the truck was. It was a hell of a poor way to have a first jump.

ALL WAS DARK IN ENGLAND WHEN WE BOARDED THE C-47, headed for Normandy. Our landing was scheduled for 1:00 A.M.,

June 6, 1944. Once we got in the air, it took a while for all planes to get off the ground and form up. It could've been thirty minutes, I don't know. I wasn't looking at my watch. Things like time, distance, height, weight—none of those mattered to me right then.

If everything went according to plan, the mission of the 101st Airborne Division on D-Day was to drop in the vicinity of Ste.-Marie-du-Mont, German-occupied France, and soften up the German troops. Our primary goal was to seize four causeways behind Utah Beach on the Cotentin Peninsula. We knew the huge action would come at Utah Beach at dawn, when some 23,000 troops from the 4th Infantry Division were planning an onshore invasion. If airborne troops were unable to secure the beach exits, the infantry division would have a horrible time trying to advance off the beach and find it impossible to move vehicles inland. Similarly, if the assault by sea failed, there would be no rescue for those of us dropped behind enemy lines. We knew the fighting would be bloody, but we had been assured it would all be over in three days. The farthest thing from our minds was that the battle for Normandy would stretch on for thirty-three days.

It took two airplanes to carry one platoon. In an airborne unit there were two officers per platoon: one leader and one assistant leader. I was platoon leader for 2d Platoon. Lieutenant Dick Winters was leader of the 1st Platoon. I had an assistant platoon leader, Lieutenant Ray Schmitz, but Ray didn't make the jump on D-Day. In the marshaling area where we spent a couple days before the jump he was wrestling with Winters and fell and injured himself. Ray was later killed in Holland.

Most of our flight across the English Channel proved uneventful. C-47s were very stark inside. A row of hard, metal bucket seats lined both sides of the plane. A heavy cable ran down the ceiling of the inside, front to back. Just before we were to jump, we'd clamp ourselves into that cable, which would pull our chutes from their bags once we jumped. There was no camp singing, no patriotic talk.

Adrenaline surged, but I didn't feel nervous. This was what we had signed up to do. Mostly, because of the roar of the plane's engines, it was just noisy as hell. About three-quarters of the way across, our crew chief came back and took the door off the airplane, leaving a hole in the side.

I took my leg bag off, stood up and shuffled to the door, and looked out. In the moonlight I could see the Normandy coastline in the distance. It looked surprisingly peaceful in spite of what I could only imagine lay ahead. Tracer bullets and antiaircraft started to appear, red, blue, and green tracers, spectacular and deadly against the night sky. As I stood in the door I turned to Sergeant Don Malarkey, a good friend and a guy I knew would go through hell for anybody. "We're really going to throw a f——— into these Krauts tonight," I yelled. Malarkey nodded and grinned.

My commission was the only thing that set me apart from other 19-, 20-, and 21-year-olds in the unit, some of whom were also college educated. Frankly, I didn't consider myself the best platoon leader in the world. I was more like a rifleman with bars on my shoulders who acted as a go-between for the company commander and my noncommissioned officers (NCOs), who interpreted the commands and got the job done. I didn't like to play poker and didn't drink, so I didn't frequent the pubs or poker games that appealed to many of the other officers. I had spent much of my off-duty time in England sitting around, shooting the bull with two of my NCOs, Malarkey and Sergeant "Wild Bill" Guarnere. In my opinion, the success of any military operation, as well as the quality of any military unit, depends a great measure on the caliber of its NCOs. I was blessed with a group of outstanding sergeants: Jim Diel, Joe Toye, Ken Mercier, Chuck Grant, Malarkey, and Guarnere.

I shuffled back to my seat and sat down for the rest of the flight. Guarnere sat a few seats away from me. He was leader of the mortar squad, which he never let you forget. Joe Toye sat a few seats away. He was an outstanding machine gunner and another good friend.

As we neared our drop zone, the weather grew overcast, and more and more antiaircraft flak began to hit near our plane. Nothing ever hit our plane directly that I was aware of. Some flak I could see exploding outside the door in the fog bank. Mostly it was just a crackling sound. I had never met our pilot, so I knew nothing about him. I assumed he was on course and would slow down enough to let us jump. What else could I assume?

We learned later that flight conditions inside some of the other planes were horrifying. Bullets from antiaircraft fire streamed inside the planes, caging the soldiers in. Ironically, all that most men in those conditions wanted to do was exit the planes and jump into the fray below. Some pilots strayed off course. Some panicked and dropped their men in the sea, drowning them all. Some flew too low—with soldiers plummeting to the ground without enough time for their chutes to deploy.

Normally a red light would flash on, and we'd have three minutes to stand up, check our gear one last time, and get ready for the jump. Then a green light was supposed to flash, which meant it was time for us all to bail out. I was jumpmaster and positioned to be first out the door. The red light flashed. *All my guys are edgy right now,* I thought, *so I'm not going to stand up and have us all standing around nervous. I'll wait a few seconds before I stand.* Before I could even blink, the green light flashed—way ahead of schedule. We had to get out of the plane—now! Something must have happened, maybe our pilot missed our drop zone.

"Let's go!" I yelled. "Go! Go! Go!"

In a flash we were standing, no time to check anything. We went out the door on the run. Parachutes unfurled and clapped open. Bullets streamed up all around us. The pilots were supposed to slow to nearly a stall so we could jump out, but our pilot must not have slowed at all. I can only assume he was in a hurry to get out of there.

The shock of the prop blast struck me with hurricane force. My jaw flew open and broke the hard plastic chin strap of my helmet liner. The outside strap held, and my helmet stayed on. I was just glad the force of the blast didn't blow panels out of my chute. My leg bag didn't fare as well. I was one of the few soldiers selected to carry the new, relatively untested piece of equipment. The bag was attached to my leg with two straps around the calf and ankle. Once you were in air you were supposed to release the straps, lower the bag with a cord, and have the bag hit the ground first—some distance away from you if possible.

As soon as I jumped and felt the opening shock, the straps holding the bag flew off over my boot. The cord attached to the bag began to feed out so fast I couldn't hold it. It was burning my hands, so I let go. The bag disappeared into the night. Paratroopers carried an average of seventy pounds of equipment. Officers averaged ninety pounds of gear. Inside the bag I had placed several rounds of mortar ammunition I was carrying for the platoon, plus all my ammunition, my grenades, my personal supplies such as a toothbrush and medical kit, and all my rations.

Worst of all, I had stowed my main weapon in the leg bag, a .30-caliber light carbine rifle. Our company weapons man, Forrest Guth, had modified it to fire full automatic, like a machine gun. I'd just hold the trigger down and let it rip—it was a deadly, capable weapon. Most of the guys carried heavier M-1s—but my job as platoon leader wasn't to be a main rifleman, someone expected to do a lot of shooting. Still, I needed to carry something that could get the job done when needed.

I could hear shots near me as I descended, but none came close. Some soldiers were shot on the way down. Some fell into land that had been flooded by the Germans and drowned. Some fell on trees, buildings, or antiglider poles. I drifted into an orchard—some sort of enclosed field with hedges all around it. My landing was good, a two-footer. Everything was eerily quiet. A few cows mooed in the distance. I was completely alone.

Attached to my chest was a circular device that was supposed to be a quick-release mechanism for getting out of the harness. Two straps came up over my legs and two over my shoulders. All fit into the device. You were supposed to be able to turn the device's dial and give it a quick thump with the back of your fist. The straps were supposed to fly off and you could step out of your chute neatly. I turned the dial and thumped. Nothing. I thumped again. Still no release. I pounded on the dial. Nothing.

I took stock of my situation. In a jacket pocket near my throat, I carried a small switchblade. I took it out and cut myself free from my chute. Strapped to my belt were a trench knife and a canteen.

With my leg bag gone, those were the only supplies I had.

Neither my first jump at flight school nor my first jump into enemy territory had gone anything according to plan. Nothing had been on schedule. Nothing had been smooth.

What could possibly come next?

· 3 ·

The Shock at Brecourt

ALMOST IMMEDIATELY, ANOTHER SOLDIER LANDED ABOUT TWENTY yards away from me in the orchard. I started over to him and made a cricket sound, the signal that differentiated friend from foe. He must have not heard the sound because he came up quick, his M-1 in his hands. Neither of us recognized each other. He was from the 82d Airborne, a completely different division than mine. That meant we were all scattered across the countryside pretty well.

In an airborne unit in 1944, a squad had about 12 men, including a machine gunner. A platoon had four squads, including a mortar squad, about 50 men total. A company had three platoons, about 150 men. A battalion had about three companies plus headquarters personnel, about 500 men. A regiment had three battalions, including headquarters personnel, about 1,500 men. A division had at least three regiments plus headquarters. The 101st Airborne Division had four regiments—three parachute regiments and one glider regiment, about 10,000 to 12,000 men total when you add in personnel. There were other categories besides that, but that was the gist of it.

I was assigned to 2d Platoon, Easy Company, 2d Battalion, 506th Parachute Infantry Regiment (PIR), 101st Airborne Division. Theoretically, I should have been running into guys from my own platoon after landing in Normandy, but I wasn't even running into guys from my own division. What were we supposed to do?

The other soldier shrugged, and we both headed out in the general direction of where we knew we were to go. Our orders had never been overly specific. Assignments would come after we landed from whoever was in charge. It was assumed that once on the ground we'd organize at drop zones at specific locations set up by the Pathfinder units. These soldiers were tasked with jumping first, in the lead planes. Their job was to set up lights in trees so we could see the drop zones and where to assemble. But the lights from the Pathfinder units were never in sight.

The soldier and I headed east, toward the beach. Soon we came across a two-lane farm road and started following that. We began to pick up other men along the way—all from different outfits. Nobody knew anybody. Sometimes guys would talk, and they'd break off together in a different direction. Some of the guys engaged in petty acts of wartime vandalism along the way, like cutting communication lines. Chief in my mind was getting another weapon, but I couldn't find one.

Soldiers were still parachuting in all around us. A few miles down the road I saw a line of jumpers falling from the sky. A swath of tracer bullets swept up into the line with an arc, cutting right through the thick of the men. Still dark out, we had no idea where the bullets were coming from. There was nothing any of us on the ground could do. Every once in a while, small groups of Germans emerged from the bushes, hands over their heads, surrendering. We weren't quite sure what to do with them, so we made them fall in with us. After a while, one of our guys came up and said he knew what to do with prisoners of war, so he took the bunch of them away somewhere.

I still hadn't met anyone from my outfit. As we hiked up the road I could see a lieutenant from D Company lying in a ditch in the distance. His leg was mangled and positioned at a strange angle. I walked over to him and crouched down. I had met him before. His name was McMillan.

"Broken?" I asked. There was no way we could carry him.

"Yeah. Krauts will get me for sure." His breath came short and choppy.

"Our medics will reach you before then."

"Maybe. Maybe not. Where's your weapon?" he asked.

"Lost it in the jump."

"Take mine. If the Krauts get me first, they might not shoot me if they see I'm unarmed."

"You sure?"

"Yeah. Take it."

Lieutenant McMillan handed me his Thompson submachine gun. Although a different configuration of weapon than what I was used to, I had seen Thompsons and shot them before. A strong sense of relief came over me. He gave me a couple of his grenades also. I thanked the lieutenant and stood up.

We walked on.

As daylight began to appear, we neared the beach. By then I was with three or four other guys, although there had been as many as twenty in our group at one time. We could hear the attack already beginning on Utah Beach—huge booms coming from the ships out in the channel. One shell flew in like a freight train and landed about fifty feet away from us. It thudded, shaking the ground, and stuck fast—a dud. If it had exploded, it would have killed us for sure.

We brushed off the experience and kept going. Artillery from the ships stationed offshore was becoming louder now and more frequent. Our group came up the road and we saw a small group of soldiers standing by a building. As we got closer, I recognized some familiar faces and exhaled. Winters was there, as were Guarnere, Malarkey,

Toye, and a few others from my platoon, along with a few soldiers I didn't recognize. Altogether, we made a group of a dozen or so.

Although we were both platoon leaders, Winters was the senior officer and took charge. That was okay by me. We weren't sure yet what had happened to Lieutenant Meehan, our company commander; we didn't know he had been killed when his plane was shot down. We could hear the German 105s being fired down onto the beach. By looking around the corner of the building, we grasped a general idea of where the big guns were. Winters ordered the machine gunners to lay down covering fire and pointed in the general direction across a field.

"Sounds like it's coming from that area," Winters said. "Compton, crawl over to that hedgerow and go see what you can see."

I give credit to Winters here. I found out later he had received no detailed battle plan other than "Take care of the fire along the hedgerows." That was it. He had already done some reconnaissance work on his own and knew the general direction of the large enemy guns. His plan, once I got back, was for me to lead the attack on one trench and him to lead the attack on another. We were situated in the privately owned farmhouse and lands known as Brecourt Manor, about three miles west of Utah Beach. Winters figured there were at least four artillery guns connected by a trench network and defended by nests of machine gunners. We didn't know it until later, but the dozen of us were up against about sixty Germans. I also give credit to the resourcefulness and skill of our men. We all put this thing together by ear.

With our machine gunners laying down fire over my head, I worked my way across the field on my belly. The field was uncultivated and flat—just grass and weeds. The hedgerow, typical of the foliage lines used to mark off fields in that area, was not too high—maybe six or eight feet, and not manicured—just a line of growth. I wasn't aware of anybody around me, but knew the enemy had to be close. Pushing through the branches of the hedgerow, I spotted a trench immediately in front of me. The trench made an L shape, with a large circle at the point of the L. I could have turned and gone either way. Immediately, I glimpsed two Germans in the end of the trench that ran perpendicular to the hedgerow. They were loading and firing one of their artillery pieces down onto the beach.

With my borrowed Thompson in front of me, I sprang through the hedgerow and jumped into the trench. Winters had told me to go take a look, then report back to him—but I figured I could take out the two Germans easily enough first. The trench was about waist deep, and I ran along it toward the Germans. They were situated in another large circle at the end of the trench, a gun emplacement about a foot and a half deep. Their German 105mm howitzer was one of the best-recognized artillery pieces of World War II. With its platform and wheels, the gun was about the size of a car, powerful enough to shoot down planes or blow up tanks. I wasn't sure what other weapons they had with them, but their arsenal undoubtedly included sidearms, grenades, and MG-42 machine guns.

Halfway along the trench I stopped running and planted myself, the Thompson at hip level. My intent was to spray them both quickly, like Jimmy Cagney in a gangster movie. The Germans heard me, stopped what they were doing, and wheeled around. Their faces were instantly full of surprise, replaced by instant horror.

Without hesitation, I pulled the trigger.

There was no way McMillan, the lieutenant with the broken leg, could've known. He hadn't fired his gun after his jump. Somewhere, perhaps on the impact of landing, the Thompson's firing pin had broken. When I pulled the trigger, all I heard was a soft *plunk*. I racked it back, and a live round popped out. My borrowed machine gun was completely useless.

I looked at the Germans. They looked at me in surprise. There were two of them and one of me. They were armed to the hilt.

I had two knives and a canteen.

· 4 ·
My "Movie Career"

I'VE NEVER CONSIDERED MYSELF A PROFESSIONAL SOLDIER.
Major Dick Winters referred to me in his memoir as one of his
"killers,"* someone who wouldn't balk when the trigger needed to be
pulled. He meant it as a compliment, and I thank him for that, but
honestly, it's a title I don't savor. When the confusion was all around
us at Brecourt Manor, when we knocked around in the muck and
blood and noise and mud, when we picked up from there and went
on to the next battle, and to the one after that, and the one after that,
I did what I needed to do, no more, no less.

If forced to give a title to myself, I'd consider myself a citizen soldier, someone who lived his life before the war, did his duty to his
country when needed, then picked up where he left off when the war

---

*Major Dick Winters, *Beyond Band of Brothers* (New York: Berkley Caliber Books, 2006),
p. 94.

was over. I was in ROTC before the war, and I stayed in the Reserves for years afterward, eventually retiring as a lieutenant colonel, so maybe I don't fit the classic mold of a citizen soldier.

When people ask me about my feelings toward the war, my response is that I was lucky. I got back in one piece and I had a great life. All it cost me was three years of my time, a small price to pay for living in this country. No one owes me anything. If your country calls you to fight, you've got a duty to go. That's all I did. I see myself as an American citizen who was willing to help out anywhere he could to win the damn war. If physically able, and if I could do anything to help, I'd be willing to go over and fight in Baghdad today.

LIKE ANYONE, MY ATTITUDES AND CHARACTER WERE FORMED ON the anvil of my childhood experiences. Some were normal, the rough-and-tumble occurrences common to any boy growing up in that era. Some would prove to affect me to the core.

I was born in Los Angeles, California, on New Year's Eve, 1921. The Great Depression was still eight years away, and America was said to be in an economic boom. But my parents certainly didn't experience any of that wild prosperity. We lived in a small apartment on Bunker Hill in downtown LA at the top of Angels Flight. Dubbed "The World's Shortest Railway," Angels Flight took riders along a 33 percent grade from the top of the hill to the bottom to the main business district. Bunker Hill was zoned for dense uses and was always busy. By 1955, Los Angeles city planners decided our old neighborhood needed a massive slum-riddance initiative. They leveled Bunker Hill to make way for modern plazas and buildings.

When we lived on the Hill, our landlord's name was Mr. Davis. He was a kindly man who helped my folks make ends meet from time to time. I was given the middle name Davis in his honor. My first name, Lynn, was always hard to live down. My mother's father was from Lynn, Massachusetts, and named Lyndley in honor of the town, so that's where my name came from. But to me, Lynn was a girl's name and always will be. To this day I sometimes receive catalogs in the mail for women's stores addressed to "Ms. Lynn Compton."

Early on, I decided to do something about my name. The LA Angels were a top-flight minor league baseball team that played from 1903 through 1957. I was a huge fan. The year I was born, the team was purchased by chewing gum magnate William Wrigley Jr., who also owned the Chicago Cubs. Wrigley couldn't get the city of LA to make improvements to Washington Park, so he built his own 20,457-seat stadium in south LA, and appropriately named it Wrigley Field. The Angels were considered among the best players around, and many of them moved on to the Cubs.

A star catcher named "Truck" Hannah played for the Angels. Truck's real name was James Harrison Hannah, so I figured if he could have a nickname, why couldn't I? One day in grammar school, I rolled around in my head the name—*Truck Compton*. Sounded tough, but I also sounded like a copycat. How about *Buck?* That was close enough for jazz. It was settled—Buck Compton was my new name. I informed all my friends that Buck was the only name I'd answer to. That was okay by them—nobody wanted a friend who had a sissy's name. Mom always called me Lynn, though.

Something that troubled me as a kid was why my folks never had any more children. One day I asked my mother. Mom said that after my father had seen her give birth, he vowed he would never put her through anything like that again. Mom was a natural blonde, petite, and always looked sharp. My dad thought she was the world—he always put her on a pedestal. I had never seen my mother scream, but the way she described to me my father's observations of birth, I could glimpse a bit of the horror. I respected my dad for his decision. It seemed like a sensitive and gentlemanly thing for him to do. My father's attitude toward my mother helped instill in me a strong respect for women. He was adamant that a true man would never strike a woman under any circumstances.

Still, I always longed for a brother or sister. If you had a brother or sister, I reasoned, there'd always be someone to turn to for support, or at least someone to talk to about stuff, particularly when the going got hard. Around that time, we moved to a small house of about eight hundred square feet on Lucerne Avenue in South Central LA. Today the property is occupied by the support columns of the southern edge of the Santa Monica Freeway, but back then it was all residential.

In first grade I wasn't allowed to walk to school by myself, but that gets hard for an independent boy. So I badgered my mother to let me walk alone. One day she caved in. The street we lived on ran down and teed into a major east–west thoroughfare called West Adams Boulevard. It had trolley lines down the center with wires above and room for vehicle traffic on either side of the trolley lines. To get to my school, Virginia Road Elementary, I had to walk to West Adams, then go east for seven or eight blocks, then cross Adams to the school. Mom was very protective of me. "Promise me one thing," she said. "That you won't cross West Adams until you get to the crossing guard."

"Okay, Buddy, okay," I answered. (When I was really little I had a hard time saying "Mommy"; I could only say "Buddy," so that was how I always referred to my mother.) I kissed her good-bye, walked half a block to Adams where I was out of her sight, stood there a moment, and thought, *Aw heck, I'm crossing here.* Each streetcar was about the length of a city bus, all enclosed, and had controls at both ends with the entrance in the middle. The motorman could drive the trolley from either end, depending on which way he was going. A streetcar passed. I looked both ways. There were no cars coming from my left. I ran across the street behind the streetcar that had passed. Just as I got to the other side, another streetcar came the opposite way.

It must have been all over in a split second. The huge yellow trolley car came out of nowhere. Suddenly it was gigantic in my face. I had no time to react. It hit me square with the metal cowcatcher low in the legs and flipped me in the air. I spun around and hit the ground, landing near the curb in the lane where automobile traffic normally passed. Luckily no cars were coming; if one had been, it probably would have killed me.

I was scared to death—a streetcar had just plowed into me. Between stops, he had to be going at least 25 miles an hour. But mostly I was scared of my mother finding out I had crossed West Adams without using a crossing guard! So I picked myself up and started running. I ran all the way to school. By the time the conductor stopped and got out to find out what happened, I had disappeared. I guess one of the investigators for the trolley company came and checked out the incident. There was a gas station nearby where my dad stopped a lot, and the fellows there knew me, so I guess they told them my name and where I went to school.

Every morning my school held an assembly before class where everybody gathered in the playground for the flag-raising ceremony. As I stood there that morning, still shaking from the hit, a couple of men in suits appeared with the principal. Sure enough, they walked straight over to me, frowning. They wanted to know my name and story. I told them I wasn't hurt. They asked a lot of questions. Mostly I just shrugged. Finally they went away. They never contacted my mother, but after a few days passed, my conscience got the best of me.

"Buddy," I said in a small voice. "I hate to tell you this, but a few mornings ago I crossed West Adams without using the crossing guard."

"Well, are you okay?" she asked.

"Um, actually, I got hit by a trolley."

My mother almost collapsed. "Oh my God, oh my God, oh my God," she kept repeating. She went completely hysterical for several minutes.

"I'm all right. I'm all right," I kept saying.

But Mom was right. The incident could have killed me, no doubt. I survived, however, and would face a much harder difficulty a few years down the road. In the meantime, I needed to go to work.

My mother's sister, my only aunt, was a switchboard operator at

Central Casting in Hollywood, the agency that hired all the extras to work at various motion picture studios. She was able to register me to work as an extra, which meant I'd always be on call to go work on a movie set, if the script called for someone my age.

Daily pay was $3.50 plus a box lunch, or sometimes $5.00 or $7.50 depending on the type of set, such as if you worked in a period piece or in a rain scene or something hard. The most common call was $5.00, which was a fair wage in those days. I gave all the money to my folks. Pop worked as an escrow clerk at the time and brought in only about $100 per month.

Casting calls came once or twice a week, and I always hated it when they did. I didn't like to miss school—it was tough after being out for a couple days to come back and try to pick up what I'd missed. The law required a teacher to be on set, and all "extra" kids needed to be in class a couple hours a day, but it was usually just busywork and never seemed to amount to much. My family needed the extra money, though, so I kept going. I was seven or eight years old when my movie career started.

One of my first calls was to work in a rain scene. A little gal a year or two older worked as an extra with me. It was a pretty miserable scene, just the two of us romping around getting wet. She was called Dawn O'Day at the time, though I think that was a screen name. When she was about fifteen she landed the lead role in *Anne of Green Gables* and eventually adopted the name of the main character, Anne Shirley, as her screen name. She went on to have a prolific career as an actress and received an Oscar nomination in 1937 for best actress in *Stella Dallas*.

I worked with a lot of kid actors who went on to become big stars, such as Jane Withers and Sidney Miller, but it didn't impress me much. I didn't like being on the sets and always just wanted to be back in school. Assistant directors all seemed to think that whenever kids were found at some public event such as a carnival or picnic, they chased each other through the crowds. Adults got the privilege of walking around normally, but we kids always had to chase each other. I didn't do that in everyday life—and the assistant directors were always on my back to run around and act crazy like they thought kids should. "Move faster!" one barked at me. "Run around more! Keep moving!" It felt forced. But of course I didn't talk back to him. I just tried to do as I was told.

One job for Paramount involved a sort of a farcical scene where a bunch of kids were playing softball in the living room of a mansion, a place where you'd never really play ball. I was the catcher. We took shot after shot, then broke for lunch. My mother and I went off the lot to eat. "We're almost at the set," Mom said to me on the way in. "Do you need to go to the bathroom before we get back?"

"Aw, Buddy, I'm fine," I said. Like so many kids, I was too busy to go to the bathroom. I must have been eight or nine—old enough to know better. We went back in, they set up the shot, and as soon as they started rolling the camera, I couldn't hold it. Of course I had short pants on like all kids did in those days, and the pee trickled down my leg. What made matters worse was that it was a close-up shot, just the batter and me. "Cut!" the director yelled, clearly annoyed. "Prop man!" The prop man ran in with a mop and cleaned up. We went back and shot the thing again. I was highly humiliated but learned my lesson in bladder control.

I worked on a set once with Marion Davies, considered one of the era's greatest silent-screen actresses, although as a kid I didn't know it. I guess a lot of scandal swirled around her, due to her being the mistress of newspaper publisher William Randolph Hearst. To me, Marion Davies was just a very nice lady, smart and self-effacing, and everybody loved to work on her sets. Whenever she finished a movie, she always had individual presents for all the kids who worked on the sets—dolls, toys, baseballs—they weren't junky trinkets, either, they were real presents. I always admired her for her kindness to us kids.

When I was about nine, I got called to do a scene on a cruise ship.

We were supposed to be sitting in a movie theater on the ship, watching a show. They placed a little girl next to me. I was very shy about girls, never having a sister, and this little girl was precocious and aggressive, throwing her arms around me again and again. This went on for a couple days. It seemed to me the most excruciating torture a young boy could imagine. I just wanted to be a mile away and sighed with relief when it was all over.

Mickey Rooney was already a big name in those days. He was just a year older than me and had made his name appearing as the title character in the *Mickey McGuire* shorts. These were a series of more than forty two-reel comedies adapted from the *Toonerville Trolley* comic strip. On one set, Mickey was my sole classmate in school. I knew who he was, but I didn't hold him in awe. He was just another kid on the set to me. We were maybe eleven and twelve at the time. He was funny and told a lot of jokes, never offensive.

On another set we were sitting in class, supposed to be doing schoolwork. The teacher sat some distance away, supposedly moderating. Really, it was more like babysitting. Mickey nudged me with his elbow and pointed to a cute girl some distance away. "Hey, how 'bout that one," Mickey said. He was definitely more interested in girls than I was at that age.

"Um, okay, whatever," I said, and concentrated back on my book.

"Wassa matter, Buck?" he said. "Maybe you and I should go sit with the dummies." He elbowed me again and pointed at another girl. I laughed. "Sitting up with the dummies" was movie slang we both knew for sneaking out of work. In the days before unions, if a studio was shooting, say, a prizefight scene, they might have two rows of seats around the ringside full of people. Behind, they'd seat several rows of dummies. You couldn't tell if they were real people or not. Mickey was just ribbing me.

Most of my afternoons with Mickey were like that—just a lot of kidding around. Some people considered Mickey Rooney a young hellion and troublemaker, but I thought he was just a fun kid who liked girls a lot. History would prove itself. Throughout Mickey's life he was married eight times, including to actress Ava Gardner.

Right around the time I knew him, Mickey Rooney met Walt Disney. Later, Mickey would claim Walt named Mickey Mouse after him. I don't know if Mickey Rooney ever proved it or not, but to me he seemed to have a lot in common with the wisecracking, mischievous mouse. Years later, the Academy of Motion Picture Arts and Sciences voted Mickey Rooney their Academy Honorary Award for his lifetime of achievement. Sir Laurence Olivier called Rooney, "The single best film actor America ever produced." I called him another kid in my class—a kid I liked just fine.

My other brush with a lifetime legend was my call to work on a Charlie Chaplin movie. Directors developed reputations, and everybody knew these directors by name. Some had reputations of being easy to work for, like Frank Capra, director of *It's a Wonderful Life*. Some had reputations of being bastards. Chaplin had the latter reputation. He was a hollerer and a screamer, a mean, miserable guy, and nobody I knew of particularly liked to work with him.

"Pay extra attention," my mom urged as we entered the lot the first day of the shoot. I had a slot on the film *Modern Times*, a movie that Chaplin had written and was slated to direct and star in as well. Talkies were just coming on the scene in a big way, and *Modern Times* would prove to be the last silent film where Chaplin would play his famous "Little Tramp" character, so maybe Chaplin was feeling extra pressure just then. Who knows?

In my scene, I played a newsboy during World War I. They gave me a bunch of newspapers to hold up that showed a headline that war had just been declared. The camera started, and I was supposed to hawk these newspapers on the street as people walked by. In silent film, you have to make broad gestures so filmgoers can read your lips and body language. I felt self-conscious. I was just not that animated.

"Bigger!" Chaplin ordered. "Yell louder! Move your arms more!"

I tried over and over to do what Chaplin said, but I was just not that type of kid. I felt silly. Chaplin kept cutting and restarting over and over. Apparently I never did get it right. Toward the end of the day he called the whole company over. It was not unusual to have a cast meeting. Chaplin went over the usual announcements, start times for the next day, and whatever. At the end of the meeting he made one statement that stayed with me forever.

"All right, everybody back tomorrow . . ." Chaplin growled with his English accent. He looked around at the cast, singled me out, and pointed his finger my direction, "Except that Compton kid. You're through!" Stunned, I wanted to sink through the floor. I wasn't making the grade, but he could have let me down easier. Little did I know that everybody felt sorry for me. Several told me so. They knew Chaplin was just living up to his reputation.

It's true, Chaplin made some strong contributions to the American cinema, but I've always been wary of him. People forget that Chaplin wasn't an American. He was from England, never an American citizen, and his true politics always lay with the left. He married author Eugene O'Neill's daughter, Oona, when he was 54 and she was just 18. Eugene was a strong left-winger and good friends with many radicals, including John Reed, who founded the USA Communist Party.

This *Modern Times* movie I was kicked out of was really a stab at the capitalist system and mass production. Chaplin might be considered an American legend by some, but I'd say his story is more that he came over here, made a ton of money, then went back to England and badmouthed the United States.

When I reached the seventh grade, I finally prevailed on my mother to let me quit the picture business. I had reached junior high and found it harder than elementary school because of all the different classes and teachers. I couldn't afford to be missing school so much anymore. My mom was fine with that. I think it was just an average day. Mom was hanging wash outside on the line when I asked her if I could quit the movie business. She nodded. I grinned. Just like that, my movie career was over.

· 5 ·

Dad's Secret

FOR MANY, THE GREAT DEPRESSION WASN'T AN INSTANT COL-
lapse. Some poor souls lost everything when the stock market crashed
on October 29, 1929, but most people, like my father, felt the decline
in fits and starts over the next several years. Pop kept his job throughout the Depression, which was a heck of a lot better than many people had it. But Pop felt it all. In the early 1930s, when I was about
eleven or twelve, the economic downturn seemed to hit the hardest.
Often at the dinner table Pop talked over the plight of people he knew
who were out of work. Sometimes he broke down and cried right
there at the table. He lacked the financial resources to help even his
own parents, who also had financial difficulties in those years.

On my mother's side, my grandfather, the one for whom I was
named but never knew, had been a deputy sheriff for LA County and
later an elected county constable. He died of tuberculosis when my
mother was a small child. Though widowed, my grandmother raised
my mother and my aunt without the aid of welfare or Social Security,

and remained self-supporting until the time of her death. When I was old enough to know her, she worked for the county recorder as a copyist. All official copies of legal documents were made by hand or on a typewriter in those days. Grandma lived in mortal fear of technology—she talked about a new demon machine called a "mimeograph," and was always afraid that the county would employ the new device and she would lose her job.

On my father's side, my grandfather operated a small barbershop in downtown LA. My grandmother was a languid, babyish Southern woman who believed that women never did anything except be housewives. The barbershop went through rough times—every business suffered in the Depression. Whenever Grandpa and Grandma came for a visit and talked about their difficulties making ends meet, my father shouldered their problems as his own. That was simply the way Pop was. I'm sure he gave them a dollar or two now and then, but he couldn't do anything major to help them out, not on his salary.

That's why he cried.

Pop had been born in Mississippi and came to LA when he was young. He met my mother at the Manual Arts High School in LA. She had been born in the city. Theirs was a rough-and-ready generation of achievers. Some of my parents' classmates and close friends later became quite prominent. Among them were Jimmy Doolittle, the general who led the bombing raid on Tokyo and later commanded the 8th Air Force in Europe in World War II. Doolittle was an early aviation pioneer. In 1929 he became the first pilot to take off, fly, and land an airplane using instruments alone, without a view outside the cockpit. Doolittle and my father boxed together at various "smokers" held in Vernon, a suburb of LA. (Smokers were intermittent club-sponsored events for men, usually held in bars or lodge halls.)

Also among my parents' classmates were Lawrence Tibbetts, a world-renowned opera singer, Frank Capra, the famous director, Buron Fitts, who became DA of LA County and lieutenant governor of California, and Goodwin Knight, the thirty-first governor of California. I grew up hearing about all these famous people, all part of the same class at Manual Arts High School. Then there was my father, a lowly escrow clerk at an LA title company. With his sensitive nature, I'm sure he felt that keenly. I think the most he ever made was $125 a month. He had served in the army during World War I at a base called Camp Kearney near San Diego. Mom and Pop had been married while he was still in the service.

Pop was a formal man. Each day when he came home from work, his only concession to informality was to remove his coat, loosen his tie, and turn up the cuffs of his shirt one width. That was relaxation to Pop. During the course of the evening, if he went to the store to pick up a carton of milk or whatever, the cuffs went down, up went the tie, and on came the coat and hat.

After I quit the movie business, I got a job caddying at a golf course named Sunset Fields. The hours were better on my school schedule, but the money was not as much as the movie business, which I felt bad about for my folks' sake. The pro in charge of the course was Paul Mangrum, brother of the famous touring pro Lloyd Mangrum. The caddy fee was a buck for a single bag and a buck and a half for a double. The pro always took a cut.

AS A KID, YOU NEVER KNOW THE FULL EXTENT OF ANY ANGST your parents might be going through. I sure didn't. Times were tough for anyone, but I considered my childhood and junior high years mostly happy. Somehow Pop would scrape together enough spare change so we could take family vacations. We never traveled outside our state, but California offered a lot to see. We camped at Yosemite National Park, Lake Arrowhead, and Big Bear Lake in the San Bernardino Mountains. Once or twice we took the boat known as "the big white steamer" over to Avalon on Catalina Island, where the Cubs used to have spring training. When the World's Fair came to San Diego, we went at least once.

My father had an Estonian friend who got himself appointed chairman of the Estonian delegation when the Olympic Games came to LA in 1932. The friend invited my dad to attend several track-and-field events at the Coliseum. Pop took me, and we sat in his friend's special box seats. I was never prouder. Pop loved football and sometimes took me to see college games. He had never attended college himself, but he developed an affinity for the Trojans, the football team from the University of Southern California. "Someday I hope you play for USC," he told me one day at their stadium. He repeated the statement several times over the years. It became a hope for him, I think, a dream—that one day his son would play college football.

That idea sounded good to me. Back then, there were no organized sports like Little League or Pop Warner available for kids, but the kids in my neighborhood were always up to something. In the streets in front of our houses, we constantly played a game called Over the Line. It was like baseball, although more informal and easier to get a good game going. At recesses and lunch hours at school we played pickup softball. I always caught barehanded and without a mask. We all did—none of the kids ever had much equipment, only baseballs and bats. Once or twice a teacher organized a game against another school, but it was never league play or anything close. Football was the same way—it was never organized, but if someone had a pigskin, we played touch football.

I was a pretty good athlete for my age, well coordinated and active. I kept my brown hair cut short, usually a crew cut, and was always sort of one of the bigger guys. If we played football, I was usually a lineman. Making friends came easily to me; I seemed to get along with everybody. My grades were okay at Mount Vernon Junior High, where I attended, and I liked math and geometry best.

I had joined a club similar to the Boy Scouts called the Friendly Indians when I was in elementary school and stayed with the program for several years. Later on I was in a YMCA program called the Commodores. When I was with the Indians we played competitive sports with the other divisions of the club. In those days the YMCA was a bastion of strong ideals and role models. Meetings were held weekly at a nearby Baptist church. Character and citizenship were stressed, as were religious ideas.

Mom and Pop were never very religious themselves. Pop's parents were Christian Scientists, the alleged healing-by-prayer-alone faith founded by Mary Baker Eddy, and they sometimes took me to the Christian Science Sunday school. But Pop was never a practitioner. His biggest separation from religion seemed to be in the area of drinking. The religion forbids it, but Pop certainly never subscribed to that.

I considered myself a pretty moral kid, but certain vices, like gambling, held an allure for me. When I was in junior high, they opened up the Santa Anita track in Arcadia and started running race results in the newspaper every day. The idea of horse racing fascinated me—the excitement and colors, the grandstands, jockeys, Thoroughbreds, and barns. There was one horse called "He Does Fly" that I liked a lot. I loved it when the caller, Joe Hernandez, yelled on the radio "There they go . . ." when the horses left the gate. I got swept up in it. Using the newspaper results, six or eight of my friends and I created a pool that we ran for several months. Every day we bet our lunch money, just nickels, dimes, and quarters, through most of that first racing season, going hungry whenever we lost.

I don't remember how we got caught. Somebody must have tipped off school officials, because one day I got called to the vice principal's office. He made me hand over my notebook with its tight columns of bettors' names and amounts: Vincent, 25¢, Frank, 50¢, Harry, 35¢, and so on. It was chicken feed, true, but we were guilty. Pools, lotteries, and yes, even offtrack betting by junior high kids were all illegal activities throughout the state. What we were doing violated Section 337A of the California Penal Code. (A few chapters later, I'll tell you how I know that.) Luckily, my vice principal kept the police out of it. Earlier, I had taken electric shop and earned a coveted spot working on my school's stage crew. It was a big deal because you got to wear overalls with "stage crew" embroidered on the back. My punishment for running the pool was to get kicked off the stage crew. It felt like the worst thing they could do to me.

Pop was never a sportsman or outdoorsman, but he had a good friend, Don Paisley, who was a good fisherman and hunter. Don had one daughter, no sons, so he sometimes took me hunting and fishing at Big Bear. Don taught me how to shoot a gun. We never went after anything large like deer or elk. Mostly it was just rabbits, ducks, and geese. I don't think I could ever kill a deer; I'm too tenderhearted about animals. The first thing I ever shot was a rabbit. I remember it well. I was hunting with a little .22 rifle and hit him right in the paw. He sat up and cried like a baby, dangling his wounded foot. We went over and put him out of his misery. It really bothered me for a long time.

As a kid, life felt mostly safe to me. But I know now that horrors are never too far around the corner. There was a lot of open space to the south of our home. This area, known as the Baldwin Hills, which is covered with homes and buildings today, was just a wilderness back then. One day a well-dressed, articulate man showed up at my school and told officials he was a good friend of Perry Parker, a prominent LA banker, whose twelve-year-old daughter, Marion, went to school there. The man described in detail how Perry had been injured in a terrible accident. He needed to take young Marion to the hospital right away, he said. He spoke so convincingly that school officials believed him.

Investigators later found parts of Marion's dismembered body all over the Baldwin Hills. Her killer, nineteen-year-old William Edward Hickman, was eventually tracked down in Oregon. He was brought back to LA, tried, and sentenced. He was hanged in San Quentin prison a few years later. That murder hit home. This was close to my home. This was my school. The news made headlines all over the country, shocking people everywhere with the gruesomeness and cruelty of the crime. But somehow you continue. You do.

POP'S SECRET WAS BOOZE.

It wasn't the drinking that bothered me so much as the sneakiness. Prohibition had been lifted in 1933, and neither of my parents was a teetotaler, but there was always friction there—a belief that one stayed away from strong drink, or at least kept drinking under wraps. One day Mom found a bottle of booze hidden in her sewing machine, where Pop had stashed it. She hit the ceiling. It was all a bit strange, our attitude toward alcohol. Mom and Pop brewed up homemade beer in the bathtub, and I'd help to fill and cap the bottles, but that was mostly for fun. Hard liquor was considered a menace.

I never saw my dad intoxicated or abusive; he never had slurred speech or hit anyone that I knew of. He just had this desire for a constant edge. I knew he had a bottle in his desk at work. Often I came across him in the garage suddenly reaching behind a box, behind a shelf, or into the closet, or into an overcoat pocket. I hated all that. Bootleggers were still common, even after Prohibition ended. The bill that President Franklin Roosevelt signed into law in 1933 initially allowed the manufacture and sale of 3.2 percent beer and light wines only. A profitable, often violent black market for stronger liquor existed for years.

It was common to overhear my father making a whispered phone call. Soon thereafter, a stranger would appear at the door with a bottle poorly concealed inside his coat. My father gave him money, accepted the bottle, and immediately hid it under the cushion in the davenport. The bottle was always clear with no labels. I never knew exactly what it was, but I knew it was whiskey or gin. One day, after watching such a phone call, I confronted my dad: "I'm going to call the police," I said. "They'll be here when the stranger gets here. They'll come out and arrest this guy. Maybe you, too."

My father sighed. "I understand your concern, son," he said. "But you won't accomplish anything significant if you do that. The stranger is only a delivery boy, not the real culprit. It won't be worth your while." I never made the call. My next ploy was to try to get rid of the booze. The next time the delivery boy arrived and the transfer was made, my father placed the bottle near the sink in the kitchen. I promptly went in and poured it down the drain.

"Oh, I wish you hadn't done that," my father said from the doorway. It was sort of a plaintive appeal. "We're having company tonight, and they will expect us to serve drinks. All you've done is cost me money and embarrassment. I know you don't like it, but I just wish you hadn't done that." He never punished me, threatened me, or struck me. He just took that quiet approach. And my father never stopped.

· 6 ·

Triumph

TRIUMPH CAN COME IN STRANGE WAYS. SOMETIMES IT COMES from the most unusual place. Sometimes it takes quite a while to see it coming, or to even know that you've hit the mark.

I had two buddies, Vincent and Bill, and we cooked up the idea of taking three girls out on a date. Helen, a girl I liked, had two friends, and so plans were made for us to see a live stage show together called *Three Men on a Horse*. I was only fifteen, but I had my driver's permit already and begged my mother to let me drive over to Hollywood for the date. My mother initially agreed, but the day before the date she changed her mind and insisted she drive us instead. Vincent, Bill, and I, along with our three dates, went to the show and for ice cream later on. My mother was behind the wheel the whole way. Talk about humiliation. Nothing ever came of those three matches.

Helen was a nice girl, though, and showed interest in going on a second date with me. My dad bought me a 1929 Model A Ford for fifty bucks, an old beater with a ragtop, so I took Helen out in it several

times once I got my official license. The first time I showed up at
Helen's house with my old rickety Ford, we were headed to a dinner
party, and her mother had made her a new dress for the occasion. Her
mother took one look at my old car, swept back into the house, and
brought out a blanket to cover the front seat. She wouldn't let Helen
risk her beautiful dress, unprotected, in my old jalopy. So much for
making a good impression on her mother.

I entered high school in tenth grade because the district operated on
a three-year high school schedule. Founded in 1873, Los Angeles High
School was the first and oldest public high school in the Greater Los
Angeles area. It was a tremendous high school, located on Olympic
Boulevard west of downtown LA. If you ever saw the opener to the old
TV show *Room 222*, which showed a huge red brick edifice—that's
the main LA High School building.

LA High School was almost like going to a college because of its
rich traditions and strong commitment to academics. They had a
large competitive swimming pool and offered water polo and swimming as school sports. They put out a daily newspaper, which to my
knowledge was the only daily high school newspaper in existence at
the time. I took linotype class and helped print the *Blue and White
Daily*. A huge seal in the floor of the main entryway greeted students
as we walked in the door. No one dared tread on the seal.

When I first walked through those great front doors and around
that seal, I doubt if I had fully thought through my motivation for wanting to play high school sports. Sports were just something I had always
done for fun. It didn't matter what sport, I'd give it a shot—football,
baseball, basketball, badminton, tennis—anything competitive, I liked
to play it. In my mind, it was a given that I would go out for sports. But
over time, a deeper reason formed. Nobody in my family had ever gone
to college. My mother never even finished high school. Attending college became my dream. I knew my folks would never have enough
money to send me. A sports scholarship was my only hope.

Getting a scholarship meant I needed to make the team—whatever team there was—I needed to be on it. For football, LA High had three teams: varsity team, B team, and C team. C was football for little guys. B was for anybody heavier or taller. Very few guys were ready to play varsity when they first got to high school. Most started at B or C level. I was no exception. I was a bigger kid for my age and started at B level in tenth grade, which I felt pretty good about, then played two years of varsity. I wasn't a starter on varsity until my senior year.

In baseball they also had three teams: tenth-grade team, B team, and varsity. The issue there wasn't size so much as ability. I signed up there, too, and played one year of tenth-grade baseball, then varsity for two years.

Playing sports meant I came into close contact with a man I wasn't so sure I wanted to get close to. Everybody in school knew coach Bert La Brucherie. He was a small guy of French descent, quite short with curly hair and tightly built. He taught physical education classes and was the head varsity football coach. We were all scared to death of him. He had a loud, booming voice and was a needler—if a kid was anything less than he ought to be, Coach Bert shouted insults at him. He wasn't all bad. He had been a star football player at UCLA and had a strong record later as a high school coach. I view him today as an earlier version of Bobby Knight, the legendary and controversial basketball coach, most recently at Texas Tech. Knight is known for his strong-arm techniques, but also revered for running a clean program. To succeed is to win his respect. That was the way it was with coach La Brucherie, too.

My first close contact with Bert La Brucherie came during eleventh grade, when I played varsity football. One afternoon at practice, Coach Bert made it perfectly clear to me why he had developed his reputation. I played offensive guard and missed a block during scrimmage. The guy I was supposed to block flashed by me and killed the play for a five-yard loss. "Whose man was that?" yelled the coach. His voice was big and booming. I raised my hand and walked toward him with my head down. *Wham!* He hit me across the side of the head. "Look up here at me!" he snarled in my face. "Are you going to miss him again?"

"No, sir," was all I said.

And I didn't.

Coach Bert always pushed us to play as absolutely hard as we could. We practiced daily, at times until well after dark. Sometimes it grew hard to see the other players on the field. Coach would throw back his head and bark: "Look for the stripes on his socks!" That was his form of humor, and as we got to know him, we laughed right along with him. Our respect for him grew as we understood his unswerving commitment to excellence.

It wasn't all blows to the head with Coach Bert. I played badminton with a good friend named Herb Wiener. Herb had a ready laugh and was an all-around good athlete. We had known each other since junior high and become close friends. Herb and I played badminton outdoors, which is not easy to do because of the wind. We played at the house of our friend Bob Thomas. He wrote articles for the *Blue and White Daily*, and would give Herb and me a plug whenever he got a chance. Bob later became a syndicated columnist for the Associated Press.

Coach Bert somehow found out that Herb and I played. His line coach, Carl Brown, also played badminton. Coach sleuthed around and found out when Herb and I had study hall, and he'd often send a note via an underclassman to get us out of class so we could play badminton with him and Coach Brown. When you got to know Coach Bert, he was quite a likable guy. His needling and yelling were sort of a persona he adopted to motivate you.

Yet Coach Bert's adopted persona was always lurking just under the surface. On game days, during time-outs, water was brought onto the field in half-pint glass bottles. Coach carried one in his hand on the sidelines and into the locker room during halftime. During one game we were ahead by a couple of touchdowns when we reached halftime. We headed into the locker room smiling, slapping each other's backs. Coach strode into the room, a scowl on his face. We all shut up in a hurry.

"You stink!" he shouted to the team. "You call that effort?!" He

threw his water bottle against the wall, shattering glass all over. We
cowered in our seats. Nothing more than total commitment to victory
would do. We might be three touchdowns ahead, and Coach Bert still
wouldn't be satisfied.

Another time during my senior year, a preseason report on high
school teams appeared in the *LA Times* newspaper describing our
team as a group of "scintillating backs operating behind a big, experienced line." Our line was indeed huge by high school standards—it
averaged more than 210 pounds. We also had some very talented
backs. Coach was not impressed. In our second game of the season
we ran up against a team from a newly opened school. They gave us
a tough game, but we were able to win by a couple of touchdowns.
After the game we were our usual exuberant selves in the locker
room. Coach called us together. He had a different opinion.

"I'd like to ask you all one question," he sneered. "Where were
our *scintillating* backs and *big, experienced* line today?" Sarcasm
dripped from his voice. It was never simply enough for Coach Bert
that we win. Something about that game demonstrated less than 100
percent effort, and that simply would not do for this man.

Do I remember Coach Bert's ideals today? You bet I do. His voice
helped push me through a lot of hard times, including the war years.
His presence became a part of me. Whatever mud or snow we were
in, if our ammunition ran low or when we didn't eat for some time,
Coach Bert was there. His voice ingrained its way into my head. I
couldn't shake that boom if I tried.

I WASN'T DOING ANY MOTION PICTURE WORK BY THE TIME I GOT
to high school, but I threw papers for extra money and mowed lawns
during summers. Times were still tough. It was the middle of the
Great Depression. Pop never lost his job, and we never went without
food. But Pop's crying at the dinner table happened more frequently.

My junior year, I didn't start yet for the varsity team. At the end of that year it was a tradition to play a football game between the juniors and the graduating seniors. The game was held, and the seniors cleaned our clocks. After the game, the guy whose locker was next to mine gave me a good ribbing. He was a senior, the quarterback, and named Frank Tatum Jr., but everybody called him Sandy. He went on to Stanford and then to a career as a highly successful lawyer in San Francisco. He was probably best known for his work with the United States Golf Association, where he eventually served as president.

"Well, next year really looks bleak for the old football team here at LA High," Sandy said right after the game. A couple of other seniors laughed and looked in my direction. All of us juniors concentrated hard on our lockers. I ignored Sandy. "Yep, the school will really have a tough time if they've got to rely on all you losers," he gibed again. I kept my mouth shut. Maybe Sandy was right. I sure hoped not. I needed to play well my senior year to attract the attention of college recruiters. But a blow at the start of my senior year threatened to take away my dream.

We didn't have the luxury of personal trainers or locker room assistants to tape our ankles. After the third game of the season, I was hit low and hard in a practice. The tackler came in solid, just above my ankle. When I stood up I couldn't put any weight on my leg. I had experienced football injuries before. Those were the days before face masks, and a few games earlier I had plowed my face into some guy's hip pad during a tackle and broken my nose. It's bent to this day. But this was different. Doctors confirmed the worst. I had broken my fibula, the small bone in my lower leg. The injury benched me for the season. My buddy Steve replaced me. I was sure all those college recruiters would pass me by.

Funny what can happen when nobody thinks you'll succeed. The season went well, much to Sandy's chagrin. Coach Bert's shouts propelled our team on, with me cheering from the sidelines. One victory followed the next. At the end of the year we boasted an undefeated record. We had made it to the City Championships. I always hoped I'd run into Sandy again someday and remind him of his remarks.

Because of the large number of high schools in the LA system, the City Championships were a huge deal. You had to beat out about forty other high schools to get there. I needed to be in that game. I hadn't played since the day I broke my leg, but I had practiced as much as I could and tried to keep in shape. Coach Bert had kept a wary eye on me over the months. Would he let me play? He nodded. I was in.

The championship proved to be a tough game; our opponents were a really rough bunch. I must have been well rested from all my time on the bench because I made a couple of good blocks. It was a close game all the way through. We ended up as city champs. The guys all played well. One of the other guards on our team was Leon Fichman. I had met him when we were kids and both worked as extras in the picture business. He went on to play at Alabama under the great Bear Bryant, and later played professional football for the Detroit Lions.

My buddy Steve came up at the end of the City Championships and thanked me for breaking my leg early on in the season. Recruiters had noticed him play throughout the year, and he knew all his field exposure had ensured him a college scholarship. "Sorry about your leg," he said, "but now I'll get the chance to go to college, too." Few of us would ever have gotten the chance to go to college had it not been for football. Playing in the championship game, as well as my record in previous years, must have been the winning combination for me. Football recruiters hit me up from Berkeley, Stanford, USC, the University of Washington, and UCLA.

During Easter break, 1939, about twenty of us from various high schools rode the Southern Pacific train known as the *Daylight Limited* up to Berkeley for a weeklong recruiting trip. Fraternities housed us, and we were given a grand tour of the Bay Area, including the World's Fair on Treasure Island. I wanted to be a forestry major. The idea of being a ranger surrounded by trees and animals appealed to me. Berkeley had a good forestry program, but after that recruiting trip I knew the school wasn't the best fit for me. The size of Berkeley panicked me. I just couldn't imagine going there. At the end of the week we each had an interview with the head coach to convince us to come to Berkeley. Since we were from the same team, my friend Herb and I went to our interview together. All through the interview, the coach referred to us as "Lem" instead of Lynn, and "Herm" instead of Herb. We could hardly keep straight faces, but never corrected him.

A football scholarship was my only hope. In baseball, we were Western League Champions my senior year, and I was voted all-league catcher. But few colleges at the time were giving baseball scholarships. I probably played better baseball than football, but I was never approached by any college recruiters about playing baseball.

In the end, the decision over which college to go to was made quite quickly. Recruiting wasn't as high-powered as it is today. Aside from the trip to Berkeley, most of it was done informally. Herb and I wanted to go to the same school, if possible. Herb had already been offered a football scholarship to UCLA, and it appealed to go to a place where I knew somebody. I sort of wanted to go to USC, because my dad always wanted me to play for them, but USC was only interested in really big football players. I weighed about 215 pounds as a high school senior, big enough for USC, but Herb weighed only about 170—not enough for USC's powerhouse program. (Herb turned out to be a hell of a college football player and USC was later sorry they didn't take him.) The football team at UCLA wasn't exactly burning up the league in those days, but surprisingly, that appealed to me as well. I knew Herb and I would get more playing time. Coach Bert had gone there, and he said it was good choice. UCLA was close to home, so I could live there and save money.

It was set. UCLA it was. My scholarship covered tuition and books. I was going to college.

I DON'T REMEMBER WHAT HAPPENED TO HELEN, THE FIRST GIRL
I ever dated seriously, but sometime during my senior year I met another girl who changed everything. Her older sister, Lorrie Star, was

in my English literature class and a very pretty girl. Jerry, two years younger than Lorrie, was the real beauty who caught my attention. She was a perky little blonde, cute as hell, with a perfect pug nose and a great figure. Still kind of shy about girls, I asked her out anyway. On our first date we went to a movie, then home—that was it. We were on and off again all that year. Sometimes we went steady; sometimes she went out with other guys if there was nothing else to do. I wasn't exactly number one on her hit parade. Jerry attracted the attention of a lot of guys wherever she went. Her mother was divorced and made a living managing apartment houses, where they lived. As time rolled on, Jerry and I became more serious. Toward the end of the year, I guess you could say we were a couple.

Los Angeles High School provided a climate ripe for opportunity. There were only one or two guys I knew all the way through high school who went sour in the end. Most of my friends and acquaintances turned out to be pretty good successes in whatever they set out to do—doctors, lawyers, businessmen—you name it. All really did well. Few of us came from wealthy backgrounds, but almost all turned out to be good citizens in our chosen careers.

In 1939, I graduated from high school. As the summer began, I felt on top of the world. I had just graduated from one of the best high schools in Los Angeles and was heading to UCLA on a football scholarship. The beautiful Jerry Star was my girlfriend. I drove a newer 1934 Ford V-8 convertible. It was a time of triumph in my life, and all the world was before me.

But triumph can come in strange ways.

Sometimes it comes from the most unusual place. Sometimes it takes quite a while to see it coming, or to even know that you've hit the mark.

· 7 ·

Horror

MY MEMORIES SELDOM COME SEQUENTIALLY ANYMORE. THEY come in bunches and snippets; I see swirls of people and places I remember. The strongest points of my life stay with me the most.

The big earthquake of 1933 has always stuck in my mind. I could never shake the impression it made on me, even as a teenager when life was so good, even when I had just graduated and didn't think anything could go wrong. I remember the quake now as if it were yesterday. The quake registered 6.3 on the Richter scale and leveled Long Beach, maybe twenty miles from our house. It wreaked havoc on the suburbs of Compton and Huntington Park. It seemed the whole city was dazed.

We were sitting in our living room early in the evening when it happened. It was still daylight, maybe six o'clock. My dad had just come home from work. We heard a terrible roar rumbling in the distance. Pop recognized it instantly. "Earthquake!" he cried. He jumped up and headed us out the back door. Fortunately, he had the presence of mind to turn off the gas to the water heater before we all went out into the backyard.

The earthquake grabbed, and the ground started rolling. Our next-door neighbors scrambled out to their backyard. Between us stood a picket fence. It felt like being on a seesaw—one minute my folks and I were up in the air and the neighbors were down, the next minute we reversed. The ground literally rolled several feet up and down. As many as 120 people died in that quake. When it stopped, we could see our house had escaped with little damage. We reentered gingerly and tried to pick up where we had left off. But the quake left us all shaken.

THE OTHER QUAKE IN OUR LIVES, THE REAL SHOCK TO OUR world, also came without warning. Afterward, we checked with doctors to see if he had a disease—something we hadn't known about. We talked with friends. We searched our memories. Nothing. Nobody had predicted this.

I'd had a confrontation with him about booze not long before. My dad and I had driven in his car to the studio in Burbank where my aunt worked. He parked in the lot at Warner Bros., then went in to see my aunt. While he was inside, I found a damn bottle of booze under the seat. The bottle didn't have a label on it, but it didn't matter, they were all alike to me. Pop was still sneaking around. Why would he continue to hide this junk—particularly in the car? When he came back, I lit into him.

"You son of a bitch!" I yelled. "You're still doing this?!" I'm not proud now of how harshly I spoke to him.

That afternoon, for first time, he stood up to me. "Don't talk to me like that," he said. "I'm still your father." He said it quietly, like he was on unsure ground.

It's not a nice memory.

I have loads of nicer memories of my dad. There's a snapshot in a family album of him in Yosemite. He's standing there feeding a deer who had strolled up to eat out of his hand. Even in that picture, Pop's got a dress shirt on with his sleeves rolled up. His collar is open at the neck, but his tie's still on. There we were at a national park, and it looked like he could be sitting at the office.

Besides going to college football games, the only other thing he did for regular recreation was shoot pool. When he worked in downtown LA, he often spent his lunch hours playing snooker. But he wasn't a man commonly at ease with recreation. As a rule, he took everybody's problems on his shoulders—my aunt's, his friends', it didn't matter. He was deeply sensitive to them all.

Another picture: In those days it was a big deal for kids to sell magazines. On your way home from school, some guy sitting in a car would call you over. He'd show you a pocketknife or something and say, "Hey—how'd you like one of these?" The deal was, if you sold subscriptions to *Liberty* or the *Saturday Evening Post* or whatever, you'd get a prize. I was always signing up for these magazine deals, and my parents always ended up buying all the magazines. I was a terrible salesman. I'd just go knock on a door and say, "Want to buy a magazine?" If the people said no, I wouldn't press them further. That was it. But my dad was always good-natured about it. He'd end up buying all my magazines. He carried everyone's problems. Even mine.

I carry another snapshot of him—this one is in my mind today. Really it's several shots, because it happened more than once. It's the one where Pop's in the bathroom doubled over, sobbing. His parents have just left our house. Again, they had given him some hard-luck story about not being able to make ends meet.

And Pop felt it so keenly afterward. He always felt it all.

THE QUAKE CAME ON A SATURDAY AFTERNOON IN EARLY JULY.

I had been up to Jerry Star's place for a date that morning and was just heading home. The road that led to my house went down a hill. As I drove down the street, I could see a police car at the bottom. It struck me as odd. I wondered what it was all about—maybe somebody had broken into our house, or maybe one of our neighbors' houses. By that time there was only one police car sitting there, but I'd find out later there had been several more. Surely they were not there to arrest anybody.

I pulled up and parked. Our house looked the same as it always had—a small, stucco, flat-roofed bungalow. It had only two bedrooms with one bath. Two strips of concrete with a grass strip in between acted as a driveway and went to the back of the house. I had to park in the street because the police car was in our driveway. Before I reached the front door, the neighbor lady ran out toward me. She had been our neighbor for years and was one of the people who had been out in the backyard when the earthquake hit years earlier.

"What happened?" I said.

She was crying, searching for words to break something to me gently. "Your father . . ." she said. "Your father . . ."

I brushed past her and opened the door to my house. My mother sat on our couch, convulsing with tears. Two police officers dressed in navy blue stood in the living room. They must have known who I was because they didn't ask me any questions. My mother came over and threw her arms around me. I hugged her for a long time.

Everything looked the same: the fake fireplace with a ceramic mantel and one of those old gas heaters inside; the old upright piano we kept in the living room for my aunt to play. I had taken lessons for a while as a kid, even played in a recital once, but I quit because I didn't like to practice—I'd rather be outside playing. I'd give anything today to be able to sit down and play piano. My aunt never had a lesson, couldn't read a note of music, but she could play all over the keyboard. She used to play and I'd sing as a kid.

Incongruously, these thoughts streamed through my mind as I

held my crying mother. I don't remember if I walked out to the garage to see things for myself. I doubt if the cops would have permitted that. They probably just described it to me, which is how I remember things today. "Why?" was all I remember saying. "Why? Why would he do this?" My mother nodded to two notes on the dining room table. The table had a flower bowl on it with two runners. Pop's notes lay on the table. They were cryptic. The note to my mother was matter-of-fact:

> *I'm in the garage. Don't come in.*
> *No need for an autopsy.*
> *Call the police.*
> *Call somebody at the office about the insurance.*

That was all he said. He didn't say good-bye, or I'm sorry, or I can't take it anymore, or whatever. No mention of any reason for this act.

The note addressed to me said:

> *I'm proud of you, big boy.*
> *I hope you beat USC.*

That was it.

He had connected a piece of garden hose to the muffler of the family car and put the other end up through the floorboard near the driver's seat. He had backed the car into the garage, closed the garage door, climbed into the driver's seat, and started the engine.

It took a while for it to sink in. When I heard of all the planning he had done to commit suicide, I knew it was no spur-of-the-moment decision. He had needed to cut the garden hose to an exact length. He had needed to carefully tape one end to the exhaust pipe with friction tape. In those days, on the driver's side by the door, there was a battery with a wooden box that he had needed to circumvent when he stuck the hose in. Pop never backed our car into the garage— that took foresight. He had even locked the garage door from the inside. It wasn't like grabbing a gun and impulsively blowing your brains out—his plan to kill himself took calculated thinking.

I WAS IN SHOCK FOR A LONG TIME.

My mother held a large, fancy funeral for him. The Reverend James Fifield officiated. He was a radio evangelist that my mother listened to sometimes, and ministered at the First Congregational Church in Los Angeles. How she got him to officiate, I don't know. But I was grateful that he came.

For the longest time afterward, it would just hit me out of nowhere. When I wanted to talk to him, and I couldn't—this feeling of helplessness would strike me with an invisible bare fist. That was the toughest part of it all. My father was gone so suddenly. The thought that I couldn't talk to somebody who was such a part of my life—it just ripped me apart. Suddenly my father just wasn't there anymore. It was a horrible feeling. My mother lived to be ninety-seven. I never had that same sense of loss when she died. We had time with her. But Pop was only forty-three.

In those first few days and weeks after the suicide, everyone we talked to was as shocked as we were. To this day nobody is sure what caused him to do it. I can only guess it was attributable to his sense of failure in overcoming the alcohol problem. The booze and the secrecy around it always caused chafing between him and my mother and me. I still bear a lot of guilt because of my conduct.

What might I say to my father if I could?

I'd say, *I'm sorry.*

I'm sorry I wasn't more respectful. I'm sorry I wasn't a better son. I'm sorry I didn't treat him with the warmth I should have in spite of his drinking problem. Certainly his good qualities far outweighed what few bad things he did with his liquor—especially considering today's atmosphere. What he did was so minor.

So yeah, I owe him a hell of an apology.

· 8 ·
Somehow You Continue

AS I WRITE THIS BOOK, I HAVE JUST TURNED EIGHTY-FIVE YEARS old. My health is strong. I still walk and drive—things that men younger than I sometimes need to give up. I continue to lead an active life. I have a radio commentary show in Anacortes, near my home. I volunteer for the Skagit County Republican Party headquarters. Four mornings each week I meet for breakfast with other veterans to swap stories and shoot the bull. On my schedule this year are a variety of speaking engagements, including two extended trips to Europe, one at the request of the U.S. government to go over and encourage troops stationed in Germany, the other to help lead tours of the battle sites of Normandy, Operation Market Garden, and Bastogne.

But strength is all relative. Sometimes the greatest signs of strength are demonstrated when you relive the hard parts of your life. I'm not a man easily given to emotion. I hate to cry. Yet there are three things that cause me to tear up today. One is when I talk about the love I have for America. The second, I'll tell you about later on in the book. The third is whenever I remember my dad's suicide.

As young people, my generation would see a lot of death. I don't think I ever grew accustomed to it. It came in darkness and fervor, by our airplanes, rifles, parachutes, and tanks. But there was something about that first death I experienced the summer of 1939 when I was just eighteen, years before the war, that stayed with me so strongly. Those first few seasons after my father died were dark indeed.

My mother needed to sell the house quickly. She received a small life insurance settlement, but, as she didn't work, we had no income. I was able to get a part-time job with the maintenance department at UCLA to help out. My friend Herb worked with me. We spent a lot of time that summer in a ravine, hoeing weeds and lugging around fertilizer. It wasn't easy work.

Mom and I soon moved into a little one-bedroom apartment on the west side of LA near the Beverly and Fairfax area. The window next to where I slept bordered on a common patio area where neighbors congregated to talk. A lot of days I'd come home and find Mom lying prostrate on the davenport, sobbing. Sometimes she spent all day and night on the couch. This was truly one of those times when it was tough being an only child.

I could always talk to Herb, but neither he nor I knew what to say. What do you talk about when your dad's just killed himself? Jerry and I continued to go out, but she was a young gal, and it wasn't like she was somebody I could ever lean on. The friend who really became a tower of strength for me was Coach La Brucherie. His strength didn't stop on the field. Several times that summer he came over to the house and encouraged me to go on. "If there's ever anything you need," he'd say, or, "If there's something I can do." He never barked at me or gave me a fight talk, not then anyway. He became an example to me of what it means to be truly strong. Even when life throws you down, somehow you get up and continue; if you can help others in the process, you do that then, too.

Eventually Mom found a job as a PBX telephone system operator at an answering service for extras and bit players who got most of their work through Central Casting. The job brought in enough money to live, but she still spent most of her at-home time crying. Sometimes Mom needed to work the night shift, which was never easy for her. With me working off hours from her that summer and trying to go to school that fall, it was a rough time for us both.

IN FALL 1939, THE YEAR I ENTERED UNIVERSITY, WHAT PASSED as a football scholarship at UCLA amounted to free tuition and books plus a four-hour-per-day job on campus at fifty cents an hour. My job was picking up trash. They gave me a gunnysack and a stick with a nail in the end of it, and told me to put in my time. To get in my four hours each day, I started at 6:00 A.M. and picked up trash until classes began at eight. I attended classes all day, then headed to football practice each afternoon. Immediately after practice, I shouldered my gunnysack again and picked up trash for another two hours until 8:00 P.M., then went home for dinner and homework. Hoo boy, I was a really big man on campus. Playing college football was nothing like it is today.

Back then, freshmen were ineligible to play varsity sports. They had a separate freshman football team, and we played against other freshmen from other universities. Usually the freshmen games were played immediately before varsity games between the same schools.

UCLA was not a football powerhouse by any stretch of the imagination. And their recruiting was something less than great the year I entered. We ended up with a freshman team of only about fifteen players. Berkeley's freshman team, by contrast, had a string of about forty. Most games, we lost. About five of us on the freshman team eventually went on to play varsity. Prior to 1939, UCLA had a fairly poor record in the Pacific Coast Conference—a ten-school district that consisted of us, USC, Cal-Berkeley, Stanford, Oregon, Oregon

State, Washington, Washington State, Idaho, and Montana. The closest UCLA had ever come to beating USC was a scoreless tie.

One of our games as freshmen was held in the Coliseum. The
other team ran out a line of about thirty-five players. Midway through
the first half, our center got injured and claimed he couldn't continue.
He was kind of a babyish guy. I don't think he was hurt as bad as he
said, and he was the only center we had, so we were stuck. I had never
played center in my life, but volunteered to give it a try.

On the first play we were backed up to our own goal line and
forced to punt. My job was to snap the ball from between my legs to
get it to the punter, who held his heel against the end line. When the
play was called, I gave the ball too much juice and snapped it over the
punter's head. The other team scored a safety. Two points. So much
for me being a star center.

The game continued. In those days a center also played line-
backer on defense—also something I had never done. The other team
snapped the ball. Everything was confusion as I tried to focus on
where the ball was. One of their blockers saw I was a sitting duck.
Their big end came off the line and blindsided me, plowing into my
knee. I never saw him coming and crumpled over like an empty potato sack. From that game on, I had knee problems that plagued me
for years. Prior to each subsequent game, I needed to splint my leg
with a sponge-rubber brace so I didn't overflex it in play.

Fraternities were big on campus, and I went through the whole
rush thing, where different frats invite you to join. My freshman year
I pledged the Phi Kappa Psi fraternity. I continued to live with my
mother and commuted to school, so most of my frat life consisted of
having lunch with my brothers each day and weekly night meetings
at the frat house. Herb was Jewish, so he wasn't allowed to join.
There were separate fraternities for Jews back then, but Herb never
expressed any interest. We were buddies; I didn't care who he was,
and the subject never came up between us.

To get in officially, you had to go through hazing first. Hazing was rigorous and continued throughout our pledge term. The existing fraternity members were called "actives." They treated you like dogs. Any active could order you at any time to bend over for a paddling. Some of the pledges muttered about it, but not too many. It was all sort of good-natured. If you resented the hazing, the existing members didn't want you in their frat. The way you got to be a member was to go through hazing with a smile on your face.

The climax of the pledge term consisted of Hell Week, a seven-day test of pain and humiliation. The week immediately preceded initiation. If you got through Hell Week, you were in. For that week, all pledges needed to live and sleep at the fraternity house. On the first day of Hell Week we new pledges were ordered to yank down our pants and sit on blocks of ice. The line of us dropped our drawers and sat, completely bare, until our undersides were frozen. After some time we were ordered to stand and promptly paddled. The wood smacked against our frozen flesh again and again. It stung like the dickens.

That first night of Hell Week we were asleep when someone barged into our room. Lamberson was a well-liked active, but sort of known as a clown, too. He wore a closely cropped buzz cut and had pockmarks on his face. "Get up!" he screamed. "Fire drill! Everybody out—now! Downstairs on the double!" We marched downstairs. Outside the fraternity house, several other actives joined Lamberson. Across the street they had started a large bonfire. Inside a stationary tub near the back door, they had dumped a bunch of garbage, then filled the tub with water. Coffee grounds. Banana peels. You name it—it all roiled together as one.

"Okay maggots—now put out the fire!" Lamberson ordered with a friendly grin. The method soon became clear: you had to suck in a mouthful of garbage water, sprint across the street, then spit it on the bonfire until it was all out. We obeyed. We sucked up old potato peelings and eggshells and ran and spat. When the fire was reduced to a pile of smoldering charcoal, we tramped back to bed. Six more days to go.

Lamberson was a highbrow transfer from Iowa's Grinnell

University and seemed to take a special disliking to me. The next morning he took a random swat at me with his paddle. "Bend over for another one, Iron Ass," he said, and gave me another swat for good measure. Anytime he saw me that day he gave me a swipe. His "special concern" for me continued throughout the week. About the second or third time it happened, I made up my mind that I simply would never react. Lamberson could whale away, and I'd never say a thing. And he did. My silence drove him madder than a hornet. As the day wore on and the next and the next, he delighted in smacking me around again and again. But I never gave him the satisfaction of showing pain.

The windup of Hell Week was something we all knew was coming. The climax was set for Friday night. It was nearly dark after football practice when I headed into the fraternity. Inside the front door, the actives were already lined up, grinning evilly. The upperclassmen blindfolded us and shoved us into the backs of various cars. I don't remember how long they drove us—it must have been several hours. They dumped us out in twos at intervals along the way.

When they dumped me and a buddy out, it was completely dark. We were beside a road somewhere. We had no idea where. There were no signs, lights, or traffic. They made sure we didn't have our wallets. The test was to make it back to the frat house without any money by noon the next day. As an added challenge, we were ordered to pick up various items along the way—a potted plant, a broom, just junk. How we procured it—that was our problem—steal stuff off people's porches or whatever.

As the car sped away, my fellow recruit looked at me and gave a low whistle. "We're really lost," he said. "Any idea where we are?"

I shook my head. We found out later we were in Silverado Canyon, more than sixty miles from the UCLA campus. "But don't worry," I said, "I've got a plan up my sleeve." We started walking. We hiked in complete darkness for several miles until we reached a small town with a roadside gas station and a pay phone out front. "What good will that do?" my friend said. "We're still broke."

I hadn't removed the tape on my wrists yet from football practice. The brothers probably thought I just hadn't bothered to change after I came off the field. "Check it out," I said to my friend, turning the tape over. Earlier that day I had stowed several quarters underneath the tape where they couldn't be seen—enough to make a long-distance call. From the pay phone I called my buddy Herb—another arrangement I had set up in advance. About two hours later he showed up at the gas station in my car. He was grinning.

"You guys really fooled them," Herb said.

"Almost," I said. "We've still got to find all that junk." Herb drove us around while we collected the items on the list. It still took us most of the night, but we reached campus the next day with time to spare. Fraternity hazing has come under fire in recent times, another victim of political correctness, but I don't believe hazing harmed us at all. When it was all over, it was a big deal to make it into the fraternity. I was happy to be in. Hazing was just part of the experience.

The day I was initiated into the fraternity was the first time I had ever worn a tuxedo. A lot of ceremony surrounded becoming an active. Everything was quite formal. We learned the secret handshakes, songs, and passwords. It was a big deal to finally wear a fraternity pin. A lot of guys gave their pins to the girl they were going steady with—it was almost as binding as an engagement. Jerry and I were too on-and-off again for me to give her my pin. I'm sure I tried a few times. She went with me to a few fraternity parties and dances. They were formal affairs often held at the Bel Air Beach Club.

One of my frat brothers was Dick Jensen, who ended up as the personal aide to General Patton. Dick was killed in North Africa. Patton had recently promoted him to captain and was said to have missed him greatly. Quite a large scene in the movie *Patton* is devoted to General Patton's reaction on hearing that Dick was killed.

Another frat brother, Tubby Simons, was killed with the Big Red One, the 1st Infantry Division, that stormed Utah Beach on D-Day.

In 1939, fraternities really ran UCLA. You couldn't get elected to any student body office unless you were a fraternity member. The radical group on campus was made up of "non-orgs," students who didn't join. They were always hanging around, passing out leaflets, protesting something or other. When Germany and Russia were allies, these radical students demanded that the United States not intervene against Germany. When the Germans attacked Russia, the radicals were in a pinch. But their allegiance was never to the United States.

BASEBALL PLAYERS IN THOSE DAYS WERE NOT RECRUITED. WE just showed up and played for love of the game. My junior year, the baseball coach, Art Reichle, found me a job working in the Hammond Redwood Mill in Humboldt County so I could play baseball for a four-team county league. We played night ball during the week and day ball on weekends. That summer I lived in company housing and ate in the mill mess hall.

Back at UCLA, our baseball team proved pretty respectable. We never won the league championship, but I was picked as an all-league catcher. One year I hit about .340. I was also team captain a couple years. All in all, I was a pretty good hitting catcher. Many years later I was voted to the UCLA Baseball Hall of Fame. I think it was mostly because of other accomplishments in my life, as I would call myself an above-average ballplayer, but never spectacular.

One of my teammates, however, truly was.

Jackie Robinson was a four-sport wonder. I played both baseball and football with him. His best sport was actually track and field, where he was a sprinter and a broad jumper. He also played basketball. He became UCLA's first athlete to win varsity letters in four sports.

Jackie transferred in from Pasadena Junior College my sophomore year. He was maybe a year older than me and wasn't the most outgoing guy in the world. We had three black players on our football team, unprecedented for the era. Kenny Washington, about a year older than Jackie, was also a hell of a good baseball player. In addition, he was also an incredible football player. In football, he rushed for 1,914 yards in his college career, which stood as a school record for thirty-four years. He led the nation in total offense statistics and became the first consensus All-American in the history of our school's football program. Kenny was one of those easygoing guys with a sense of humor. Everybody liked Kenny.

But nobody will forget Jackie.

In 1947, Jackie signed with the Brooklyn Dodgers and became the first black man to play Major League Baseball. He won the Rookie of the Year award that year, despite being harassed by both players and fans because of his color. Two years later Jackie won his first National League Most Valuable Player award. He eventually played on six World Series teams and in 1962 was inducted into the Baseball Hall of Fame. Throughout his career he earned six consecutive All-Star Game nominations. He retired with a .311 batting average, which continues to place him in the top 100 highest batting averages of all time.

Though Jackie and I were teammates at UCLA, I can't claim that we were ever close friends. Jackie kept more to himself. One incident sticks out, though. I'm not proud of it, but it was true to the boys-will-be-boys atmosphere prevalent on a lot of college sports teams. On a train ride up to Berkeley, Jackie sat opposite me playing cards. It was football season, and a lot of other students were on the train as well as team members. Some joker barged into our car and shouted, "Hey, Elaine's on the train—they got her up in a berth. She's up for any-body." Elaine, a UCLA coed, had a reputation for being easy. I looked at Jackie and gave him a wink. "You wanna go?" I said. I wasn't a Goody Two-shoes, but it wasn't something I would've actually done, either.

Jackie didn't smile at all. He looked at me and said, "Hell, if I did, they'd lynch me."

We kept on playing cards.

Jackie was a supporter of Martin Luther King Jr. and a strong civil rights proponent. A Congressional Gold Medal and the Presidential Medal of Freedom were awarded posthumously to Jackie for his civil rights activities. He died in 1972 at age fifty-three from heart problems and diabetes complications. On April 15, 1997, the fiftieth anniversary of his debut as a professional baseball player, Major League Baseball retired his jersey number, 42, in recognition of his accomplishments both on and off the field. In 1999, *Time* magazine named Jackie Robinson one of the top 100 most influential people of the twentieth century.

I PLAYED BASEBALL WITH ANOTHER GREAT PLAYER ALSO, TAK Kobayashi. He was a Japanese kid, a center fielder, and a highly capable ballplayer. Through no fault of his own, he didn't stick around long.

When World War II broke out in 1939, with America's stance on isolationism and neutrality, mostly we kept focused on our studies and university life. For those first two years, World War II was considered "Europe's war." We watched it, but not very closely. I first heard that the Japanese had attacked the American naval base at Pearl Harbor when I was lying in my bedroom in the apartment shared with my mother. It was December 7, 1941, and some neighbors were standing on the patio outside my window discussing the attack with low, angry voices. The bombing killed more than 2,300 Americans, destroyed the American battleship USS *Arizona,* capsized the USS *Oklahoma,* damaged 21 other U.S. ships, and demolished 180 aircraft.

The next day, December 8, under President Franklin Roosevelt, Congress declared war on Japan. Three days later, on December 11, Hitler declared war on the United States. Italy soon followed, along with the other Axis powers. For the United States, World War II had officially begun. Because of his race, my teammate Tak Kobayashi was taken in a roundup of all Japanese in America and placed in an internment camp. Our coach, a reserve military officer, tried every angle to keep Tak excused from confinement and enrolled at UCLA, but was unsuccessful.

I had joined the ROTC for two years when I enrolled at UCLA, like all male freshman students in state universities were required to do, then opted for two more years in order to get a commission as an officer in the Army Reserve. I didn't know of anybody who was bothered by having to do two years of ROTC. Our education was being subsidized by the American taxpayers, so none of us considered it unreasonable to give a couple of years' military training in exchange for it. When I hear today of major state universities trying to bar armed forces recruiters on campus—that strikes me as unconscionable.

After the Japanese attacked Pearl Harbor, the climate in America changed almost overnight. There was a lot of concern that the Japanese would follow up Pearl Harbor by bombing the United States mainland. On campus, everybody's outlook suddenly got very serious. We all knew active duty lay ahead. The only question was which branch of the service a guy would go into. Nobody I knew talked about going to Canada to get away from it or any other evasive strategies. (In fact, Canada had already been in this war for two years before Pearl Harbor.) Everybody I knew expressed a willingness to go. I was already in the upper divisions of ROTC, so I didn't run down to the recruiting center to sign up, as many guys did. It was just a matter of staying prepared, waiting for the orders to go.

The war would change our lives in ways we could never dream. But at first we were caught in a lull. Though war had been officially declared, our lives stayed virtually the same for nearly a year while the existing military was deployed. It was a season of change, of buckling down, of trying to anticipate what lay ahead. Right around that time my mother began dating one of the clients of the answering service she worked for. He had been a well-known cowboy actor in the Tom Mix era, but he received mostly bit parts now and blew all his money on booze. Out of respect for my mother, I tolerated the guy, but secretly couldn't stand him. A few years later, when I was away in the service, she married him. He was an obnoxious drunk until the day he died.

I doubt if we will ever know the full extent of the ways my father's suicide affected us. That one dark action cast a pall over years of our lives, but life demanded to be lived. In those first few years after it happened, I don't remember if I ever made a conscious decision to keep going forward. Perhaps it was Coach Bert's strong presence in my life that motivated me. Or the activity of sports, studies, or fraternity life. Perhaps it was even partially the pull of responsibility I felt to defend my country.

Somehow I continued.

· 9 ·

Train for Georgia

IN DECEMBER 1941, RIGHT AFTER PEARL HARBOR, OUR FOOTBALL team took a long train trip to Gainesville to play the University of Florida. All the talk was of war. We all knew we were going to go, we just didn't know when. For those of us in ROTC, our first task was to finish the course. Another train trip east would soon speed me to my destiny.

I completed my junior year in spring 1942, worked that summer, then entered UCLA in fall 1942 as a senior. Moving to the varsity football team two years earlier had made life a little more comfortable. The campus jobs got easier, and I was allowed to eat at the training table, which helped with expenses.

That fall, our football team really hit its stride. Maybe the anticipation of war helped fuel us forward. The few freshmen, who had once struggled to even make up a full team, had been augmented in subsequent seasons by additional recruits and junior college transfers; 1942 proved to be the best season in UCLA's history to date. We had a crackerjack quarterback named Bob Waterfield, one of the all-time great T-formation quarterbacks. He married actress Jane Russell his senior year and went on to have a great career with the LA Rams, later coaching the team.

With Bob leading us that fall, we defeated team after team. People started calling us "unstoppable." For the first time in UCLA's history, we defeated powerhouse USC. Then we triumphed over the University of Washington to win the Pacific Coast Conference. That meant one thing: we were headed to the Rose Bowl. Nicknamed "the grand-daddy of them all," the Rose Bowl was considered the most prestigious college football game in America. For me, living in LA and being close to the Rose Bowl made it even bigger in my mind. I had even ushered at the Rose Bowl a few years as a high school football player, so getting to play in the game as a college senior was an exceptional thrill for me.

The Rose Bowl is played every year on January 1. It had been played the previous year right after Pearl Harbor in Wallace Wade Stadium in Durham, North Carolina, due to fears that the Japanese would attack major West Coast cities. But this year, 1943, it was back in Pasadena, where the game had been played since 1902.

Herb and I celebrated my twenty-first birthday, December 31, 1942, in the Vista Del Arroyo Hotel in Pasadena, which overlooks the Arroyo Seco, the canyon that encompasses the site of the Rose Bowl. My birthday itself wasn't extravagant. We didn't go out partying or drinking or anything. We had the biggest game of our lives the next day. We needed our sleep.

Game day dawned early. No matter who you are, you always have butterflies in your stomach before a big game. I sure did. The nervousness abates after the first few plays, but it's always there in the beginning. Herb and I headed to the locker rooms and suited up with our teammates. Coach gave us a few last words. Nothing compared to the moment we finally came out on the field. We exited the tunnel to the roar of a hundred thousand people thundering in the stands. We had played in big games before, but this was the first time UCLA had ever been to the Rose Bowl. The crowd cheered itself hoarse.

After the coin toss, the game started slowly, with active defense on both sides. Slowly, the opposing team, the University of Georgia Bulldogs, ground us down. Every time we ran a man in motion, Georgia slanted sideways. We had never been up against a defense that good. We had a hell of a time making our running game go.

Georgia ran the same play a few times, where their halfback acted like he had the ball and ran through a gap in our middle. When he came through the line, the quarterback lobbed him a pass. It was a fake move. It worked once or twice for several yards. As the guy calling the defensive plays, I decided to drop back and tackle him the next time he came through, even though I knew he didn't have the ball. Next time he ran through I hit him hard. The umpire behind me called me for defensive holding. It wasn't critical to the game, but it meant I couldn't keep stopping that play the same way.

I shook it off and forgot about it, but it's funny what sticks with a person. In about 1960, I was in the DA's office and the phone rang. The voice said, "Mr. Compton—I'm a doctor with the University of Tennessee Medical School. I was the umpire in the Rose Bowl when you played Georgia. You know, all these years I've been troubled by that call I made when I called you for defensive holding. I think I was wrong. I apologize." We both had a good laugh about it.

Georgia also had a huge end, George Poschner, who stopped everything that came his way. Poschner was All-American, and drafted in the eighth round by the Detroit Lions in 1943. I met him later at Fort Benning, where we both attended Officer Candidate School (OCS). Sadly, he lost both legs during the Battle of the Bulge. I feel honored to have known him and played against him in the Rose Bowl.

In the end, the Bulldogs beat us 9-0.

The Rose Bowl marked the end of that season of college life for me. I don't remember if the notice came in the mail or by phone, but a few days after the Rose Bowl my military orders were issued. It was the middle of my senior year; I had just turned twenty-one. College, football, baseball, girlfriends, Ford V-8s—all of life, for the time being, would have to wait.

Those of us from ROTC met at the old Union Station in LA and boarded a train for Georgia, site of the Infantry School at Fort Benning. We knew this was it. We were going to war. Back in the summer of 1942, I had been scheduled to spend a summer on active duty at a military base as a prerequisite for getting a commission, but because of Pearl Harbor, the army canceled that—none of the bases was available. So as we came close to finishing our four years of ROTC, they rerouted us to Fort Benning to take the regular Officer Candidate School course. From there we'd get our commissions and a post somewhere in active duty.

My buddy Herb had decided to go into the Navy, so he wasn't at Union Station with me. We had been good friends for years, played on the same teams, gone to the same university, dated within the same circle of girls, but war was the point where we said good-bye. Thankfully, he made it through his combat years okay. He later married a Jantzen bathing suit model and became a lawyer. We reconnected after the war and kept in touch for decades. As I'm writing this book, I've just received word that Herb has passed away. Our ranks are really getting thin these days. Three of Herb's family members phoned me with the news. I honor his memory.

STRANGELY, NONE OF THE GUYS AT THE TRAIN STATION THE DAY we pulled out looked all that nervous. It must have been the sense of duty we were feeling. We had been waiting for our call, and this was it. This was our responsibility to go and fight.

My mother was in tears, of course, when she said good-bye to me. At the time, it didn't feel as difficult for me to say good-bye to her, but years later, after becoming a parent myself, I can't imagine what it felt like for my mom to know her only son was heading to war.

Communication was not nearly what it's like today, either. Letters took a long time coming. Every parent's worst fear was receiving a telegram with a star on it.

"Write often," Mom said as I boarded the train. "Please take care of yourself, Lynn. *Please.*"

The train whistle sounded. We were off.

Young men heading off to war often have no idea of the darkness that lies ahead. We certainly didn't, anyway. The atmosphere on the train bordered on a party. Guys told jokes and swapped stories. We snacked, wisecracked, and played cards. Some dozed, read magazines, or looked out the window. At New Orleans the train stopped. Somebody got off and came back with a mess of shrimp. I loved shrimp and ate my fill. I supposed it had been boiled—it tasted fresh anyway. A few hours later my stomach started to do flips. Sweat broke out on my forehead. I made trip after trip to the bathroom.

The rest of the train ride was a blur.

It was a cold, windy afternoon, nearly evening, when we finally lurched into the station at Columbus, Georgia, our final stop. It was one year after America officially had entered World War II, and American flags flew all over town. Trucks were set to cart us from the train station to Fort Benning, but the trucks were at the other end of the city. Someone told us to start walking, and we ended up walking the entire length of downtown Columbus to reach our rides. We were all in civilian clothes still, dressed in overcoats and carrying suitcases. My gut was cramped from the shrimp, and I kept a sharp lookout for restrooms. By the time we reached the trucks, it was dark.

The trucks took us to some barracks and deposited us. It was the middle of the night by then. Our only order was to go to sleep. We stumbled to the barracks we were shown and opened the door. "Why do you have to make so much damn noise?" a voice yelled in the darkness. Inside were a bunch of Regular Army personnel, not happy about having their sleep disturbed. We groped around to find empty bunks.

"Shut up and go to sleep!" yelled another. "Bunch of college punks." I found an empty bunk at last, got undressed in a hurry, and lay down. I still felt like I was moving. My sleep was fitful and disturbed for the rest of the night.

To become an officer in those days you either went through OCS, came from the United States Military Academy at West Point, or received a battlefield commission, but those were quite rare. The officers coming out of OCS, like I soon would, were derogatively referred to as "ninety-day wonders," or "shavetails." The nickname shavetail reaches back to the beginning of the cavalry. When green troopers first arrived, they were given a horse with a shaved tail. Other riders would see the tail and give the greenhorns extra space in which to operate.

I didn't care about the nicknames. To get to go to OCS was a hell of a lot better than a lot of assignments. And in my book, the training we had done all those years in ROTC counted for something. But the military is all about proving yourself—as an individual as well as a group. There were hierarchies even within the OCS. A lot of the guys in OCS were Regular Army enlisted men sent there to become officers. They were professional military personnel who had already gone through basic training and spent time as soldiers—some had already spent as much as a decade in the military.

To them, those who came from ROTC were just a bunch of college kids with no military experience at all. ROTC certainly didn't count for much in their eyes. The only reason we were at Benning was because we missed the summer camp program and had been rerouted here. The professional military guys made it perfectly clear we were the low men on the totem pole. The next morning, there were enough guys up and moving around so that everybody was awake by the time the bugle sounded. The regulars all had uniforms. All we had were our civilian clothes. They eyed us disdainfully.

"Nice tie," one sneered at me. "Did your mama pick that out for you?" When he wasn't looking, I took it off. A number of other regulars made similar cracks at the other new recruits. We were ordered to fall out on a muddy piece of ground next to the barracks, where we all mingled in with the Regular Army personnel. Most of the new guys looked at the ground, or out of the corners of their eyes. Our suits and coats were a disgrace. Never did I want to wear a uniform more.

· 10 ·

To Get a Uniform

THEY TOOK ROLL CALL ON THE MUDDY GROUND, THEN DISMISSED
us. That was about it. For the first few days at Benning, surprisingly,
we didn't do anything. No training. No running. No push-ups. We
just hung out.

We were placed in what was called a *casual battalion,* a category
used to house men until enough were present to make up a new class
to start a training course. A class was about the size of a company, as
many as 150 men. So until the Army got enough guys and had the facilities and instructors ready to make up our class, we simply waited.

It took several days to get everything in place. It seemed like an
interminable amount of time. At last a class was formed, and we were
taken to our permanent barracks, just single cots, about fifteen guys
to a building. A few more days passed before our uniforms were finally issued. They were regular olive drabs (ODs)—green wool pants,
shirt, and jacket, sturdy brown captoe shoes. The uniforms were
scratchy but great for the cold weather. No weapons were issued right

away. Shooting training began, and we were able to use weapons there.

Our status in Officer Candidate School felt strange. We were neither fish nor fowl. We weren't sworn in yet as soldiers, but we were officially on active duty with a unit. We didn't have rank yet, and we dressed like privates. It would take the full ninety days at Benning until we received our commissions.

Fort Benning is a huge facility, just acres and acres of sites with all kinds of military activities going on at the same time. Throughout the grounds are multiple sections of bleachers and grandstands with expanses of ground in front. Most days we sat in the bleachers with instructors below who demonstrated all sorts of things—hand-to-hand combat, sharpshooting, bayonet use, how to move as a convoy, how to fight as a platoon on attack or defense. We took notes and had tests, like any school. We were trained how to be lieutenants in the infantry—platoon leaders. It built upon the training we received in college.

Some people are surprised, even disappointed, to learn that what I went through at Fort Benning was nothing like the intensive physical training the guys endured at Camp Toccoa. Really, I never went to boot camp. If you've seen *Band of Brothers*, or read the book, you'll remember the men of Easy Company shouting, "Three miles up, three miles down" while running up and down the legendary Currahee Mountain, sometimes twice a day. Though the military put together the 506th Regiment at Toccoa, its officers were drawn from several sources. I was one of the 506th's officers who came from somewhere else. I got a bit of the intensive physical training later when I went to jump school, but compared to the guys at Toccoa, I had it relatively easy.

I don't want to make it sound like we weren't prepared at Benning. Though the regulars made fun of the guys who came from ROTC programs, we had done quite a bit of physical training as part of ROTC, including marching, close order drills, and tactical maneuvers in the hills around UCLA. I was also still in good shape from baseball and football season. But, true, our training had a different focus. Boot camp was about taking a guy off the street and creating a soldier out of him. What we went through at OCS was training to be leaders. We had about an hour of physical training each day at Benning, but it was nothing like obstacle courses or extreme marches. We weren't being trained to be foot soldiers. We were being trained to command.

Parts of the OCS training were very demanding. You could get "washed out" of the OCS program for a lot of reasons. If you flunked a test or got sick or couldn't perform one of the requirements—you were gone. No questions asked. There were certainly a few incompetent men who became military officers, but they were the rare exception. For the most part, the military produced solid, high-performing leaders. I knew a few guys who didn't make it. During my tenure in OCS, a member of my squad was a Regular Army enlisted man from the Newfoundland Base Command. He was a crusty sort, well tattooed, and enjoyed a night out on the town whenever he could swing it. I liked the guy, and one evening he asked me to join him on a trip into town.

There were two cities that military men from Benning frequented— Phenix City, Alabama, or Columbus, Georgia, separated by the Chattahoochee River. Phenix City had a reputation of being a real sin city, filled with prostitutes and cheap booze halls. Columbus had the reputation of being just a regular Southern town. I felt relieved when my buddy said he was going to Columbus. But as soon as we hit the city, he headed straight for the tattoo parlor to get another tattoo. "C'mon, Compton," he said. "You're in the Army now."

I thought it over for a minute, then shrugged. My father had a tattoo of a star on his forearm, blue with half of the points shaded in— I suppose from his World War I days. I was still pretty stuck on Jerry Star, my high school sweetheart—I was positive at the time that she was the love of my life—so I asked the tattoo artist to put a blue star on my left arm with the letters J E R R Y around the star. I don't recall if I telephoned Jerry or wrote her about it. Neither do I remember her reaction when she found out. I was certainly not imagining then that the romance would ever fade. You've got to be careful of the tattoos you get in your youth.

When we got back to base, over the next few days my friend's new tattoo turned colors it shouldn't have. He was diagnosed with blood poisoning and began to miss classes. Finally he was booted out of OCS. A tattoo cost him his commission.

About a month into the program, I nearly met a similar fate. One morning I woke up with itchy red bumps all over me. Was it spider bites? Mosquitoes? A reaction to wool? The bumps scratched like hell. My forehead felt hot, too. I tried to scratch as inconspicuously as possible.

"Compton, what's the matter?" said the guy next to me. He was somebody who had shown he could be trusted, so I carefully pulled back my shirt to show him the bumps. My friend shook his head. "I'd recognize those anywhere. Had 'em myself when I was a kid. You've got yourself a case of the measles, Buck."

I stood up and began to put on my uniform. "Don't tell anybody," I said. "If I report for sick call, they'll pull me out of classes and I'll have to go back to square one." He didn't tell, and I rode it out. Apparently nobody else caught it. Sitting still through classes was a real challenge, though.

We finished our three months of training and received our commissions. I was a second lieutenant and wore a single gold bar on my shoulder. My new uniform was identical to any other officer. The "Class A" or dress uniform consisted of an olive drab wool garrison cap (a foldable wedge cap with straight sides and a creased crown that sloped to the back where it was parted), olive drab wool trousers, an olive drab wool shirt with a khaki cotton tie, an olive drab wool four-button tunic, and russet brown Type I service shoes. You have to buy your own uniforms as an officer. You were given a clothing allowance as part of your pay, but it didn't cover everything you needed to buy.

There was no real sense of unity in my graduating class from OCS. It wasn't designed to be that way. We all knew we'd be scattered to various places soon. Some were guys I had known from UCLA, but the guys came from all over. I enjoyed getting to know those from different schools, and for the most part they were all great guys. As soon as we graduated, we received our orders to report to the units to which we had been assigned. Most of my classmates were posted to various infantry replacement centers around the country.

Right when OCS ended, I was given ten days off (called a "delay in route") between OSC and my assignment. If I hurried, I could just make it to California and back for a visit home. Standing in a commercial airport for the flight home, I wore the uniform of a commissioned Army officer, but I sure didn't feel very important yet.

"I'm sorry, sir," said the airline attendant, "you've been bumped off your flight by a priority passenger." I shrugged it off and went in search of other travel arrangements. Such bumpings were common. Finally, I wrangled my way back to California by a series of bus rides and trains. Every ride I caught on that trip seemed to be on the oldest equipment possible. The train I rode on for most of the way had been pulled out of Weyerhaeuser retirement. It had cement floors and old gaslight lamps. No air-conditioning. It was so hot on the trip home, I opened the window and sat for extended hours on the hard, upright bench seats. At the end of the ride I had a lapful of soot from the engines. Travel took so long I was able to spend just two days at home. Mom was sure happy to see me. I tracked down a few friends from school and took Jerry Star out once or twice.

The ride back to Benning proved less eventful. My assignment, for some reason, turned out to be the 176th Infantry Regiment, a Virginia National Guard outfit, the unit providing the demonstration troops back at Benning. They were housed in brick buildings at the main post. It was no great assignment. I wasn't leading anything or in charge of anyone. The 176th consisted of three battalions and was commanded by a full colonel. I was just a lowly second lieutenant, one of the many. My first assignment was to lecture classes in aircraft recognition.

The war had started, and I had my uniform. My contribution to the war effort would be to hold a bunch of model airplanes each day for an hour or two in front of a group of maybe forty guys. It wasn't quite the action I had imagined.

· 11 ·

Decision of a Lifetime

IT WAS EARLY IN MY COMMISSION WITH THE 176TH AT FORT
Benning. Just another average day as a soldier in the United States
Army.

I woke up late, yawned, stretched, shuffled on my ODs, and me-
andered down to the mess hall for breakfast. There was no reveille at
sunrise for me, no predawn ten-mile hike. Pancakes were piled high
on my plate, and I downed them with syrup and butter, eggs and
toast, orange juice and coffee. Breakfast over, I strolled over to the officers' club, where there was an indoor pool, donned my trunks in the
locker room, and took a leisurely swim. I showered off, got into clean
gear, taught my class for an hour, then did whatever the hell else I
wanted for the rest of the morning.

Then I got some lunch.

Then I kicked around all the rest of the afternoon.

Then I got set to play baseball in the evening. I'd be playing outfield in a first-class ballpark with a good-sized grandstand, well lighted for night games.

Just another day in the Army for me.

Yep. And that's about all I was doing, too.

IT HAD ALL BEGUN DAYS EARLIER WHEN I REPORTED TO COLONEL Cox, commanding officer of the 176th Infantry Regiment. The exact meeting was quite short. He greeted me briefly, turned me over to his adjutant, and left the room. The adjutant looked me over and told me to report to company headquarters. When I walked into company headquarters, I was greeted by the personnel officer, just the lowly corporal who happened to be sitting behind the desk at the time.

"Lieutenant Compton," said the corporal. He shuffled papers behind his typewriter. "It says here your orders are to conduct aircraft identification classes."

I nodded.

"We've also got you down to play baseball," he said. "You're supposed to go see the manager."

"Baseball?"

"Yeah. You're to report to the ballpark tonight at 1800 hours. That's about all I know."

The corporal didn't give me much more information than that. I had to fill in the blanks in bits and pieces to learn what was going on. It turned out my orders were to be a member of the regimental baseball team, which played in a league on base. A number of professional ballplayers, including major leaguers, had joined the military and played for the league. We played day games on weekends and night ball during the week. On the team I joined, another guy was already assigned to play catcher, my usual position, so I played outfield instead. I didn't mind playing a different position. The guys on the team were all quality players and it felt good to get out on the field again.

Having a quality regimental baseball team meant bragging rights for a commanding officer. It wasn't as bad as I'm making it sound. Baseball has always been America's pastime, and the war years were no exception. A high percentage of major league players had joined the military (one estimate puts it as high as 90 percent), and star players were viewed as a valuable recruiting and morale tool as the country joined together for war. Everybody helped out wherever they could. Even Hillerich & Bradsby, makers of the famous Louisville Slugger baseball bats, turned their wood-turning skills to the production of stocks for the M-1 carbine rifle. Virtually every significant American military installation around the world boasted a formal baseball team. Officials sponsored hundreds of exhibition contests, and most soldiers I knew enjoyed going to as many games as they could.

Various branches went to great lengths to best their rivals. The Navy ended up with Gene Woodling from the Indians, Virgil "Fire" Trucks from the Tigers, and Lynwood "Schoolboy" Rowe from the Dodgers. Among the players in the league at Fort Benning were Ewell "The Whip" Blackwell, the Reds' starting left-handed pitcher, and Bob Ramazzotti, the Cubs' star infielder. Each branch of the service aimed to collect the best cadre of major leaguers in an attempt to secure the best team.

If you were a good baseball player, it was hard to do anything in the military except play ball. Nearly all baseball players were prevented from seeing combat. The great Joe DiMaggio, as well as Hank Greenberg, the Tigers' star power hitter, were among the many ballplayers who asked for combat duty but had it denied. Bob Feller from the Cleveland Indians was one of the few baseball players whose combat request was granted. He was chief of an antiaircraft gun crew of the USS *Alabama* and was decorated with five campaign ribbons and eight battle stars.

Included among the athletes at Fort Benning was Bob Waterfield, who had been our star quarterback at UCLA. Bob talked to me one day about organizing some football games on base with him coaching and me assisting. I went over to his house where his wife, Jane Russell, served us snacks and hovered in the room where we planned our coaching strategy. Jane was a real looker. Together with Lana Turner and Rita Hayworth, Jane embodied the popular "sweater girl" look of the era, and many servicemen had pinups of her. Bob seemed totally engrossed in the playbook he was mapping out. I remember thinking that if I were married to Jane Russell, I'd never give football a second glance.

I was over at the Waterfields' house several times while at Benning. Once, Bob asked me to escort Jane to a dance. He had to be on night maneuvers and didn't want her to go alone. Jane didn't want to miss the event, so Bob asked me to go and run interference for her. So I took Jane Russell to the dance. She was a very nice lady, very classy and well spoken, not a tramp at all, as she's sometimes portrayed. She spent most of the dance talking to some fellows from the University of Georgia who had played in the same Rose Bowl as me. Years later Jane founded the World Adoption International Fund, an organization that pioneered adoptions from foreign countries by Americans. She also started the Hollywood Christian Group, a weekly Bible study at her home for spiritual seekers in the movie business.

For my part, the only military duty I was required to perform in the 176th was a one-hour class each morning in aircraft identification. I'd hold up models of the A6M2 Zero, the main fighter plane of the Imperial Japanese Navy, and the Nakajima Ki-43 Oscar, the Army fighter plane, which was even lighter than the Zero, and point out a few of each plane's characteristics. For instance, the Zero was armed with two 20mm cannons, had a long range, and climbed quickly. It wasn't hard stuff.

But the longer I played baseball for the military, the more discontented I became. I understood the big picture of baseball boosting morale, both to the military men and the country. But to me, there was a larger task that needed to be done. I certainly didn't want to

ride out the war Stateside holding up airplane models for new recruits. I wanted to head overseas.

From talking to the guys on base, I knew our commanding officer
would block any application for transfer made by a ballplayer. But
there were two situations where the CO was powerless. First, if you
applied for flight training. Second, if you applied to be a paratrooper.
Flight training took a full year to make it up the ranks from cadet to
pilot. I thought the war would be over in a year—we all did. But jump
training only took a month. That left only one option.

Some people will say I was crazy for wanting to go to war. Sometimes it's tough even for me to put myself inside my own head. My decision hinged on my competitive nature. It doesn't matter what's
involved, I want to win. For instance, I've never been one to simply
run around a track or do calisthenics in the morning. I've got to play
handball or racquetball—some sort of game that requires a measur-
able challenge or skill. And whenever I play something, I play hard.
Not obnoxiously. I simply like to succeed. I even enjoyed taking tests
in school to see what kind of score I could get. So when it came to the
military, in my mind we were being trained to fight a war. Overseas
was where the action was. I didn't feel content sitting around in the
backwoods being a waterboy for someone else to play the game. I
wanted to be in the action. I wanted to win.

I don't think anybody criticized my decision for signing up. I
doubt if I told my mother the ramifications of what I had done. I had
graduated from OCS in May 1943. I was in jump school by July. All
in all, I played baseball for six weeks. Long enough to know I wasn't
doing what I needed to.

There were no brochures or anything to explain the program. I
didn't know anything about being a paratrooper. Although the idea
had been around for some time, the actual practice of using parachutes to drop troops into battle positions was a relatively new technology in 1943. I had met only one paratrooper before. Back at
UCLA, Sal Matheson, a brother of a guy who played center with me,

came back to campus one day. He was a couple years ahead, had already graduated, and joined the paratroopers. I talked with Sal a bit and remember admiring his uniform. He went on to have a long career in the military and eventually retired as a major general.

The paratroopers already had an impressive reputation. Airborne officers were already considered to be among the Army's most valuable officers. The drill sergeants who got you to that place were yellers and pushers—they let you know who was running the show. But they were good physical specimens themselves, and never asked you to do anything they wouldn't do themselves. I had heard a story of a paratrooper drill sergeant named Fioritto, a small guy but in incredible shape, known for his rope-climbing abilities. He had been in a training plane with his class when the plane encountered engine problems. He helped shove all his men out the door safely before riding the plane down in a ball of fire. That act of giving his life for his men made an impression on me I'll never forget.

But truthfully, when I signed up for the paratroopers, I had no idea what I was getting myself into. My biggest goal was to get transferred out of playing baseball. I must not have had a fear of heights, because the idea of jumping out of planes didn't bother me. What would my life have been like if I hadn't made that decision? I probably could have spent the rest of the war Stateside, getting up whenever I wanted, eating long meals, swimming at the officers' club, and being a morale booster in the outfield.

Sometimes, however, you take the route least expected.

· 12 ·

Wearing the Wings

FALL IN!

The drill instructor (DI) went man to man down the line of Jump School candidates, inspecting us to see if we had everything in order. He was a well-muscled military regular, and our ranks didn't matter; the DI rode us all like recruits in boot camp. We weren't in Jump School as a unit. We were just a bunch of individuals who volunteered, all mixed in together.

Standing next to me was a full Army colonel, Colonel Cato. Anybody who wanted to join an airborne unit, even to command one, needed to go through Jump School the same as anyone else. His brother was E. Raymond Cato, chief of the California Highway Patrol, a very big name in California at the time. Colonel Cato was a West Pointer—it seemed like fancy company for me to be in. But anybody who wanted to wear the wings needed to be a qualified jumper—that meant going through Jump School first.

As the sergeant moved from the colonel to me, I hoped he would pass me by quickly, but no such luck. The DI gave me a once-over and leaned into my face. *"When did you last shave, Lieutenant?! When?!"* he shouted, inches from my nose. I decided to come clean immediately. "Last night, Sergeant," I said. I knew I was busted. It was a rule that you had to shave every morning before inspection. The night before I had been so tired, I'd decided to shave then instead.

Nothing escaped the sergeant. *"You have exactly seven minutes to get to that barrack, shave, then get back here!"* he shouted. The sergeant marked his watch. *"Go!"* He and I both knew it was a next-to-impossible timeline. I sprinted both ways. Nothing scrapes up your face like trying to shave in a hurry. I got back with half a second to spare, just in time to head out on a fifty-minute run. The hot Georgia sun beat down on us. We kept a good pace. Although it was early morning, the humidity already felt like an ocean of warm vapor all around us. By the time we got back to the instruction area, we were soaked through.

"Gather round. Time for push-ups. Give me fifty. Now!"

The DI got down with us, and we all counted off together. There wasn't much these DIs wouldn't do, and anything they asked us to do, they had done first. They had a lot of credibility in our eyes. Some were screaming bastards, but most were professional military leaders, and their goal was to get you to the other side alive. A lot of military training is designed around how to instill self-discipline in a recruit. Good DIs teach that by example. For instance, it might be 102 degrees outside, with the mosquitoes biting like crazy. You might all be standing at attention. You'll want to swat those mosquitoes, but you can't move. The mosquitoes will be biting the DIs as well, but they won't swat them, either, simply to demonstrate self-discipline. It might sound like a stupid thing to let yourself be bit by a mosquito, but self-discipline fosters confidence. If you can't handle a mosquito bite, you can't handle anything.

The night I shaved at the wrong time was near the end of the first week of Jump School. I swore it was the last time I'd ever try to get away with anything. I just wanted to get through and get my wings. Parachute classes were located right there on the grounds at Fort Benning. Training consisted of four stages referred to as A, B, C, and D. A-stage was entirely physical. Each day involved dawn-to-dusk physical training. We'd head out for a run, then come back for a half hour of calisthenics. Multiple sets of push-ups and grass drills might be the case, followed by more push-ups, rope climbs, and jumping jacks. Each day was varied.

We also practiced a variety of martial arts and hand-to-hand combat techniques. We learned chokeholds and how to take a man down. Those who weren't already physically fit fell away immediately. It was nonstop exertion all day long in the sticky Georgia heat. Sometime during A-stage we were deep into a set of "Indian clubs" when my eyes got blurry. Indian clubs were a popular exercise device of the era. They were shaped like bowling pins and weighted at the ends. They loosened and strengthened your arms and shoulders and could be deceptively strenuous. We swung them around in various patterns until we nearly keeled over—we did them so long the clubs felt almost hypnotic after a while.

I was in good physical shape from football season but wasn't used to the humidity of Georgia in the dead of summer. As we stood in formation swinging the Indian clubs for all they were worth, a DI walked by me. They normally walked through the ranks as we did our exercises; this was nothing unusual. "What's the matter, Lieutenant?" he asked. "You look woozy." His voice was crisp, but he wasn't shouting this time.

"I think I might be going to black out," I said, just as the darkness closed in around me. There was little sympathy in Jump School, but having men pass out from heat or exertion during training was not uncommon. A DI's goal was never to kill you. The sergeant ran to get me some salt tablets. In California, I had never heard of salt tablets. At Benning, they kept dispensers of salt tablets on the sides of buildings.

B-stage involved more physical training and jumping from low heights, such as from a mock fuselage door of a C-47 into a sawdust pit, or from a tower about thirty feet high. You wore a harness attached to a slack cable that glided you to the ground. At Jump School you got to know everything about parachutes—how to pack them, wear them, adjust them, rely on them—the works. You learned all the techniques needed to accomplish a mission with absolute confidence—how to stay loose, get ready for impact, let your legs absorb the shock, roll, and collapse your chute quickly, release your harness, unsling your weapon, and deploy into position.

C-stage involved more physical training and dropping with a fully open chute from the tall towers.

D-stage was five live jumps from a C-47.

The first three stages were fairly uneventful for me. On the last stage, when I jumped out of a plane for the first time, the shroud lines threw a couple of half hitches around my ankle and I had to get untangled before I reached the ground, which I described in detail in the first chapter.

All in all, I survived, graduated, and finally got my wings, the tiny silver parachute with wreaths around it. The Army Parachutist Badge, or "jump wings," is awarded to all soldiers in any service who complete U.S. Army Airborne School. It signifies that the soldier is a trained Army parachutist and qualified to conduct airborne operations. I wore mine with pride.

Following Jump School, I attended a short course on demolitions. It was a couple weeks long. Pretty much everybody took one of two extra courses: demolitions or communication. Communication was learning Morse code. I didn't think I had the mind for dots and dashes, so I signed up for demolitions instead. They taught us how to use detonators, blasting caps, and fuses—that type of stuff. Few things on the battlefield have the efficiency and destructive power of explosives. Demolitions were used to clear obstacles such as rock or rubble, construct craters, and sometimes as a weapon to destroy buildings or the enemy. You were taught to compute the amount of explosives needed for specific tasks, how far away you'd need to be when a blast occurred, and how to shape the charges that triggered the explosions.

Following demolitions I was assigned to the 515th Parachute Infantry Regiment, stationed in the aptly named "Frying Pan" area of Fort Benning. When the sun beat down, which seemed like always, this flat, hardpatch dirt area of the camp simply sizzled. My unit soon became part of the 17th Airborne Division. We were transferred to Camp Mackall, North Carolina. My commander thought I should take a course in chemical weapons training and sent me to Edgewood Arsenal, Maryland. Following the training, which didn't amount to much, I was sent back to Mackall.

While I was with the 17th, I met again Jack Singlaub, also with the unit. We were in the same year at UCLA and he was a friend of mine. He was number one in our ROTC class of 1943. I was number two. When I returned from chemical weapons training in Maryland, Jack was no longer with the 17th. In my absence, representatives from the Office of Strategic Services (OSS) had come to our unit, and Jack had volunteered. The OSS was a wartime intelligence unit formed by General William Donovan, which later evolved into the Central Intelligence Agency (CIA).

Singlaub went on to have quite a career. During World War II he led a mission that rescued four hundred Allied POWs from a Japanese camp on Hainan. He became a highly decorated OSS officer and major general in the Army. Singlaub was one of the founding members of the CIA and was active for more than forty years in overt and covert operations. He headed CIA operations in postwar Manchuria during the Chinese Communist revolution, led troops in the Korean War, managed the secret war along the Ho Chi Minh Trail in Vietnam, and worked with the Contras in Nicaragua.

Singlaub eventually became chief of staff of the United Nations Command in South Korea. He was forced to resign from his command in 1978 after criticizing President Jimmy Carter's plans to reduce the number of troops in the area. By contrast, Singlaub enjoyed a good relationship with President Ronald Reagan and worked over the next years to establish a variety of anti-Communist resistance movements in Angola, Mozambique, Ethiopia, Laos, Cambodia, Vietnam, Nicaragua, and Afghanistan.

Amazing—the people you meet when you're young.

WHILE I WAS WITH THE 17TH AT MACKALL, ORDERS CAME THAT would change my life forever. It would prove to be one of my luckiest breaks, though I didn't know it at the time.

The orders were to join the 101st Airborne Division, already stationed in Aldbourne, England. I didn't know anything about the unit or the intensive training they had already received at Camp Toccoa. I didn't know, either, why I was suddenly assigned to them. The only possible connection I've been able to make in subsequent years is this: A guy at UCLA I played football with had an older brother named Sal Matheson—he was the guy whose uniform I had admired. Matheson had been in ROTC and had left campus to become a paratrooper. When he came back to campus one day, I talked to him and we developed an immediate rapport. He was in regimental headquarters with Colonel Robert Sink, regimental commander of the 506th Infantry, and told me years later that he had seen my name on some list and was responsible for my transfer to the 101st. Matheson later became a major general.

It didn't matter to me then. New orders in hand, I went to the point of embarkation at Camp Kilmer, New Jersey, then departed from the Port of New York on the *Queen Elizabeth*. It was December 1943, and we were set to cross the frosty North Atlantic, unescorted, in five days.

The *Queen Elizabeth* was a steam-powered ocean liner of the Cunard Steamship Company that had been outfitted to carry troops across the Atlantic in World War II. Painted gray for wartime maneuvers, she was the largest passenger ship afloat at the time. I don't know of any large-scale troop movement across the Atlantic that involved airplanes in those days. We all went across by sea.

Conditions on the ship were cramped for everybody—all around each wall iron-hung bunks were stacked four high. As many as sixteen bunks were crammed into staterooms designed for two. But because I was an officer, I was berthed above the waterline and had it better than many. There's an old military saying—R.H.I.P.—Rank Has Its Privileges. That was certainly true on the *Queen E*. I can't say I suffered mightily on the voyage. Officers ate in the ballroom, a large open room with columns and two-story ceilings. As soldiers, it was quite an ornate place to eat.

But every day I witnessed a depressing sight. I felt so sorry for the guys. Each afternoon they'd do a drill where everybody had to assemble on the top deck. The *Queen E* is huge. A lot of guys were jammed into the bowels of the ship, three or four decks down. I never went down to the very bottom myself, but I understood that as you went lower, conditions became progressively worse. My job during the daily drills was to stand at one of the hatchways on one of the lower decks to expedite traffic up the ladder. Some of the guys were absolutely green around the gills when they came up. Just miserable. I silently thanked God I didn't have to be down there, with my tendency to motion sickness. Even the *Queen Elizabeth*, big as it was, rolled side to side with a constant slow sway. I would have been sicker than a dog if I had been down in the bilge.

Arriving in the United Kingdom, the ship sailed into Scotland's Firth of Forth, a big inlet navigable by oceangoing vessels, and dropped anchor. Troops were off-loaded by shore boats, placed on trains and trucks, and moved to southern England. My destination was the little village of Aldbourne, the location of E Company of the 506th Parachute Infantry Regiment. My first job would be assistant platoon leader of the 2d Platoon. This was it. This was why I quit playing baseball and volunteered to be a paratrooper.

I was set to join Easy Company. My life would never be the same.

· 13 ·

Joining Easy Company

YOU HAD TO EARN YOUR WAY IN.

When I got off the ship, a train took me inland as far as Birmingham, the largest of England's core cities. I hitched a ride farther south to Swindon, a city of canals and industrial streets, then caught another ride to Aldbourne, the picturesque little village where E Company was housed. Aldbourne was a town you'd see in postcards. Located in a small valley, the village had a town square dominated by a large church. The surrounding countryside was ideal for military training with its forests, creeks, and green fields.

On the last leg of the journey, I was all by myself. Clouds covered the December sky, and wintry showers fell almost nonstop. When you show up at an unfamiliar place, all you notice at first are stares. I got the feeling immediately that the men of Easy Company did not think too highly of "outsiders." They had already been through much together, even though they had yet to see combat. It wasn't that the men expressed outright mistrust of me. Nor were they hostile or even unfriendly. They simply wore the confident look of a group of soldiers who were close-knit, proud, and well trained.

When I arrived in Aldbourne, I asked around until I found Lieutenant Meehan, the company commander, who directed me to the platoon leader, Pat Sweeney, a second lieutenant like myself. My orders were to be Sweeney's assistant. "Compton," was all he said at first. One eye looked permanently cocked. "C'mon," he motioned with his hand. "This way."

As Sweeney took me over to the officers' quarters, I noticed he walked with a bit of a limp. How he got into the Army with that, I never knew. I had heard of guys rejected for much less. Sweeney pointed ahead. "Stow your gear there," he said. Officers were quartered in a large, two-story manor house at one end of Aldbourne's town square. The officers' mess was also located in that building. The soldiers of 2d Platoon, to which I was assigned, were billeted in stables built around a courtyard next to the officers' quarters. Other enlisted men were billeted in nearby Quonset huts, lightweight tubular buildings made of corrugated steel. The whole area looked damp and clammy.

Aldbourne was a farming town and primitive by 1940s standards. The house where I was billeted had belonged to a private citizen before it was requisitioned, as per military agreements between the American and British governments. The house had no running water. Inside, a stone washbasin sat on top of a woodstove. The only way to heat water was to pump it into the basin, start a fire, and heat it on the stove. Taking a bath would be next to impossible. After showing me the quarters, Sweeney took me over and introduced me to Lieutenant Dick Winters, leader of 1st Platoon, and Lieutenant Harry Welsh, his assistant.

Welsh was a guy you instantly liked. He had a fiery, scrapper look to him. He was a teacher back home, so I knew he had a compassionate side to him as well. Months later, after D-Day, Welsh became leader of 1st Platoon. One day, some time later, he and I were talking together at company headquarters, and the radio was tuned to the Armed Forces Network. A newscaster reported that the Russians were making great advances on the Eastern Front.

"If the Russians keep it up, we might not be called on for another jump," I remarked.

"You better not root too hard for the Russians," Welsh said. "We're going to have to fight them after this is all over." History proved Welsh prophetic. It has always impressed me that he predicted the Cold War even back then.

Winters was from eastern Pennsylvania and had grown up with a strict Mennonite background. He was a hard worker, serious, and had paid his own way through Franklin and Marshall College, where he had been a business major. Winters became an officer the same way I did, by going through OCS at Fort Benning, although we were not there at the same time. He traveled from Benning to Toccoa and was one of the original members of Easy Company.

SO MUCH HAS BEEN WRITTEN OVER THE YEARS TO DESCRIBE Easy Company, I hesitate to write anything here for fear of duplicating what's already been said. If you are new to the subject, I recommend reading Stephen Ambrose's book *Band of Brothers,* or watching the video series by the same name, which traces Easy Company from its formation through the end of the war.

Briefly, Easy Company, or E Company as it's commonly known, was made up of about 150 guys. The company was divided into three platoons; about forty fighting men in each platoon plus support personnel. Easy Company was one of nine companies that comprised the 506th Parachute Infantry Regiment (PIR), which had about 1,500 men. The 506th was part of the 101st Airborne Division, which had at least ten thousand soldiers.

Most members of Easy Company today, including myself, are strangely both honored and embarrassed at being singled out for all the attention we've received over the years. Really, we became famous only because Stephen Ambrose, while a history professor at the University of New Orleans, was a neighbor to Walter Gordon, who had been a corporal in E Company during the war. If Walter Gordon had been in A Company or D Company, or probably any other company for that matter, *Band of Brothers* would have been written about a different group of soldiers. We were probably not the most decorated, verifiably not the most wounded, did not suffer the most killed (although one statistic puts our unit's casualty rate as high as 150 percent), and did not have as many days of contact with the enemy as some of the other companies of our division.

That said, Easy Company still comprised a stalwart and elite group of men. I doubt if anyone would ever describe E Company as "average." Throughout the course of the war, the unit encountered situations that required extraordinary bravery, as many units did. I am honored to be included in their ranks. But when I officially joined Easy Company in December 1943, it took me a while to feel like I belonged to this group.

Easy Company, together with the 506th, had been formed at Camp Toccoa, Georgia, in 1942. At that swampy rural site, men from all walks of life—volunteers all—assembled to learn how to become paratroopers. They had marched an unbelievable 120 miles from Toccoa to Fort Benning, where they went through Jump School together. By the time I reached Easy Company in England, they had already trained together for nearly two years. I felt a bit envious that I hadn't gone through Toccoa with all the guys. They talked about it often and referred to their experiences there. And of course, the men had a common bond with their hatred of Sobel.

Back at Toccoa, Easy Company had been led by Captain Herbert Sobel (portrayed in the *Band of Brothers* miniseries by David Schwimmer). Sobel was known for his excessive strictness, often revoking men's weekend passes for petty infractions and heaping up additional physical training on them during weekends and evenings. He once brought a court-martial against Winters for failing to inspect a latrine. Sobel's extreme training tactics paid off in some ways—he ended up creating a hardened and highly physically fit company. From all the tough training they received, Easy Company could boast the finest performance record in the regiment.

Yet Sobel's men believed he lacked tactical and combat skills. After several of Sobel's noncommissioned officers refused to fight under him, believing him unfit to follow into battle, Sobel was reassigned to the Chilton Foliat Jump School, where he became a parachute instructor for noncombat officers. Lieutenant Thomas Meehan, a transfer from B Company, took over for Sobel.

I never met Sobel personally, and it's been controversial as to whether Sobel was truly as inept as the miniseries made him out to be. Sobel's second son, Michael Sobel, has spoken out in his father's defense in recent years, and most veterans I know respect Michael for doing that. My good friend Don Malarkey, who was with Easy Company from the beginning, insists that Sobel had his good points. Sobel's contributions helped mold Easy Company into the formidable fighting force it came to be.

Easy Company had been deployed to England at the end of August 1943, nearly four months before I joined them. Just before the company boarded the ship to cross the Atlantic, Sobel wrote letters to loved ones back home on behalf of his men. I have a copy of one of those letters in my files today. It shows a side of Sobel that perhaps isn't talked about as much. It's written in cursive on a Company E letterhead and reads:

27 August 1943

Dear Sir:

Soon your brother-in-law, Pfc. Robert Van Klinken, will drop from the sky to engage and defeat the enemy. He will have the best of weapons and equipment and have had

*months of hard, strenuous training to prepare him for suc-
cess on the battlefield.*

    *Your frequent letters of love and encouragement will arm
him with a fighting heart. With that he cannot fail but will
win glory for himself, make you proud of him, and his
country ever grateful for his service during its hour of need.*

*Herbert M. Sobel, Capt.,
Commanding*

ANOTHER LETTER, WHICH FELL INTO MY HANDS AROUND THAT
same time, was short and sweet.

    This one was from Jerry Star, my high school sweetheart, and
came to me while I was at Aldbourne. It wasn't exactly a "Dear John"
letter, but it may as well have been. Jerry conveyed the impression
that she was not exactly waiting for me to get home. The letter was
friendly, but I wanted more than a friendship. I walked out of the
mess hall, letter in hand, shaking my head. Malarkey saw me and
shook his head as well. He looked like he understood immediately—
he was in the same boat with a girl he was dating back home. We
spent a lot of time commiserating with each other. He and I and Bill
Guarnere became fast friends and spent a lot of time in our off hours
at Aldbourne, just hanging out talking.

    In my early days after arriving in Aldbourne, I don't think I fully
had a grasp of what was expected of me. Sweeney soon got transferred, and I became the leader of 2d Platoon. Lieutenant Ray
Schmitz became my assistant. Our platoon sergeant was Jim Diel,
who later earned a battlefield commission.

    So there I was with the elite 101st, and my own military experi-
ence only involved ROTC, OCS at Benning, a short stint with the
176th Infantry where I played baseball, and a couple of training
schools. I looked after my guys wherever I could, but much of the

time I kept my own counsel and relied on my noncommissioned officers (NCOs) to get the job done. I had very little contact with anybody outside of E Company. Some officers from D and F companies were billeted together with us, so I knew a few others. But mostly I had contact only with my men and the other officers of E Company.

It was a strange relationship with my men at first. I don't think I did too much "leading." Don Malarkey, Bill Guarnere, Joe Toye, and my other NCOs already knew how to run things pretty well without me. I thank those three for making me feel welcome to the unit right from the start. Mostly I'd just say things like: "Hey Guarnere, we're supposed to be doing so and so." And he'd go and do whatever needed to be done. I just sort of stood around and watched them perform. I never found any occasion to administer any discipline of any kind or chew anybody out, the way some officers do.

Conventional military doctrine frowns on having too close a relationship between officers and enlisted personnel. I understand the reason behind it, and do not challenge it today. But I must say that I got along with many of the enlisted personnel in my platoon just fine. They were all guys about my age—20, 21 years old, some of them just out of college just like me. I was supposed to hang out with other officers only, but it wasn't in my nature to be anything other than myself or hang out with people whom I didn't like. I didn't enjoy playing poker, and I didn't drink, so I didn't frequent the pub or the poker games that appealed to many of the officers. Once I came out of the officers' mess and noticed a group of our soldiers having a craps game inside a big empty glider box situated in the stable area. I walked over and watched. Dinner was just over and it was still daylight. There wasn't any television to watch in those days.

"Hey Lieutenant—you want in?" said someone in the game. I think it was Johnny Martin, a staff sergeant and all-around good guy.

"Why not?" I said. I threw down some pound notes and *faded the shooter*. English money didn't mean too much to us. We were used to

American greenbacks of course, and the English money felt like Monopoly money to us.

I lost.

Winters, who was not company commander at the time but a fellow platoon leader, observed my conduct and took me to task. The issue wasn't gambling. It was being overly friendly with enlisted men. In the video series, Winters and I are riding in a jeep when he reprimands me. (Winters is portrayed by actor Damian Lewis.) He also tells me the reason for the reprimand. But in real life, I already knew the reasons, and we were just standing around when he chewed me out.

"What were you doing?" Winters asked.

"I dunno," I said, "it was just a bunch of guys. We were having a good time." This next line is verbatim. It's always struck me as a strange remark—

"If you like 'em so much," Winters said, "why don't you move out of the officers' quarters and go sleep with them." (He meant "sleep" in the sense of "bunk" with them, not in a sexual connotation.)

I got a little hot under the collar. "Maybe I will," I retorted. "I have more in common with them than I do with you." The truth was, Winters was correct. I was wrong. Looking back, I probably would have done things differently. I don't hold myself up today as having been an exemplary officer. I didn't think I was then, either. The military reason for officers not being overly friendly with enlisted men is that when you're all in combat together, an enlisted man might not immediately obey an order if it's coming from an officer he considers a friend. Likewise, an officer may balk at giving an order, particularly a difficult one, if he's on too good of terms with an enlisted man. And orders need to be given in the military. That's a fact.

But I've never found it easy to order anybody around. I'd rather ask someone for something than demand it. I'm sure that came out in my demeanor as an Army officer. In the end, I've never felt that my attitude toward my men resulted in any lack of discipline or insubordination on their part. It was not in my nature to be anything other than myself. If I consider somebody a friend, enlisted man or otherwise, I don't hide it.

Winters and I were never close friends through the war years, but were always respectful of each other. We both had a job to do and did it. Simple as that. Winters later recommended me for the Silver Star, which I'm grateful for. In later years we've seen more of each other at company reunions and become closer. I'm thankful to know him today. For the most part, everybody in Easy Company seemed to get along okay, although there was always the usual friction that happens when people live in close quarters.

I didn't actually see this event, but news of it spread quickly all over camp. A couple of cooks lived in some Quonset huts nearby. The cooks were not paratroopers, just regulars assigned to the battalion. They were known for gambling a lot. Somebody got the idea that the cooks were cheating in cards and tossed a white phosphorous grenade into their hut at night. The explosion could have killed them. Turned out there were no injuries, but it was a pretty serious event. We never found out who did it.

In later years, Malarkey (portrayed by actor Scott Grimes in the miniseries) has credited three things that helped me become accepted as a part of Easy Company at Aldbourne. I don't know if I agree with him or not, but I'll list them here for the record: my size (I was built stockier than most paratroopers were in 1944, and I guess it's tough to disrespect someone who's bigger than you); my reputation as a football and baseball star from UCLA (I disagree with the word "star," but that's the word Malarkey uses); and the fact that I was pretty easygoing by nature. I wasn't the average officer, and I guess the men liked that about me.

You can take all that for what it's worth, but that's what Malarkey says anyway.

ONCE WHEN WE WERE IN ALDBOURNE, I WAS RUNNING IN A field, twisted my ankle in a gopher hole, and snapped my fibula, the same injury I'd had in high school. It healed pretty fast and I could walk on it pretty quickly. Good thing. Something huge was building, and I wanted to be a part of it, whatever it was going to be.

Each day, great formations of bombers flew overhead, as high as you could see in the sky. Thousands of them, all headed for Europe. They came back at night, some limping home with one motor out, straggling through the air. They were bombing the hell out of the enemy, softening up the coast. The planes were stationed all over England. They rendezvoused somewhere over England, we never knew where, and passed over us in Aldbourne. They were pretty well formed up by the time we could see them. The numbers of them were just staggering. I looked up into the sky with my mouth open whenever they flew over. I knew even then that American industry could be a key factor in winning the war. The ability to produce ships, tanks, planes, and rifles in the short amount of time that we did was simply astounding to me.

It was probably April or May 1944 when we went on a large-scale maneuver on the south coast of England. I remember looking at a map of that coast and comparing it with a map of the north coast of France. You could see they were almost a mirror image. The terrain we were operating in was almost identical, so you could almost pinpoint where the company was going to eventually end up.

At the end of May, all of Easy Company moved to an encampment at Upottery Airfield near Devon. Tension grew in anticipation of what we knew would soon come. We went through days of extensive briefing, and were shown maps and sand tables and instructed to memorize everything we saw. Our specific mission in Normandy soon became clear.

Gathered for the operation in early June 1944 were Allied land, air, and sea forces in what would become the largest invasion force in human history. The operation, given the code name Overlord, was to deliver five infantry divisions to the beaches of Normandy, France. The beaches were code-named Utah, Omaha, Gold, Juno, and

Sword. This operation would mark the start of the Western Allied effort to liberate mainland Europe from Nazi occupation. Altogether, some 2 million people from twelve Allied countries were set to take part in the operation; about 156,000 would see action on June 6. By June 30, more than 850,000 men, 148,000 vehicles, and 570,000 tons of supplies had been landed on the Normandy shores.

When meteorologists predicted a temporary break in the stormy weather that gripped the week preceding D-Day, General Eisenhower gave the final order that put the vast operation in motion in the early morning hours of June 5.

General Eisenhower's message was as follows:

Soldiers, Sailors and Airmen of the Allied Expeditionary Forces: You are about to embark upon the Great Crusade, toward which we have striven these many months. The eyes of the world are upon you. The hopes and prayers of liberty-loving people everywhere march with you. In company with our brave Allies and brothers-in-arms on other Fronts you will bring about the destruction of the German war machine, the elimination of Nazi tyranny over oppressed peoples of Europe, and security for ourselves in a free world.

Your task will not be an easy one. Your enemy is well trained, well equipped and battle-hardened. He will fight savagely.

But this is the year 1944! Much has happened since the Nazi triumphs of 1940–41. The united nations have inflicted upon the Germans great defeats, in open battle, man-to-man. Our air offensive has seriously reduced their strength in the air and their capacity to wage war on the ground. Our Home Fronts have given us an overwhelming superiority in weapons and munitions of war, and placed at our disposal great reserves of trained fighting men. The tide has turned! The free men of the world are marching together to Victory!

*I have full confidence in your courage, devotion to duty
and skill in battle. We will accept nothing less than full victory!*

*Good Luck! And let us all beseech the blessing of
Almighty God upon this great and noble undertaking.* *

Just before the jump, we had some time on our hands at Upottery.
Lieutenant Ray Schmitz and Winters got into a friendly wrestling
match, and Schmitz rolled over and hurt his neck. Hurt as he was, he
wasn't able to make the jump. That meant I didn't have two officers
in my platoon as others did. Winters and Welsh led 1st Platoon. Lieutenants Warren Roush and Fred "Moose" Heyliger led 3d Platoon. It
was just me and Diel, my platoon sergeant, leading 2d Platoon.

For Easy Company, June 6, 1944, dawned the same as any day.
We knew we were going to be part of something big, yet only history
would show how big the day would become.

---

*See http://www.eisenhower.archives.gov/ssa.htm, accessed May 21, 2007.

· 14 ·

Beyond D-Day

WITH OUR MACHINE GUNNERS LAYING DOWN FIRE OVER MY head, I worked my way across the field at Brecourt Manor on my belly. We had all made the jump into Normandy the night before, June 6, 1944, as I described in detail in chapters 2 and 3. This was it. We were really in the thick of things now.

Pushing through the branches of the hedgerow, I spotted a trench immediately in front of me. The trench made an L shape, with a large circle at the point of the L. I could have turned and gone either way. Immediately, I glimpsed two Germans in the end of the trench that ran perpendicular to the hedgerow. They were loading and firing one of their artillery pieces down onto the beach.

With my borrowed Thompson submachine gun in front of me, I sprang through the hedgerow and jumped into the trench. Winters, now acting as company commander, had told me to go take a look, then report back to him—but I figured I could take out the two Germans easily enough first.

The trench was about waist deep, and I ran along it toward the Germans. They were situated in another large circle at the end of the trench, a gun emplacement about a foot and a half deep. Halfway along the trench I stopped running and planted myself, the Thompson at hip level. I had never killed a man before but knew what I needed to do. The Germans heard me, stopped what they were doing, and wheeled around. Their faces were instantly full of surprise, replaced by instant horror. Without hesitation I pulled the trigger. All I heard was a soft *plunk*. I racked it back, and a live round popped out. My borrowed machine gun was completely useless.

I looked at the Germans. They looked at me in surprise. There were two of them and one of me. They were armed to the hilt. I wasn't.

Immediately from behind me I heard bursts of submachine gun fire. Earlier when I had crawled across the field, I hadn't seen Guarnere sneaking across after me. I've never been sure exactly when Wild Bill joined me. He may have just sprinted across, bold as ever, as soon as I reached the hedgerow. Bill had jumped in the trench behind me and was now firing by my side toward the two Germans. One went down right away. His body crumpled over, lifeless. The other German started running across an open field away from us. I yanked out a hand grenade and hurled it in his direction. I threw it reflexively. The grenade was right on the money. It detonated in the air right above the German's head, killing him instantly.

That was my first kill. Ask me today what it's like to kill a man in combat and I don't say much. I have no idea who he was, what he did outside the war, or if he had a wife or family. You just don't think. A man is trying to kill you, and you either need to kill him first or be killed waiting to assess the situation. Any decisions I needed to make had been solidified long before that. I doubt if the choice I made to throw the grenade was even conscious. A sense of duty had long since taken over. We knew what our orders were, and we followed through as best we knew how.

If anything, I felt stupid because my submachine gun didn't work.

I'm sure I could have been more effective if it had. Somebody wrote somewhere that I eventually got the borrowed Thompson working again, but that's not true. It had a broken firing pin, and I tossed it aside. I got another weapon somewhere and fired the hell out of it, but I don't remember where or from whom I got the other gun.

I have spotty memories of the action at Brecourt after that. I wish I could walk you through it sequentially, but it's all sort of a blur. I will say this: Our attack on Brecourt has been written up in military textbooks as a model small-arms assault, but nothing seemed very by-the-book about it to me. Mostly, it seemed like ad-lib fighting, developing strategy as we went along. Maybe that says it all. The American military man is taught ingenuity. If he's thrown into a chaotic situation, he figures out how to dig his way out.

Our specific task at Brecourt was to take out a battery of German guns firing onto the second causeway leading off Utah Beach. I couldn't tell you the exact progression of how we accomplished the mission. I never knew how many German guns we were supposed to take out—I couldn't tell you now or then if there were one or four or twenty. The only one I actually saw was the first gun we took out. I was never aware that we had any specific task other than to survive. We were getting shot at with a lot of machine gun fire. Nobody quite knew where all the machine gun fire was coming from, or what exactly we needed to do to neutralize it. Most of the time we hunkered down in trenches trying to avoid small-arms fire. In the course of Brecourt, somebody stuffed some ammunition down the barrels of those German guns—and that accomplished the mission. But it was never a big, planned, coordinated maneuver. It was all seat-of-the pants to me.

At one point, Lieutenant Bob Brewer, another guy, and I were taking quite a bit of machine gun fire. We spotted an empty gun emplacement, maybe twelve feet in diameter, and jumped in, bullets still streaming over us. A German wooden ammunition box was in the hole. On top of the box lay a German potato masher grenade. Somebody bumped the box, the grenade rolled off, and the pin fell out, which meant it was going to explode in a hurry. I saw it and yelled to the guys. There was nothing we could do. We couldn't jump up because we were getting too much machine gun fire overhead. All we could do was flatten ourselves against the embankment and brace ourselves for the blast. The grenade exploded in a shower of dirt and smoke. When the dust cleared, we looked around. Remarkably, nobody had a scratch.

Later on, someone in a book described the potato masher incident like this: "Buck was fooling around with a grenade and it went off." But that's not how it happened at all, and the person who wrote about it wasn't present when it happened. That description bothers me.

At another point during Brecourt I was crouched in a trench, trying to work my way down toward where this machine gun fire was coming from. A big tall kid came down the trench and ran by me. He had served as a waiter in the officers' mess, where I knew him, but he wasn't in my platoon and I didn't know his name. From the trench, I saw him spin around and sprint back toward me. He took a bullet in the back and collapsed in front of me, dead. Later, I found out he was Private First Class John Hall of A Company. He had coached the regimental basketball team. Two other soldiers from D Company were also lost at Brecourt. From Easy Company, Robert "Popeye" Wynn was wounded and evacuated back to England, but he recovered and joined us later just before Operation Market Garden.

A lot has been written about the infamous brass knuckles incident that happened in a lull during the fighting, with controversy surrounding exactly who did the hitting and why. You can take it for what you want, but this is my account: I saw it firsthand and gave our guy hell for doing it. Malarkey says I threatened the guy with a court-martial, but I don't remember that. I was too mad. I won't name the guy today. He doesn't deserve the recognition.

It happened back in a cleared area where we initially entered the trenches. Some of our guys had a German prisoner. The prisoner stood with his hands up, crying, probably afraid we were going to kill him or something. One of our guys, a desk jockey from headquarters, had an old trench knife with brass knuckles on the end of its handle. He came up full of bravado and belted the poor kid in the mouth. The German began bleeding all over and spitting out teeth. Probably broke his jaw. It was senseless. The prisoner wasn't offering us any resistance. I grabbed our guy by the arm, spun him around, and told him to get his ass out of there. We didn't need his crap.

I don't remember when victory was at last declared at Brecourt. All the German guns were eventually destroyed, and Winters must have ordered a fallback to our original starting point. History has shown that troops landing at Utah Beach had an easier landing due in part to what was accomplished at Brecourt. I'm happy about that. If our actions saved any of our boys' lives, that's part of what we were there to do.

Later on, some of us received medals for Brecourt. I received the Silver Star for valor in face of the enemy. But success in a military operation always feels short-lived. You shoulder your rifle and move on from there to the next battle.

THE DAYS OF PRECISE FRONTS, WHERE SOLDIERS FROM OPPOS-ing armies lined up in rows facing each other, were long since over before World War II began. Precise fronts are certainly long gone in the wars of today. With battle lines not clearly drawn, your enemy hides and disguises himself. And when that happens, accidents are bound to occur. I don't justify accidents. I only acknowledge their reality in combat situations. That said, an incident happened just after Brecourt that pains me to discuss, but it needs to be talked about. Secrets have power over us. Only when secrets are revealed can truth be known and freedom brought about.

Still in Normandy, Private Joe Liebgott and I were patrolling our way along some hedgerows at dusk. Across the field was another hedgerow, maybe fifty yards away. Two soldiers were skulking along, sort of hunched over, working their way along the other hedgerow.

Both soldiers wore German camouflage ponchos. One guy carried a German Mauser rifle, which I could tell because a Mauser has a silver disk at the side of the butt where the strap attaches. I spotted the ponchos and the rifle's silver disk, figured for sure they were Germans, and called Liebgott over. He came back; we both drew down and shot the soldiers. When we reached the bodies, we turned them over, saw their faces, and looked at their dog tags.

They were both Americans.

We had shot and killed a couple of our own.

Mere words will never convey the horror we felt.

The fact is that they were taking a huge chance, running around with German equipment on. They should not have been wearing the ponchos, nor carrying the German guns. We had no way of knowing they weren't Germans, unless we had gotten really close to them. And running over to confront them, fully armed as they were, wasn't going to happen. I don't say that to justify myself. There is a sense of guilt that will always be part of the war for me. It's the guilt I feel from making mistakes. It's the guilt I feel because I survived. Surviving a war is such a tricky thing. Why does one man live through a chaotic situation when another man doesn't? Another time I was standing on a road, talking to a couple of other officers, and a random mortar round came in and hit right underneath us. The explosion knocked me flat on my face. I didn't get a scratch. Why?

McMillan, the guy from A Company from whom I got the busted Tommy gun in Normandy, survived his injury and went on to fight in Bastogne. He was lying well covered in a foxhole when a random piece of shrapnel about the size of my little finger hit him in the chest, killing him instantly. Why did he survive one attack only to get killed in another? Particularly in a situation as random as that? Out of all the horror of war, the guilt of survival is one of the things that haunts me most to this day. I will never know why I survived when so many others did not. When it comes to understanding any of this, I have long since given up trying.

· 15 ·

Carentan

I HAVE SKETCHY MEMORIES OF THE BATTLE OUTSIDE CARENTAN, which happened a few days after D-Day. Geographically, Carentan sits at the corner of Utah and Omaha beaches. Basically, controlling Carentan was the key to controlling an important road network. The Allies wanted to funnel troops and tanks through Carentan into Europe. We reached a section of the town's outskirts that had been taken over by the battle-hardened German 6th Parachute Infantry Regiment, led by Colonel Von der Heydte. His orders, so they say, were to defend the town to the last man.

All I know is that we spent a lot of time sitting up on some high ground looking down on the town. It was a pretty well-protected position. Our boys from behind us shelled the bejesus out of the town with artillery. The shelling lasted a couple of days, maybe more. It was hard to see anything. I could see explosions landing everywhere in the town, and a big church tower. But it was hard to see any detail.

Overhead flew American P-38s, the distinctive fighter-bomber

planes with twin boom engines. They were nicknamed Yippies because of the whistling, whining sound they made coming through the
air. It was always a welcome sound to hear those guys zooming across
the sky. As long as they were up there, you knew you wouldn't encounter any air problems from the enemy. In World War II, America
had command of the air—no question about it.

In those days, if a company commander wanted to give an order
to an officer, he could either send a runner to have you come back to
headquarters, or he could send a runner to tell you something directly.
I didn't have a radioman in my platoon, so sending runners was the
usual way of communication. Winters was our company commander
by then, as Meehan had been killed on D-Day. Winters would have
been receiving his orders from Colonel Strayer, the battalion commander. There were still some guys from the 82d mixed in with us at
Carentan. We hadn't yet fully gone back to our original companies.

For some reason, one night we were told to get out on the road,
walk down toward Carentan, then take a right turn and go around
the town. It was dark and we hiked single file. Nobody quite knew
exactly where we were going or what we were supposed to be doing.
Somebody lost sight of the guy in front of him, so we got split in half.
The action made no sense to me—to move a whole battalion in single
file where your contact depended on seeing the guy in front of you—
it went against everything we had been taught. Then the word came
down to turn around and go back to where we had just come from,
up on the hill. To this day I can't tell you what happened.

So we sat on the hill for some more time. We took a bit of
shelling, but it wasn't bad. We were pretty well dug into our foxholes.
A day or so later they told us to move down into Carentan, so we
went off down the road again. It was daylight this time, not night,
and we walked straight in. The place was a shambles—crumbled
buildings, dead Germans lying all over. We just walked through it all.
Carentan was like a ghost town, just a vacant city. Some units way
ahead of us must have done all this and moved on. Or it may have

been caused by the barrage of artillery rained down on the town. I don't know.

They show Carentan in the series like it was some big, high-powered battle, but I never saw any of that—not on the way in, anyway. When we walked through, we didn't have to fire a shot. It was already slaughter alley. We walked down the main street and out the other side. It may have been a half mile, I'm not quite sure, but I'd estimate we saw a dead body every ten feet or less. Most of the bodies were pretty well mutilated, heads blown off, blood all over, that type of thing. I didn't see any townspeople anywhere, but there may have been some still around, hunkered down in their basements.

It's impossible to ever truly sense the mood of your men. We didn't act overtly victorious, probably because of all the gore and carnage, but I'd say we probably all felt like we had won one. Without a doubt, it looked like the town didn't belong to the Germans anymore.

We moved beyond Carentan into farmland area. Suddenly we heard the *rat-tat-tat* of small-arms fire aimed at us. Dirt spattered around us like hailstones. We fanned out into the hedgerows and fired back at the Germans. I lost track of time. The fighting was pretty intense, with a lot of yelling and confusion. We fired at anything we could see—rifles, bazookas, a couple of German tanks. Everybody fired back and forth—it was kind of a standoff. We couldn't lose this skirmish after our guys had taken the town. We were all just trying to figure out what to do next. Finally some American tanks showed up, and we made way for them. We were sure happy to see them. They finished up for us while we pulled back into town.

All was quiet back in Carentan. We spent several days there. Guys bunked down wherever they could. Some were in storefronts. Some of us officers were in one of the little hotels. We spent several days doing nothing before orders came to return to Utah Beach. We hiked back to Utah, got aboard one of the Navy's Landing Ship, Tanks (LSTs), and prepared to head back to England. Malarkey had found an old government-issue Harley motorcycle somewhere. Just before we got on board, he asked me if he could take it back with him to England. I didn't care. These guys had all been through a rough spot. My thought was whatever helped them out was okay by me. In the officers' quarters on the LST, I remember thinking the Navy had it pretty nice. They broke out some ice cream for us. They had it right there in the refrigerator. I hadn't seen ice cream in a long time.

All told, Easy Company had been in France for thirty-three days. When the final numbers came back, we had lost sixty men. Grief always comes in mixed bouts. You feel sad for the guys who didn't make it. But you know you've got to keep going, too. Aboard the ship, motoring back to England, I breathed a sigh of relief. It felt like we had made it through one round. For the time being at least, we were on our way to some sort of normalcy.

WE SPENT THE LATTER PART OF SUMMER 1944 BACK IN ALD- bourne. Everything felt pretty quiet. We heard some talk of the war soon being over. When we weren't training, I spent my time writing letters back home and shooting the bull with Malarkey and Guarnere. One incident that happened during this time still bothers me a bit. In the *Band of Brothers* miniseries, Lieutenant Lewis Nixon is depicted as an all-around swell guy. Even though Nixon (portrayed by actor Ron Livingston) is shown to have some faults, for example, he has a drinking problem, he's also shown as Winters's best friend and confidant.

I must say, however, that Nixon was never a particular favorite of mine. Apparently he did not care for me, either. Nixon had been a Yale man and always struck me as a bit of a highbrow. He jumped at Normandy and had been promoted to battalion intelligence officer shortly after Carentan. One day soon after our return from France, he and I were having a casual conversation when he gratuitously remarked that he had no use for "jocks," directing his remark at me. He considered us "stupid" (his words) for spending all our time in college practicing and sweating while he spent all his time out "partying."

Then out of the clear blue he announced he was appointing me as battalion physical training officer. That meant I had the duty of taking the battalion on an hour-long run each day. The order wasn't really within the scope of his authority, but he had no trouble getting the battalion to issue an order to that effect. I had no problem as physical fitness officer, and I had no problem with leading the men on a daily run. But when the order was issued, it prescribed two types of uniforms for this particular activity. For the enlisted men, the uniform was to be T-shirts and jump pants. For officers, the uniform was olive drabs. I was the only officer who would be making the run, which Lewis knew.

Picture it: There I was running each morning, sweating my butt off in a long-sleeved woolen shirt, woolen pants, and a necktie. Five hundred guys ran the course dressed in normal fitness gear, and one officer—me—led the group, dressed up like a damn peacock.

All thanks to Lewis Nixon.

Take that for what it is.

MOST EVERYBODY GOT SOME LEAVE TIME THE SECOND TIME WE were in Aldbourne. I decided to take a short trip up to Loch Lomond, Scotland. Lieutenant Bob Brewer and I headed out together and made a stopover in London on the way. While walking through Hyde Park, one of the largest parks in central London, we heard one of the German V-1s overhead. The V-1 was a pilotless monoplane powered by a pulse-jet motor. It carried a one-ton warhead. The Germans had developed rocketry early on and were in the practice by then of launching V-1s indiscriminately at London's civilian population. Londoners had apparently gotten used to the bombings, because everybody around us seemed to know what to do. But this was the first one that Brewer and I had ever encountered.

We could hear the vibration of the V-1's drone as it came on. Then sudden silence, which meant the bomb was ready to drop. Brewer and I hit the grass. The bomb hit a building a block away and exploded. There wasn't a ton of damage, but it felt pretty brutal. It gave us a taste of what Londoners had learned to live with.

The trip continued without incident. Brewer and I wore our uniforms the whole time, and the Scottish people were very warm and friendly. We housed in a small bed-and-breakfast, and the people who ran it had an automobile and some gas (I don't know how, because rationing was in effect). They took us on a tour of Dunoon and up to the Holy Loch as well as to Loch Lomond. Some American soldiers had it in mind to be anti-British, anti-Scottish, whatever—the idea being that we were over there to save their skins. But I never felt that. I felt we had a common bond with the British. They were fighting valiantly for their country. I never ran into any Brits who were anti-American, either. Even at Aldbourne, they'd invite us over for dinner every now and then.

I liked Brewer a lot. He was from California, where he had attended a military school in the San Fernando Valley. He also had his commission through an ROTC program, so we always had a lot to talk about. Right after D-Day, word came out that Brewer had been hit between the eyes with a piece of shrapnel and killed. But when I got to Aldbourne after Carentan, there was Brewer with a scab between his eyes and in fine form. Later, in Eindhoven, Brewer was making his way across an open field when a sniper's bullet hit him in the neck. The bullet went through his jaw and out the other side. He lay on the ground, blood spurting out of his jugular. Word came down the line again that Lieutenant Brewer had died. After I had been hit, I went to an American hospital in Oxford, and there sat Brewer, sitting in bed reading. He had two little scabs on his neck.

"Brewer!" I said, "I thought you were dead again!"

"Not a chance," he said, grinning.

Brewer stayed in the service and had quite a long career with the CIA.

All in all, the months we spent in Aldbourne for the second time were fairly quiet. We had several aborted missions—I can't even remember where they were to take place. General Patton and the Allied forces were making such fast progress across Europe that they were overrunning their targets with ground forces. We kept training, too, but it wasn't overly difficult.

When guys don't have enough to do, sometimes they get into trouble. Ours were no exception. One morning I looked around, and Malarkey and Guarnere weren't there for morning assembly.

"Anybody seen these guys?" I asked my platoon.

Nobody had.

I shook my head. "Well, everybody wait here," I said. "I'll run up to the barracks to see if I can find them." I walked up the road out of town to the house where the sergeants bunked. I walked in the barracks and gave a low whistle. . . .

I will digress at this point and not mention exactly what I saw. Truth is, I don't know the details of what had actually transpired. I didn't really care then or now, and over the years various versions of this story have come out, so who knows? But this is fact: Guarnere and Malarkey were in the house, as well as two other sergeants. And there were two attractive English girls in the house, too, both in various stages of undress. So you can make your guesses as to what exactly went down.

I glared at the guys. "You're supposed to be at assembly," I said. "You better get these girls out of here or we're all going to be in big trouble. The officer of the day will be coming around to inspect soon. If he catches you, you'll really get it."

"Okay, okay, we will," they promised.

The officer of the day was a rotating assignment. You put on a sidearm and walked around inspecting stuff. That day it was Lieutenant Thomas Peacock, not one of my favorite people. He was a debater at Washington State and had always struck me as sort of a prissy guy. I headed back to the assembly. A short time later, Peacock strode down the hill.

"Hey Tom," I said, "did you do the inspection of my sergeants' barracks yet?"

"Yes," he said flatly.

"How was it? Okay?"

"You know what I found," he growled.

"Tom, let's talk. Can you just forget about it and not report it? They're all good guys. They just got back from the front. Cut them some slack, will ya? Nobody got hurt."

"It's my duty to report it," he said. "I'm officer of the day."

So he did.

Peacock told Winters. Winters put Malarkey and Guarnere on kitchen duty, which was quite an embarrassment for them. Winters also made Guarnere go into the town square at night and give close order drills to imaginary squads. Which meant that Guarnere had to go about hollering "forward march" and "about face" and junk like that to nobody except himself. It was a humiliating punishment.

I went to Winters privately and asked him not to do this. He insisted. I guess as company commander he had to do something, but I was pretty sure that under the Articles of War, Winters couldn't impose that type of punishment on a noncommissioned officer. He needed to bust them down a grade first. You simply couldn't have a sergeant peeling potatoes or doing any of that humiliating crap.

Winters eventually relented and lifted the punishment. He wasn't about to bust them—Winters was too smart for that. Malarkey and Guarnere were too good NCOs to be demoted. They had already earned the respect of the men in the field. The men would probably have done something faster for them than they would have for either Winters or me. You kind of get the impression that I'm not too much of a disciplinarian. You're probably right about that.

· 16 ·

Market Garden

gland.

"All right, Lieutenant, nice and easy now," said Technician Fourth Class George Luz from behind me in the bar. I adjusted my shoulders, sniffed the smoky air with the composure of a UCLA physical education major, and aimed the dart square at the bull's-eye. Wobbly, the dart hit the black on the edge of the board, far off its mark.

"Tough break, said Luz condescendingly, "you're having a tough night." He shrugged. "People have tough nights."

Bull Randleman puffed his cigar and cleared the board for us. It was all just a ruse.

"You know, it's a good thing we weren't gambling," I said, shaking hands with the replacements who beat George and me.

"Yeah, we would have got killed," Luz agreed.

"Hmm, you want to bet?" suggested one of the replacements. "Pack of smokes?"

"Naw, I'm not much of a gambling man," I said, shaking my head. Luz agreed. Then, as if changing my mind, "Well . . . first one to hit the bull's-eye wins?"

"Why not?" suggested the replacement.

"Two packs?" I offered. "Want to make it for two?" He nodded. I took aim.

As if on cue, Luz interrupted: "Lieutenant, you gonna shoot lefty all night? Just curious . . ." he turned to the replacement and pointed at me—" 'cause he's right-handed."

"George," I said, a big grin on my face, switching hands, "what would I do without George Luz?" I threw the dart in for a perfect bull's-eye.

The replacements had no choice but to pay up.

THAT SCENE OPENS PART 4 (TITLED "THE REPLACEMENTS") OF the *Band of Brothers* miniseries. I'm an old Hollywood boy—I understand that things have to be dressed up for the stage—but in real life, that scene never happened. There are a few other places as well where I need to clarify what truly took place and didn't. This book is my life story, and as I tell it from my perspective, stories may not always gibe with how I've been portrayed. My intention in clarifying some items from *Band of Brothers* is not to denigrate it in any way. Stephen Ambrose interviewed a lot of men from Easy Company, but it's not like he singled me out to interview me in-depth. My contact with Professor Ambrose involved about one thirty-minute phone conversation, mostly about Brecourt Manor. The other parts of the series that portray me were made up from anecdotal stories told by others. I can't vouch for something somebody else said.

People ask me all the time if *Band of Brothers* is accurate, and I always say yes—generally. *Band of Brothers* was designed to show the war through the eyes of the combatants, to show how you could take guys from all over the country and from all walks of life, train them, and make a good fighting unit out of them. It portrayed well the overall flavor of war and the men who fought in it. I'm very happy with how *Band of Brothers* turned out, and I encourage anybody to read the book or watch the series.

That said, I never went into the Blue Boar Inn—not once. I didn't drink, mostly because of what had happened to my father, and I didn't start smoking until much later in my life (I smoke a pipe today), so I would not have been concerned then about winning two packs of smokes. I never played darts with Luz, either (I don't even know how to play darts), though I liked him a lot. Luz was one of my favorite guys; he could mimic people and keep a whole crowd laughing. I did hang around with enlisted men quite a bit—that part is accurately portrayed. I always felt more comfortable with them than I did with officers.

In the video series, Carwood Lipton, the new Easy Company first sergeant, interrupted all of us in the bar to make an announcement about Operation Market Garden.

"Hate to break the mood here boys," he said, "but we're moving out again."

The noisy bar was suddenly quiet.

In real life, I don't remember who made the announcement or where it was made. But the sudden change of mood was accurately portrayed. An announcement came that we were going to fight again—no doubt about that.

It's funny. People ask me about Operation Market Garden, and I really don't have much to say. It was a great landing in broad daylight. No mixups. We landed where we were supposed to. We assembled where we were supposed to. We set out toward the objective we had been given: a bridge over the canal. We got there a little too late. The Germans blew it up before we got there.

That was Market Garden.

Some may accuse me of shrugging off my war experiences, but that's not how I see it. On the outside, I think sometimes I appear offhanded about the war—I don't glorify the time I spent in active service. I'd never hold any of us in Easy Company up as perfect or say that we didn't make mistakes. I try not to dwell too much in the past. So I guess I focus on the surface somewhat; perhaps that's how I cope better with my memories. I ask for your patience as I unravel my life and try to remember the bad as well as the good. When you go through something as brutal as combat, your memory has a way of being selective. You do not want to remember everything, and it takes work to dig deeper.

Just before we jumped into Holland, there's that scene in *Band of Brothers* where Sergeant Don Malarkey goes to pick up his laundry. That's one scene that did happen in real life, and Malarkey talks about it to this day. One of the laundrywomen asked him to take back some clothes for some other men to save them a trip in, and started handing him stacks of clothes. There were many stacks of un-claimed laundry—and Malarkey realized the truth. All those guys hadn't picked up their clothes yet because they weren't around any-more. Lieutenant Meehan, whose plane went down on D-Day, Salty Harris, Sergio Moya, Robert Bloser, Everett Gray, Richard Owen, Herman Collins, George Elliot . . . all men with loved ones waiting for them to come home—girlfriends and wives and parents and chil-dren. On June 6, Easy Company had jumped with 139 officers and soldiers. When we pulled off the line June 29, we had 74.

Maybe that's why I sometimes appear offhanded about the war to-day. It's not true indifference; it's just how I deal with it. I don't think what I personally did in the war was any big deal. The men who didn't come back again, so that we can enjoy the freedoms we hold today—the men who gave life and limb for us—they are the real heroes. I don't want anybody venerating me for my military service. Venerate those who live with injuries today, and those who didn't come back.

WE JUMPED INTO HOLLAND FOR OPERATION MARKET GARDEN ON September 17, 1944.

Once again, the sky was dotted with green-gray chutes. We landed together as a unit in a grassy field. No one was shooting at us this time, at least that's how I remember it. I hit the silver circle clasp on my chest that popped me out of my chute and joined up with my platoon. Our assignment was to take the bridge near Eindhoven that ran across the Willamena Canal. The theory was that we'd create a corridor up through Holland across the Rhine River and into Germany. British armored forces would make this fast run up there. Before the Germans knew what hit them, the British would be into Germany, behind the Siegfried Line.

Between World Wars I and II, Germany and France each built fortifications along their borders facing each other—big concrete defenses with underground tunnels. One was the Maginot Line, on the French side. The other was the Siegfried Line, on the German side. The border between France and Germany was a highly occupied, armed, fortified area on both sides. It didn't make a good place to try to go from France to Germany by ground. Because of these fortifications, the Allied plan was either to go up through the lowlands of Holland into Germany, or down through the high ground around Strasbourg. It didn't make a lot of sense to make a frontal assault against the Siegfried Line.

So General Montgomery developed this plan that they would take three airborne divisions of British and Canadian troops combined, and these divisions would bear the brunt of the crossing up at Arnhem. The combined troops would jump up at the bridge at Arnhem. The 82d would jump farther down the road at a place called Nijmegen, where there was also a bridge over a river. And we were to take the bridge at Eindhoven that ran over the Willamena Canal.

It was a well-thought-out plan in my estimation. But something happened to throw a monkey wrench into things. Maybe it was Murphy's Law—everything that could go wrong did go wrong. Several theories abound. One is that somebody in the Dutch underground tipped the Germans off. Another is that planners hadn't taken into account some obstacles along the way that slowed up Allied forces, and they got bogged down around Nijmegen and didn't get to Arnhem fast enough. In any event, the Germans attacked at Arnhem and just slaughtered the British and Canadians who were there. The armored force that was supposed to get up there to do the work didn't get there in time. And the thing was a failure.

In the meantime, Easy Company received another assignment to defend and spread the width of the corridor—northeast up through Belgium and Holland. On the way into Eindhoven, we were traversing an open field and came under attack. That's where Brewer took that shot in the neck from a sniper holed up in some buildings off to the right. The sniper fire hadn't been enough to make us dodge around much. We thought he was too far away to be effective. Mostly we were just ignoring it. Sort of random, the bullet that hit Brewer.

With Brewer loaded up and headed off to the hospital, we continued into Eindhoven. A strange sound filled my ears. I heard it before I saw it. First came cheering, then music—a strange cacophony of jubilation. The Dutch had been under German occupation for nearly five years, as Germany's first lunge of the war had been through the Low Countries—Holland, Belgium, Luxembourg, and into France. Just before we arrived, Eindhoven had been freed. The streets of Eindhoven were jammed with citizens. They shook our hands and slapped our backs. They offered us food—fresh milk and fruit. I didn't notice women kissing soldiers randomly, as was portrayed in the series, but it could have happened. All ages crammed into the streets. We continued through the town on a wide street where the buildings come right down to the edges.

In the series, Winters, Nixon, Welsh, and I observe some Dutch women getting their heads shaved by force. A member of the Dutch resistance tells us it was because the women had slept with German soldiers. But I never actually witnessed anyone getting her head shaved. All I saw was a lot of people lining the streets and handing out food. We were well received in the town.

One small scene is still vivid in my memory: Toward the edge of the city, a little girl came toward me, motioning me to come to her level. I bent down. She reached up quickly and pinned a little rag doll on my uniform. She didn't say a word, but just offered me this small tribute, then disappeared into the crowd. I still have that doll, packed carefully in my garage.

We didn't see any snipers inside the city. We weren't necessarily wary. Maybe it was a misplaced ease. I just figured it was another one of these cities that the Germans had abandoned—or the citizens wouldn't have been out there. They probably knew better than we did what was happening in their town. We continued through Eindhoven and on to Hegel, the next village up the road. You know that feeling you get when it's too quiet? That's what it felt like. Just the road and a light wind, sky, and clouds.

Unknown to us, a German Panzer unit had formed a half-moon defense ahead of us. Without warning, machine gun fire zipped in like hail. I scrambled to spread out our platoon off the road and behind a barn. We needed a protected area where we could dig in and defend.

"Get down! Get down!" I kept hollering to my guys.

Standing momentarily in the middle of the farmyard, with my side turned to where the firing was coming from, suddenly I felt like somebody had hit me in the butt with one of those wooden paddles from fraternity hazing days. I didn't see it or hear it. It just felt like a swat. The force of it knocked me off my feet. I went down forward on my knees, which was peculiar because the shot had come from the side. It didn't really even hurt. The blast just banged me and down I went.

I lay on my belly and quickly tried to assess the situation. I knew I had been shot—it couldn't have been anything else. The wound lay somewhere below my lower back, which concerned me when I envisioned pieces of my spine getting blown away. But I could still feel all my extremities, so I knew I wasn't paralyzed. I didn't reach around and feel blood or anything—I didn't want to.

We were still getting a lot of fire at close range. The shots were raking back and forth over the top of a hill. I figured it would be better to stay down than try to move. Several of our other guys also got hit. Chuck Grant took one. Some guy—can't remember who—just got rifled by machine gun fire. I hoped the other guys had all made it to cover. If I just lay there and thought about it, I knew somehow I'd get out. I'm not trying to feign bravado, but I wasn't worried. I didn't think I was going to die. Somebody would come along to get me soon. It would probably hurt to walk, but lying there, it wasn't too bad.

Gene Roe, our medic, ran up right away. Within a matter of seconds he was right beside me. Bullets still zipped around us. Roe was fearless. He dumped some sulfa powder on my wound to prevent infection.

"Where's your medical kit?" he said.

"Don't need it. Don't want the morphine—hate needles."

He shrugged. "Okay, Lieutenant." And he went to the next man.

In the video series, Malarkey and Toye are crouched next to Roe when he helps me. I tell them all to get out of there, to leave me for the Germans because I'm too heavy for them to carry. That might have happened. But I don't remember saying that. It couldn't have been five minutes later—a jeep was right there. It had to be somebody else's, because our company didn't have any (we didn't jump with any jeeps). It might have been British or from some ground forces. In the movie they had me in the back end of one of those GMC trucks, but I'm pretty sure it was a jeep.

So they cut the seat out of my pants, stuck a bandage on it, and threw me over the hood of the vehicle. I wasn't strapped on or on a stretcher or anything—more like a deer across the hood of a car. Somebody wrote somewhere (it's in the video series this way, too) that some of my guys ripped a door off a barn and dragged me to safety on that—that could be true, and I thank them if that's how it actually happened, but I just remember being on the metal hood. What I do remember is how embarrassing it was as we started heading for the hospital. All these GIs were coming down the road in the other direction. We traversed slowly, which offered them a prime look at my backside.

"Hey Lieutenant, what were you doing with your butt in the air?" one called. The gibes came all way down the road. It was a prime opportunity for enlisted men to barb an officer. All I could do was grit my teeth. They got a lot of fun out of needling me as we traveled to the hospital. With me gone, I think Sergeant Bill Guarnere took command of my platoon. We still didn't have an assistant officer, ever since Ray Schmitz hadn't made it to Normandy. I don't think we had another officer in my platoon. I couldn't tell you why. I wasn't worried about my platoon, anyway. Your platoon wasn't going to flounder without you. Somebody would assume command, or they'd join up with somebody else.

Market Garden was supposed to be a short mission, but Easy Company was eventually in Holland for eighty days. When we jumped that sunny day in September, we had 154 men. By the time Easy Company left for France in November, a third of the company was either dead or wounded.

Traveling to the hospital on the hood of a jeep, my war was over. Or at least my part in Operation Market Garden was anyway. After we had parachuted down to the field, about all I had done was walk into a town and out the other side.

It didn't feel like much.

· 17 ·

Wounded

WHENEVER YOU GOT A GREASY BULLET IN YOU, YOU NEVER KNOW what sort of damage was done. As the jeep motored toward the hospital, I wondered how far we had to go. The road was paved, but I sure wasn't very comfortable on the hood. I was glad, actually, for the pain. Pain lets you know something is wrong—and if you know something's wrong, at least you still know you're not finished yet.

We arrived at a British-controlled hospital back in Eindhoven. It was pretty well filled with casualties, both civilians and soldiers. They loaded me onto a stretcher and set me down in the hallway to wait. That was a good sign. My injury couldn't have been that terrible if they didn't rush me into surgery immediately. Or maybe they were just filled. Hard to tell in the bustle of the hospital hallway. Suddenly a British corpsman rushed by and stopped at my butt.

"This is going to hurt a bit," he said, and jabbed me with a tetanus shot, right next to the wound. *Yowie*—that needle hurt worse than getting shot in the first place!

Your mind kind of drifts while waiting in a hospital. The blood coming out of my backside had been pretty well stanched by the bandage, but I wasn't sure how much I had lost in the time it took to get off the field. I guess anytime you get hit, you wonder if it's enough to get you sent home. Sure, I wanted to go home. We all wanted to go home. But I was pretty sure this wound wouldn't be the one that would do it. Strangely, I didn't feel disappointed. I couldn't tell you exactly why. I guess I was still in the mode of duty. I was pretty sure I'd heal and get sent back to the line. From there, who knows what would happen?

The hospital at Eindhoven didn't do much more than check me out and see that I could make it to another hospital. So they loaded me up again and sent me to a British field hospital someplace in Belgium. This one was a mobile complex—just tents and cots all over. I couldn't tell you the conditions of the hospital—all I really saw was the entrance coming in, my cot, and the exit going out. They operated on me and took out the bullet, which had lodged in my buttocks on one side.

It was kind of a strange wound. The bullet went into one cheek, across the top of my crease, and into the other side. There's not too much space between the marks. An inch higher or forward and it would have hit my spine. It could have been awful in almost any other direction—if the bullet hit my hip or pelvis, or lodged in the femoral artery—I would have been really messed up. But it just happened to hit in the perfect spot.

The bullet was a .30-caliber, about an inch long and as round as your finger. It could definitely kill you if it hit in the right place. My injury was caused by one bullet, making three holes: an entry, then two below my lower back. They had to cut into the other cheek to take the bullet out. So it's really one bullet, four holes (the video series shows Guarnere making a kindhearted joke about it as he loads me on the truck). Come to think of it, a lot of guys have made jokes about that over the years.

Surgeons gave me a general anesthetic. When I came out of it, I was lying on my cot in the field hospital and looked over at the guy next to me. I rubbed my eyes in disbelief.

"Mickey? Is that you?" I said.

"Buck? Of all the people to meet. I can't believe it."

Mickey Panovich had played basketball at UCLA and was a great guy. He'd been hit in the ankle, badly, and was set to go back to the States. A real million-dollar wound. I wrote a buddy of mine back at UCLA, Bob Wolcott, about the incident. At the same time, Mickey wrote to Wilbur Johns, UCLA athletic director and basketball coach, about the incident. Funny, neither one of us knew the other had written. Bob Wolcott was a writer for the school newspaper and got hold of Mickey's letter. He already had mine, and he published both in the newspaper. The article appeared in the *UCLA Daily Bruin* in October 1944. The letters are still posted on Internet sites today. They read:

*Bruin Paratroopers Compton and Panovich Injured in Holland,
Meet in Hospital*

Written to Bob Wolcott '42
Dear Bob:

Just got your latest letter about ten minutes ago. The conditions under which I received it will probably surprise you. As you know, we were in Holland, and on Wednesday, the 20th of September, I got hit by a couple of slugs from a Jerry machine gun. I was crossing through a yard behind a farm house and was hit from the side. It felt like I had been hit with a pitched ball, not a sharp pain at all. Well, both arms went up in M.G.M. style, I fell on my face, and they have been carrying me ever since.

I was evacuated through the channels of the British 2nd Army to Brussels. From there I was flown by R.A.F. Douglas C-47 to England, and here I am taking it easy in a nice American hospital. Radio, etc. Nice looking nurses.

When I came out from under an anesthetic in a hospital in Diest, Belgium, I looked over and there was Mickey Panovich in the next bed! He was shot through the lower leg. He's O.K. though.

Your accounts of football certainly give me a case of nostalgia. I'm really determined to come back and play my last year of ball. I listen with interest to the broadcasts of the scores. I read in the Stars and Stripes about the thriller with SC. What I'd give to be back in school playing ball! I really believe I have a good year left in me.

Be sure and tell Wilbur and Babe and Ray and Bob Waterfield and all the gang hello for me and good luck in the season. I've actually gotten so I feel at home in England, although I miss UCLA and all the old friends. But I've been over here a year now.

Well pal, the nurse is coming to give me a treatment, so I guess I'll have to close. Remember to remember me to all the boys you see.

As ever,
BUCK COMPTON

Dear Wilbur,

Well—I've gone and done it!—Got myself shot while in action. I guess you know where if you've been reading the papers.

It all happened while I was out in front too far while going into this big city first. A bullet ricocheted to my front, went through my right boot barely grazing my ankle and then hitting my left calf chipping the tibia and making quite a hole—it could have been a lot worse, Wilbur, and I consider myself very lucky indeed.

We were cut off in front so far that we were being fired

at from all sides. We were in a house that we'd just captured when mortar fire set it on fire, so we started to crawl back to our own lines. It took me 3½ hours to make it. Snipers and machine guns had us zeroed in all the way. I still don't know how I made it back. I blacked out and lost quite a bit of blood.

The Jerrys are very dirty fighters and don't believe in coming out and fighting it out. They'd rather snipe at you and retreat—they get better results that way. So much has happened during the past days, Wilbur, that it would take a book to tell it all. I know I'll never forget it. Buck Compton got hit too and he'll be all right.

One morning I awoke in a British evacuation hospital and who was next to me but "Buck!" What a coincidence—we both felt better having each other to talk to. Just heard the news that S.C. tied us 13–13! I guess old Bob Waterfield is doing pretty well, eh? Lots of luck to your basketball team, Wilbur, and I hope I'll be out there for spring practice next year—I should be all right by then.

Sincerely,
MICK
*From Lt. M. J. Panovich**

AFTER BELGIUM, AS I WROTE ABOUT IN THE LETTER, THEY TOOK me to a civilian hospital in Oxford, England, to recuperate. I don't remember if they flew me or took me by boat. The hospital was very nice. Nice buildings, nice nurses. Several other soldiers were there.

---

*http://www.hbo.com/apps/band/site/client/stories/curated_story.jsp?exid=490, accessed June 4, 2007.

Nice guys. Most were ambulatory. Whenever I got my bandage changed, they'd all come gather round my bed and make gibes, because it was always done by a female nurse. The guys always seemed to have a card game going, poker or whatever. I tried to get in several times just to kill the time, but all I had with me were Dutch guilders. For some reason I couldn't get the money changed. The guys never let me into the game, either. I'd come around and say, "Aw, come on you guys, let me play."

"Naw, take your GD guilders out of here," they'd say, "We don't want 'em."

We had some fun in the hospital.

Eventually I got so I could walk around. From the time I got hit until the time I recuperated was about a month. Maybe a little more.

When I returned to Easy Company, the guys were out of Holland and based at a French army post just east of Rheims. The mood was that the war was winding down. The Allies were making some great advances across Europe. Heading to Japan was always a possibility for us, but for the most part, Rheims was very much a garrison mode. Nobody expected that we were going to do any more missions in Europe.

When we were stationed at Rheims, a young lieutenant, Charles Thirlkeld, joined us. He was a graduate of the Citadel and had previously served at Supreme Headquarters, Allied Expeditionary Forces, which was Eisenhower's headquarters. Thirlkeld had been involved with planning the invasion and liberation of Europe.

When he joined Easy Company, Thirlkeld brought with him some of the plans, which by then had been declassified. They showed that the planners had missed calculating the recapture of Paris by only six days—an amazing accomplishment when you think about it. It's popular today in some circles to make fun of the military, to talk about "military intelligence" as if it's an oxymoron. But when you understand all the planning and logistics that went into that operation, it was clearly a vast undertaking. That the Allied planners could come so close was impressive.

Thirlkeld, unfortunately, was killed January 3, 1945, just a few feet from me at Bastogne, a hole the size of a grapefruit blown through his back. He was the son of a general. After he joined Easy Company, this was the first combat he had seen.

WHILE IN RHEIMS, SOMEBODY CAME UP WITH THE IDEA OF PUT-ting together a football game between the 506th and the 502nd, another regiment in our division. The game was set to be played on Christmas Day. We nicknamed it the Champagne Bowl. I was appointed coach of our team. I don't remember where the equipment came from, but evidently we scrounged some up somewhere and started practicing daily. I didn't have any thoughts about designing original football plays, but basically used the same system we had used at UCLA. It took a couple weeks to get the team off the ground and get them up to speed. The team was making pretty good progress when one day we were called off the practice field and told to report to company headquarters in full field equipment, ready to go. It was mid-December, 1944, and our breath hung smoky in the late autumn air.

In the series, it shows all the guys watching a John Wayne movie when the announcement comes. Dick Winters, who's become a captain by now, has just pulled up a chair behind me and asks me how I'm doing. I don't answer at first—you don't know whether I'm mesmerized in the film or lost in thought. The scene implies that cracks were starting to form in my psyche. My personality is depicted as introverted and withdrawn, and the suggestion is that being wounded in Holland has seriously affected me. Truthfully, my wound had been relatively painless and non–life threatening. In Rheims, I was feeling perfectly fine and totally focused on coaching the regiment's football team. I never attended a movie on base—I don't know if they even showed any.

Regardless of where we were when the announcement came, the new operation soon became clear to us: one more round of combat.

Hitler's troops, whom we thought had been retreating, had launched one last full-fledged attack, in the Ardennes Forest, cutting off supplies and separating British and American troops. Taking advantage of the cold and fog, Hitler had attacked the sparsely deployed troops around Bastogne, a small but essential town that had seven roads leading to it. The Germans called it a "road octopus." Bastogne was a prized possession for any advancing army.

For now, all we knew was that Bastogne would be our next battle. History would later show it as one of the key stages of the Battle of the Bulge, the largest engagement ever fought by the U.S. Army. In the end, almost 20,000 U.S. troops would lie dead. We were outnumbered three-to-one, and newspaper reports would later refer to Easy Company as "those battered bastards from Bastogne."

For me, Bastogne would be the last combat I would ever see.

· 18 ·

My Last Battle

FROM RHEIMS, THEY LOADED US ON TRUCKS HEADING FOR THE front line. Rumors circulated that the Germans had broken through already, but details were sketchy. We bounced and jostled in the truck for more than a day. All was dark when the trucks screeched to a halt and let us out a few miles from Bastogne. I could feel the temperature dropping. It hadn't snowed yet, but I knew it soon would.

We were wearing basically the same uniforms we had worn in Holland. Aside from new wool overcoats, no other cold-weather gear had been issued. Our boots were just regular leather ones, not designed for snow or rain. Our feet got wet and stayed wet. We had no long underwear or woolen socks. We were given "fart sacks"—lined sleeping bags, which were pretty sturdy but not specially designed for cold weather. Some of the guys had turned in their guns for repairs after Holland and hadn't received them back yet. Off the truck, I ran through my guys, making a quick inventory of what kind of ammo they had.

"One clip and a couple grenades," said Sergeant Malarkey. "No carbine ammo at all. In other words, squat." The other guys answered similarly. This was a hell of a way to jump into a fight.

We could see a lot of fire off to the right. There was obviously a lot of stuff going on in the high ground. You couldn't make it out in the dark, other than seeing a lot of fire and explosions. Word came to head down the road on the Bastogne–Foy highway. We started to walk. We hiked for some time. After a while the sky began to grow gray with the dawn. It's strange, when you're heading to fight a battle, to see men—men in the same army as you—walking the other way, but that's what we began to see. As we were heading up, they were heading down. Some were without weapons. Some were bloody. All had their heads down. I don't remember which division it was, but it had been overrun.

"Where are you going?" I asked one.

"Just *back*," was all he said.

Stories began to surface. Some of our troops had apparently abandoned their tanks, which the Germans had taken—so we were to be on the lookout for our tanks blowing up things they shouldn't. The Germans were merciless, others said—they came out of nowhere, there was no way we could win. Our guys began to ask the retreating soldiers for whatever we could scrounge—ammo, food, warmer clothes. Hell—they weren't going to need the stuff wherever they were going. But we sure could use it.

We hiked east of Bastogne and ended up in the woods, where we were told to dig in a defensive line. We dug our foxholes. The dirt was cold and stuck in clods on our trenching tools. Overhead the clouds grew darker. A smell of snow and smoke was in the air. There wasn't much we could do. The orders were to defend our position. Ammo was short, so we weren't supposed to fire unless a large group of the enemy was upon us.

So we sat.

The first while was all quiet. A day and night passed. Then another.

We knew the enemy had circled around Bastogne. We were basically closed in. Ice formed on mud puddles. Constant fog made visibility a problem. Then snow began to fall. It fell slowly at first, then all at once, almost blizzardlike. It stopped as quickly as it began. Everything stayed frozen. Several nights, about all we did was stay in the woods in our foxholes. We got shelled once in a while—not heavily, but they fired a lot of antiaircraft at us. The tracers hit the trees with a lot of clatter. It was just fireworks and noise and didn't do too much damage. Mostly all it did was keep us awake. We got to the point where we were always on edge. Not jumpy, just alert—constantly ready to act. Always tense. The atmosphere was unsustainable, I knew. It was the type of uneasiness that could make a guy crack before long.

We changed positions several times, digging new holes wherever we set down. At night you could often hear noises. Vehicles moving. Tanks. It all sounded ominous, all this mechanized stuff moving. Next morning we never knew what to expect—tanks coming at us or what. Our feelings were boxed up with watching, listening, always expecting something that never came.

Mostly we just sat.

Some small-arms fire came.

Some shelling.

But never the big attack we always anticipated.

A sunken road ran between us and a platoon of Germans. Woods grew on both sides of the road. We dug foxholes in the woods and kept cover—us in our woods, the Germans in theirs. Several nights I took a few of our guys up close to the road and set up a listening post. We'd send one guy across the road to the German side and two others on the American side with the phone, just listening. Listening. Just trying to hear anybody coming through. We'd trade off sleeping and listening to this phone. Guys would think they'd hear something, but it would never turn out to be anything.

For a few days we set up another listening post in an open area near the town of Foy. We'd only man the post at night. I'd head out there with one other guy and the two of us would sit out there trying to hear anything. Sergeant Bill Guarnere sat with me on many of those nights. He was much more softhearted than he ever let on. In the series, it shows us together in a foxhole. In the background we can hear the Germans singing "Silent Night" not far away from us. I hand Guarnere a picture of my girlfriend back home, lamenting to Bill that she was finished with me—just in time for Christmas. I don't remember that ever happening—the singing, or the picture incident—but this often did: Bill and I were supposed to take turns staying awake and sleeping. Often I'd wake up and he'd say in his South Philly accent, "Aw, go back to sleep, Lieutenant. I got it." I'd protest, but he'd always insist.

For days, there was hardly any action. We existed in the tension of trying to be on the alert all the time, trying to keep warm. At night, German planes sometimes flew over, lighting the place up with flares. We never knew the reasons. The flares hung in the sky for a long time. You could see the man in the foxhole next to you, his dirty face, the rings under his eyes, the tight grip he kept on his rifle. Constantly we anticipated a large-scale nighttime attack. But day after day, night after night, it never came.

One day, broad daylight, we were sitting up in the woods getting snowed on when we spotted a German ambulance crawling toward us on the road. We tensed and grabbed our rifles. Nobody said anything. The ambulance pulled up even with us and stopped. The back door opened. Out came a German soldier. He had no gun, so none of us made a move. Then out came another and another. They stood with their hands up, surrendering. This was a surprise. We had all thought we were the ones surrounded.

As we began to interrogate the German soldiers through a translator, one turned out to be from the German Navy. Another was from the Luftwaffe. The guys in the back of the ambulance represented a conglomerate of people that had been cobbled together. It didn't speak well to the caliber of the German Army by then. According to the reports we had received, we were supposed to be facing some of their top units. I guess they weren't the ones surrendering. Years later I returned to Europe with my family to tour some of the battle sites. While in Europe, I played a round of golf. My caddy had been a German paratrooper in the war. He spoke some English and told me stories of how bad the German soldiers had it at times. Once they were getting ready to make a jump but didn't have enough gasoline to get the airplanes off the ground. Toward the end, it got pretty disastrous in Germany.

It got hard for us, too. Unrelenting pressure infused the atmosphere in the snowy woods. It wasn't like anybody could clock out and take a day off to recharge. We never had a moment when we weren't on the alert for shelling. Every night we faced shifting sleep, nightmares, and cold. Every morning we faced again the gray dawn of war. Our ammo grew lower. The heavy fog meant we wouldn't be getting resupplied with air drops anytime soon. I instructed my guys not to fire at anything they didn't absolutely need to. Some of the guys began to wrap their feet in burlap, then pour water on their feet to let it freeze over. The ice provided a type of insulation. Every once in a while we'd hear about a guy who took his boots off on purpose, just to let his feet freeze so he could go home. We heard of one or two who, in desperation, put bullets in their feet for the same reason. This was no way to fight a war.

Just before Christmas, 1944, we got word that the Germans had closed the circle around Bastogne. This meant that the 101st Airborne was now completely surrounded by the enemy. Dick Winters said once that being surrounded was no problem for paratroopers—we were used to that. For me, it's hard to describe the feeling of isolation. The heavy fog meant that we were cut off from any help from the sky. We were alone, out in the woods, surrounded, with desperately low supplies. We were in day-to-day survival mode. Build the occasional fire. Melt some snow. Find something to eat. Cook it in your helmet. Stay out of harm's way. Just do what you need to do to get through the day.

In places, the snow lay halfway to our knees. We received orders to take off our boots once a day and massage our feet. A couple guys tried it and it only made matters worse, so I never enforced the order. We were supposed to shave every day, too, but it was pretty hard shaving in the bitter cold. I didn't care if my guys grew a full beard or not. My feet had turned blotchy and gray by then. One minute they were burning and tingling, the next there was no sensation. I knew trench foot was setting in. You tried to keep your feet dry. You kept two pairs of socks and tried to wash one and dry it around your neck at night, but your feet were always cold, always wet. There wasn't much anybody could do about it. By the way guys were walking, I knew a lot of them were feeling the same thing. I'd move from foxhole to foxhole trying to stay positive, saying things like, "Keep those toes moving, guys." Like that did any good.

Two days before Christmas, I woke up and looked up from my foxhole. The sky seemed different than I'd seen it for a long time. Then it dawned on me, it wasn't overcast. I grinned. Joe Toye, a good friend, was hunkered down next to me.

"Look at that," I whispered. "UCLA blue."

"Listen—" Toye said quickly. "Planes. I hear planes."

It was an early Christmas present none of us expected. American C-47s dropped food, blankets, ammunition, medicine—the works. Some of our guys went to pick up the gear. The Germans spotted us and opened fire. If I remember correctly, everybody made it back.

It was either that day or the next, the Germans delivered an edict to General Anthony C. McAuliffe, demanding our surrender. A one-page flyer from the general had reached us the day before Christmas, explaining the story. Beneath a "Merry Christmas" greeting, General McAuliffe had written:

24 December 1944
    What's Merry about all this, you ask? We're fighting—it's cold. We aren't home. All true but what has the proud Eagle

Division accomplished with its worthy comrades the 10th Armored Division, the 705th Tank Destroyer Battalion and all the rest? Just this: We have stopped cold everything that has been thrown at us from the North, East, South and West. We have identifications from four German Panzer Divisions, two German Infantry Divisions and one German Parachute Division. These units, spearheading the last desperate lunge, were headed straight west for key points when the Eagle Division was hurriedly ordered to stem the advance. How effectively this was done will be written in history; not alone in our Division's glorious history but in World history. The Germans actually did surround us, their radios blaring our doom. Their Commander demanded our surrender in the following impudent arrogance:

The Germans had written:

> To the U.S.A. Commander of the encircled town of Bastogne.
> The fortune of war is changing. This time the U.S.A. forces in and near Bastogne have been encircled by strong German armored units. More German armored units have crossed the river Our near Ortheuville, have taken Marche and reached St. Hubert by passing through Hompre-Sibret-Tillet. Libramont is in German hands.
> There is only one possibility to save the encircled U.S.A. troops from total annihilation: that is the honorable surrender of the encircled town. In order to think it over a term of two hours will be granted beginning with the presentation of this note.
> If this proposal should be rejected one German Artillery Corps and six heavy A.A. Battalions are ready to annihilate the U.S.A. troops in and near Bastogne. The order for firing

will be given immediately after this two hours' term. All the
serious civilian losses caused by this artillery fire would not
correspond with the well known American humanity.
—*The German Commander*

The German commander received the following reply:

22 December 1944

To the German Commander:
N U T S!
—*The American Commander*

Nuts! We all had a good laugh about that one. Rumor had it that
when the translator had relayed the information to the German commander, he had been asked to explain what *NUTS!* meant exactly.

"Go to hell," the translator said. "The Americans are telling us to
go to hell."

On New Year's Day, 1945, the day after my twenty-third birthday, a few of the guys asked me if they could fire a couple mortar
rounds at the Germans, just to let them know we were still here and
the worst was still to come. I said yes. Not because it was my birthday. My guys had asked me, and I didn't give a rip about much of
anything by then.

IN PART 7 OF THE SERIES (TITLED "THE BREAKING POINT"), IT
shows Sergeant Bill Guarnere and Edward "Babe" Heffron in a foxhole, wondering if I was about to take a step off the deep end.

"You've seen him," Heffron says. "He's all wound up like a
spring."

"He's fine," Guarnere says. "It wasn't getting shot [in Holland]
that got him, it was being in that hospital. I been there—okay? It ain't

pretty. Besides, once he was up and moving around, he was his old self again. I'm telling ya, Buck Compton's fine."

In real life, the events surrounding this time of the war are perfectly clear in my mind. This is what I remember:

One day in early January the anticipation we had been feeling for so long was shattered. Very suddenly, broad daylight, really bad shelling started coming in—big, heavy stuff. *Ka-Boom! Ka-Boom! Ka-Boom! Ka-Boom!* Landing on us was the most shocking display of firepower I had ever seen. It was absolutely merciless. I yelled to the guys—*Incoming! Find cover!*—something like that. Shrapnel flew and shredded every which way. Bursts of dirt and snow exploded all over. You could feel the ground bounce. You could taste gunpowder in your mouth. It was all very close. Thirlkeld was only a few feet from me. What he was doing aboveground for so long, I never knew, but he didn't make it—we had been in the woods for so long you got used to the lulls. The shelling blasted away tree branches; huge limbs fell with thuds all around us. I could hear someone yelling, "I'm hit! I'm hit!" For some time, all was complete chaos.

The shelling stopped almost as suddenly as it began.

I think I was the first out of my foxhole, because I remember being the first to scream at what I saw. "Medic!" I hollered for all I was worth. "Medic!" Nobody seemed to be within shouting distance. I have a hard time explaining today how narrowed the focus is of anybody in my position. A platoon leader is down pretty low on the officer scale. Most of the time, no matter where we were, I was unaware of the bigger picture. My focus was a ditch or a road—just the fifty-yard stretch of land around me.

When I got up to survey what had happened, I couldn't believe how my fifty yards had been ravaged. It looked like slaughter alley—huge trees blown down, ground ripped up, a whole bunch of guys lying all over the place, some motionless, some gasping, unintelligible words coming out of their mouths. It's a terrible thing to see your guys like that. Death was everywhere. These were the first heavy losses we'd taken at Bastogne.

In the series it shows me coming out of my foxhole to survey the damage. I scream for a medic, then drop my helmet and just stand motionless. In the next scene there's a fury of activity around me while I'm sitting on a fallen tree with my head in my hands. Then it shows me lying on a cot in a field hospital. I'm in the fetal position in tears with Malarkey next to me, trying to read me a letter from back home to cheer me up.

I appreciate the series for doing that (even though all but one of those scenes were fictionalized) because it shows the progression of a soldier who suffered from combat stress reaction, commonly known as shell shock. Truly, there were men in World War II—in any war—who are so affected by the horror of their experiences that they break under pressure. But although I was affected by the horrors of Bastogne, I do not believe I was clinically shell shocked, as the series portrays me. In real life, while I was hollering for the medic, trying to figure out what to do, I remember two distinct thoughts:

How are we going to help the wounded guys? We were so alone out there. Company headquarters, battalion headquarters—they were all far away.

My second thought was: *Maybe this is the time the Germans are really going to get us all. They've been softening us up. Now, this is it. With all these guys wounded, what the hell are we going to do to fight back?*

Truly, it was an impossible sight to take in—to know what to do, to know how to help. I had seen men die before. I had seen men get wounded before. But this was different. This was unprecedented gore.

More than a dozen of our guys lay bleeding in the snow. Guarnere and Toye, probably the two toughest guys in the unit, had both taken it bad. Toye had gotten hit first. I guess Guarnere had crawled out of his foxhole after him, trying to drag him to safety. In the process, Guarnere had taken one as well. Both were missing legs. Our medic, Eugene Roe, got to Toye first and tied a bandage around what was left. He gave him a large hit of morphine, then went to Guarnere to do the same. Toye had only recently returned to our unit from an aid station where he got his arm patched up. He and Bill were good friends of mine. Deep red smears were all over the ground.

Dick Winters wrote in his book (not critically of me) that I suffered a serious mental trauma after the shelling and simply "walked off the line."* He was at battalion headquarters at the time and not present in the area of my platoon, so his information came secondhand. I mean no criticism of him by clarifying the facts.

In truth, I did not "walk" off the line.

I ran.

---

*Dick Winters, *Beyond Band of Brothers* (New York: Berkley Caliber), p.183.

· 19 ·

The End of the War

I RAN TO GO FIND DIKE.

I ran about fifty yards in the general direction of our company command post, yelling for medical help and personnel support to deal with the wounded and the fact that in our area, "the line" had essentially been wiped out. I wanted Dike to get hold of battalion and send troops to help us. I didn't know how widespread the attack had been. Dike was my only link with higher headquarters.

When I didn't find Dike, I exploded in rage. I'm sure other people saw me blow up. That may have led some to believe that I was cracking up.

But here's the backstory to that: A few months before we went into Bastogne, Lieutenant Winters had been promoted again and transferred to battalion headquarters. A new guy, Lieutenant Norman Dike, was made commander of Easy Company. Dike's father was a judge in New York City (I didn't hold that against him); Dike had attended Yale and had good connections with General Maxwell

Taylor, commander of the 101st Airborne Division—all that is probably what got Dike the position. In my mind, and I think in many of the men's minds, Dike came to us from out of nowhere.

In Bastogne, I was soon the last officer still with the company who had been with Easy Company since Normandy—Fred "Moose" Heyliger had been hit. Lieutenant Warren Roush was someplace else. Lieutenant Harry Welsh had come to Bastogne but was severely wounded on Christmas Day. The Army has its systems for promotions. Usually the systems are fair, but sometimes they can rankle a guy. In the series, it shows Winters and Nixon dealing with the fallout of some of Dike's lack of leadership. Winters and Nixon wonder aloud who else might command Easy Company. Winters says, "[Compton's] the only real choice. Buck's a real combat leader, but you know, I want Easy Company to have at least one experienced platoon leader." I don't know if Winters actually said that or not. What got me wasn't so much that I believed I should be promoted to Easy Company commander—I just couldn't stand Lieutenant Dike.

Dike came across as a haughty, Ivy League, aristocratic type of guy. Behind his back, some of the guys called him "Foxhole Norman." I secretly wondered if Nixon had a hand in his transfer. Both were Yale guys, and Nixon never liked me—it was probably all just crazy stuff in my head, but that's how my thinking was going by then. Out in Bastogne, Dike kept this huge foxhole, about as big around as a bedroom. It had a covering on it and a fire going constantly. He'd sit there, smoking his pipe, holding high levy with various platoon leaders. Reporting to Dike felt like kneeling before his throne.

So when I ran to find Dike after the hard shelling had hit and failed to locate any sign of him, I was furious. He was always somewhere else than he needed to be. From the command post, I returned to the gore at the platoon area. Medical help appeared not long after, and I did, as depicted in the series, sit down on a fallen tree and cry. It was a cry prompted not only by grief and sadness, but also by anger arising from the frustration I felt toward Dike. I was not shell shocked or suffering from any mental condition other than what I have described.

I have no clear memory of exactly how or why I traveled from my platoon a short time after that and reached regimental headquarters. At that time, I had an opportunity to express my frustration and anger. Colonel Sink, commander of the 506th, was a soft-spoken and kindly Southern gentleman whom I admired very much.

"Feet hurt?" he asked.

My feet hurt like hell. Frostbite and dampness had lodged their way into my skin time and time again, all sorts of veins spidered their way across my feet—but there was no way I was going to nod my head.

"Well, you've been through a lot," the colonel said. "I think you could stand a rest."

"A rest? Sir?" I was limping—hell, we were all limping—but I could still walk. I shook my head.

"A rest," the colonel repeated, this time more firmly. "I think you need a rest, Lieutenant."

That was it. I was taken off the line.

For the most part, today the Band of Brothers is like a large, extended family. The survivors meet at reunions annually to swap stories and catch up. Most of us are the best of friends. But every once in a while one or two of us have a drink too many—that may have been the case with Lewis Nixon at a reunion in Dallas a few years back, so I'll cut him some slack here. I wasn't at his table when this happened, but he, along with Harry Welsh, Don Malarkey, and Mike Ranney were sitting there, and Nixon called me a coward.

"Is that right?" Malarkey asked. "And how many Silver Stars do you have?" That shut Nixon up like a clam. He was at Normandy, but hadn't fired a single shot the whole war. Battalion headquarters personnel are generally quite a distance removed from the fighting. Honestly, back at Bastogne, I was worried about leaving the line. Colonel Sink's "suggestion" about getting a rest was not exactly a direct order. I don't know if I could have talked him out of it or not. If I had to do it all over again today, I would have tried to resist his decision.

They took me to a hospital in Belgium to treat my feet. Somehow I managed to get out and hitch a ride back to the guys in Bastogne. Maybe Winters gave me permission, I don't quite remember. I knew I wouldn't be allowed to stay on the line, but I don't know—I guess I just wanted some closure.

I hesitate writing this next bit, lest I appear self-important, but I include it because it speaks of a friendship with Don Malarkey that has lasted to this day. It also speaks well of my men. If one of their own could make it out—well, they were happy for him. That's true brotherhood.

With a driver waiting for me, I walked through the snowy woods in the direction I knew my platoon was. Malarkey found me first. We exchanged pleasantries and caught up with the bull. Soon, it grew time for me to leave. I cleared my throat and paused. I wasn't sure how to phrase what I still needed to ask.

"Don, there's something I need to know," I said at last. "What . . . uh—what do the other guys think of me?"

Malarkey didn't hesitate. Not for a minute. "They think you're a hell of an officer, Buck."

"Really?"

"Really. They all wish you the best. Honest."

I looked down. When I looked back up, Malarkey was saluting me. I saluted him back.

There was maybe a split second of silence between us. I turned in the snow and headed back to the jeep.

Malarkey turned and headed back to the line.

FOR REASONS I NEVER KNEW, LIEUTENANT DIKE WAS RELIEVED from his duties in Bastogne a few days after I left the line. He returned to division headquarters, was eventually promoted to captain, and made General Taylor's aide. Lieutenant Ronald Speirs was put in command of Easy Company. Speirs had been with Dog Company and was a skilled field officer.

Altogether, Easy Company spent more than a month on the line at Bastogne. We had arrived with 120 men. When Easy Company left, it had about 60. The Battle of Bastogne is sometimes described today as a rescue mission—that General Patton broke through the lines to save the encircled 101st. No member of the 101st has ever agreed that the division needed to be rescued. Easy Company was repositioned. Whatever is said in the end, the Battle of the Bulge was an Allied success.

After my time in the hospital in Belgium, I was sent to another hospital in France. I was moved from room to room on a stretcher, my bare feet always hanging out in the air. When my feet got better, they sent me to one of these transfer camps that help guys get reconnected to their units. I was set to head back to the company, which I heard was somewhere in Austria by then.

I had some time to kill in Paris and walked into the American Express office one day. It was a three- or four-story building and had been commandeered as a military command center for the troops stationed in and around Paris. The office was said to be a good place for troops on leave to find something to do—such as tickets to a show. All around the walls in the main-floor lobby were signs of different people who worked in the building and the various jobs they had. Out of sheer boredom, I started reading through the lists. My eye landed on one name.

Chuck Eisenmann.

I'd recognize that name anywhere. Chuck had been a ballplayer with the LA Angels, and I had played against him a few times when I was in college. Chuck was a good pitcher and had a whale of a good curveball. I hadn't seen anybody I knew for some time, so I took the stairs to his office and knocked on his door.

"Well, Buck Compton!" he said. "Come on in—how ya doing?"

Eisenmann was one of these Sergeant Bilko types who knew how the system worked. Different hotels around Paris billeted military men according to their rank. Eisenmann was a captain but was somehow living in a hotel where colonels were housed. We sat for some time in his office while he described his new job in Paris, providing athletic facilities for troops on leave. He also managed a baseball team and was pitcher for the team.

"Where you heading to, Buck?" he asked.

"I'm on my way back to the 101st Airborne," I said. "They're somewhere in Austria last we heard."

He shrugged. "How'd you like to stay here and go to work for me?"

"Thanks, but I'd rather go back to my unit," I said.

He looked directly at me. "War's almost over, Buck," he said. "We're sure about it this time. Germans are finished. Your unit's probably not even up to much right now. You could go sit on your ass and play cards all day or do something for the troops here."

"I don't know," I said. "I've got my orders."

"Hell," said Eisenmann. "I'll take care of that."

Eisenmann got up from his desk and walked across the hall. I could hear him say something to somebody about an *urgent need* to get some orders cut. A short time later he walked back in. "Your transfer's ready," he said. "You're stationed in Paris now, Buck."

That was all it took: Wander into a building somewhere. Look up an old friend. One short conversation later. Life completely changes.

My combat days were finished for good.

IN HINDSIGHT, I WISH I HAD RETURNED TO THE OUTFIT AND RE- sisted Chuck Eisenmann's offer of a transfer. I wish I had just gone back and rode it out with Easy Company. Maybe then there would be no need today to explain all this stuff about my mental health. I find that all a bit torturous. But you can't change history.

Eisenmann quickly turned much of the reins over to me. My primary task became running the athletic program for American troops in Paris. My job affected virtually every soldier who came to Paris—which was most of them at one time or another. I also played for

Eisenmann's baseball team, the Seine Section Clowns. We played with and against a lot of major league players, including the Cardinals' star pitcher Murry Dickson and Dave Koslo from the Giants.

Anything a soldier needed in the way of athletics, I organized it. As the months stretched on, I secured a multitude of facilities in and around Paris for the troops to use—golf courses, tracks to run around, swimming pools, stadiums. I also coached a football team and set up various games against other teams. The games were advertised in *Stars and Stripes* and mostly soldiers attended the games. Eisenmann had found some semipro boxers in the military and arranged some fights that I helped out at. Once, we arranged for some German POWs to make a ball field. It wasn't hard work, and I figured it was nicer for them to be outside than sitting around locked up.

In early May 1945, we got word that Hitler had committed suicide. A few days later, on May 7 and 8, the Allies formally accepted the unconditional surrender of Germany. That meant that the war in Europe was officially over. On V-E (Victory in Europe) Day, all of Paris just went wild. People turned out en masse for parades. Civilians and soldiers danced in the streets. Allied flags were flown in a group under the Arc de Triomphe. When darkness came, it seemed like all of Paris was still aglow in lights.

I continued to run the athletic program in Paris. The series shows me rejoining Easy Company at Eagle's Nest, but that never happened. Don Malarkey came and visited me once for several days in Paris. Things were going well, he said. I missed the guys, but figured I was being more useful where I was.

About three months after Germany surrendered, as the world knows now, nuclear bombs were dropped over Japan. On August 6, 1945, "Little Boy" was dropped on Hiroshima. On August 9, "Fat Man" was dropped on Nagasaki. A week after that, on August 15, 1945, Emperor Hirohito accepted the terms of the Potsdam Declaration, the document that outlined Japan's surrender. The formal Japanese surrender took place on board the USS *Missouri* in Tokyo Bay,

September 2, 1945. President Truman declared that day V-J Day—
victory in Japan (although it's now celebrated on August 15).

World War II was officially over.

To say we were all happy is an understatement. But there was still
work to be done. It takes a while for any war machine to disband,
and nothing changed for us immediately.

When my orders finally came to go home in December, I had been
on active duty for three years—from January 1943 to December 1945.
When I thought about what we had gone through during that time, I
just shook my head. We had been through Normandy, Brecourt Manor,
Carentan, Market Garden, and Bastogne. Survival seemed so implausible, but some had made it in the end. I was one of the lucky ones. Today,
when people thank me for my service, I figure three years of my time is
a cheap price to pay for living in this country. Nobody owes me a thing.

Worldwide estimates of casualties from World War II range from 50
million to 70 million people dead. To put that into perspective, that's like
wiping out all the people in California and Texas, the two most populous
U.S. states. Think of all the people who live in major cities such as Los
Angeles or Houston. To me, those numbers are just staggering. Reports
say it's hard to pinpoint exact casualty numbers because so many died
from secondary reasons such as starvation and disease. Though they
were both on the winning side, the Soviet Union is said to have suffered
the most casualties, with more than 25 million lost, and China lost about
11 million, many of them civilians. Some 5 million ethnic minorities
and 6 million Jews were murdered in Nazi concentration camps. The
United States and Britain each lost about 450,000 people. For the Axis
powers, Germany lost about 7.5 million; Japan lost about 2.6 million.

As a result of the war, the United States and the Soviet Union became the world's leading military and economic powers. The strained
relations between these two superpowers morphed into the Cold
War, which would define global politics for decades to come.

For me, in December 1945, I got cleared to leave Paris.

I was heading home at last.

· 20 ·

Return to Normalcy

HOW DO PEOPLE RETURN FROM THE HORRORS OF WAR AND SIM-
ply pick up where they left off? After World War II, I think we all
tried to return to life as we knew it, the best we knew how.

For fourteen days in late December 1945, I pitched and shud-
dered across the North Atlantic for the trip home. We rode aboard a
"Victory" transport ship, a class of ships mass-produced primarily by
the Kaiser Shipyards during the war years. It was smaller than the
Queen Elizabeth, which had brought us over. Some outfits came
home as a unit and were disbanded all at once. Some people, like myself, came home as individuals. Chuck Eisenmann rode on the ship
home with me. Other than him, I didn't know anybody on board.
Eisenmann went on to pitch for the San Diego Padres, the White Sox,
and the Brooklyn Dodgers. In later years he trained German shep-
herds. His dog, London, was featured in *Life* magazine and starred in
a long-running family television show called *The Littlest Hobo.*

Seeing the Statue of Liberty took on new meaning for me as we steamed into the Port of New York. We were free in this country, really free, and even after all I had experienced in Europe, I felt more than ever that freedom was worth fighting for. From New York, I was processed for travel to Fort MacArthur in San Pedro, California. In short order I was relieved from active duty and placed on Reserve status (I stayed in the military Reserves for the next twenty years or so, serving a weekend each month and two weeks each year, eventually retiring as a lieutenant colonel). A couple of my buddies from school met me in San Pedro. They had been in the service but got home ahead of me. They picked me up and drove me to my mother's house. Mom was sure happy to see me. I was happy to see her, too.

It was January 1946 when I finally arrived home from the war. Prior to heading overseas, I had been in university for three and a half years, from fall 1939 to January 1943, and needed at least a semester more to finish my degree, probably two. I reentered UCLA for the spring semester and tried to return to normalcy the best I knew how.

At first I found it pretty easy. I still had a year of baseball and a year of football eligibility. My old high school football coach, Bert La Brucherie, was now head coach at UCLA. Football was over for the year, but I got hooked up with baseball right away. I bought a 1942 Ford with money I had managed to send home—both military pay and money I had won from shooting craps. All in all, I had about four thousand dollars, a good chunk of money for those days. The car I bought was pretty stark, though. I don't think it even had a radio in it.

With butterflies in my stomach, I called up my old sweetheart, Jerry Star. She had written me in England to say things were all over between us, but I wondered if things had changed since then.

"Buck?" she said on the phone. "You came home?"

"Uh, I was kinda wondering if you wanted to go out sometime," I said.

The line was silent for a minute. "Sure, why not," she said. "Why don't you pick me up this Friday at eight o'clock."

Just like that, Jerry and I were dating again.

Five months later, Jerry and I were married.

Our courtship was a whirlwind. We went to shows and night-clubs. Our wedding, in May 1946, felt a bit rushed, I think, but everybody was happy. I was happy. Jerry's mother was happy. Jerry was willing. We didn't "need" to get married—it wasn't one of those things. In those days you got married and had kids. Everybody did. All my friends and classmates were getting married. Jerry and I were 24 and 22—that was old enough to tie the knot.

Friends toasted us at our wedding ceremony at the Chapman Park Hotel in LA. Jerry and I took a honeymoon up to Santa Barbara. Places to live were hard to come by, but Jerry's mother managed apartments and found us a one-bedroom apartment to move into when we got back. It had a pull-down bed, a kitchen, a dinette, and a bathroom. Everything in the apartment was very tiny.

Home from the war. Back at school. Marriage. All just normal. My life was looking up. I had memories I didn't want to have, of course, and every once in a while when I closed my eyes I saw things I didn't want to see. But nobody really talked about the war—not in depth, anyway. You certainly wouldn't talk to anybody about how you felt about things. Nobody did that. You just kept going.

I didn't sit around trying to figure things out, either.

When UCLA let out that spring, I got a shot at my dream. Earlier I had met a scout. We renewed our connection, and somehow I obtained permission to try out with the LA Angels baseball team. The Angels were in the Class AAA Pacific Coast League and a farm team for the Chicago Cubs. The Angels also had a farm team in Spokane, Washington, in the Class B Western International League. I went down to Wrigley field for batting, catching, and infield practice, trying to make the cut. The players were all good, but as tryouts progressed, I was holding my own.

On June 25, word came that would shake the athletic community nationwide. The Spokane team was traveling by bus over the Cascade Mountains when a driver drifted into the wrong side of the rain-slicked roads, causing the bus to swerve. The bus skidded out of control, crashed through a guardrail, and hurtled down a steep slope, where it caught fire. Eyewitnesses said that an hour later the bus was only a twisted steel skeleton. In the end, seven players were killed and nine injured. Among the dead was first baseman Vic Picetti, described as the most promising young player on the Pacific Coast that season.

It was a horrible tragedy. Yet club owner Sam Collins decided to finish the baseball season, believing the boys themselves would want the game continued. The only question now was where to find replacements. I got the call. It wasn't the ideal way to make it into professional baseball, but it was still my dream—every boy who has ever played baseball's dream—to make it into the big leagues. The job would mean a move to eastern Washington, and it would mean some years of hard work still before I made the majors. But this wasn't college ball anymore. This was the pros. The offer included a $1,000 signing bonus and $300 a month. It wasn't a lot of money, even in those days. Would I accept?

"Absolutely not," Jerry said, back in our apartment. "There's no way I'm going to pack up and move from Los Angeles to—where did you say—*Spokane*? And we can't live on three hundred dollars a month, Buck."

"Jerry," I said quietly, "this is my dream."

"You're twenty-four years old now, Buck—that's pretty old to begin a career in baseball. Particularly at a farm level. I like the idea of you playing sports well enough—football, anyway—but you'll be riding all over the country on a bus, always trying to make it to the next level. Do you really want to do that?" Yes, I did. I wanted to play baseball, but Jerry was probably right. To be a catcher in the majors, conventional wisdom said you had to put in about five years in the minors first. I would have emerged at age twenty-nine, probably over the hill.

When I turned down the offer from the Spokane Indians, I knew that ended any chance I would ever have of playing professional sports. Playing professional football was out of the question—the leagues just weren't the size they are today. A few guys like Bob Waterfield went on to play in the pros, but very few of the guys I played college football with ever did. One day in the mail I received a questionnaire from Boston's pro football team, asking about my interest level in playing pro ball. It wasn't the same thing as an offer, merely an inquiry. I filled it out and mailed it in, but never heard from them again.

WITH SCHOOL OUT FOR THAT YEAR, I NEEDED A JOB. THE STU-dio business at the time was all closed union, closed shop. You couldn't work unless you belonged to a union. And you couldn't get into the union unless you were the son of a union member. Somehow Coach Bert pulled some strings and got me in for the summer. I became a day laborer, the lowest on the ladder, and went to work on the "nail pile"—knocking down old sets, tearing apart old scenery, and mixing and hauling plaster from which the skilled plasterers made new scenery.

Word came that the industry was short of "juicers" (slang for electricians), as every member of the Studio Electricians Union was already employed. I applied and received a union permit to work as an electrician. I didn't know anything about the industry, but rigging sets with the necessary lights and electrical hookups was better than working on the nail pile any day. For several weeks I worked at Eagle Lion Studio, where they were filming *Arch of Triumph* with Ingrid Bergman and Charles Boyer. I never did get used to working in a union. One day we were sent to a stage to load a number of large coils of cable onto a truck. I picked up a coil and headed for the truck when the union shop steward stopped me cold.

"Set that down immediately," he said. "Two men need to carry that coil."

"It's not heavy," I said. "I can handle it."

"Set it down—now!" he growled. "You're working us out of a job."

We moved to another site that involved loading a bunch of small spotlights onto a truck. I picked up one in each hand and again was ordered to carry only one at a time. This would have never happened in the military. A few weeks later one of my fellow crew members suddenly found himself out of a job. He had worked at the same studio for six years but was still on permit for some reason and could not get a card in the electricians' union. The guy who took his job was a cardholder. All the cardholder had to do was walk on the job site, flash his card, and take the job of the noncarded guy. So much for my experience with union labor. It all offended my sense of fairness.

My little old gray-haired mother, while working as a switchboard operator at a studio, crossed a picket line once. She belonged to the office employees' union, but they weren't on strike. The carpenters and plumbers were. These big old workmen came up and started hassling her, rocking her car and stuff. They were actually trying to turn the car over with my mother in it. She was scared to death. I wanted no part of the unions.

In the fall, I was glad to go back to UCLA. I had a few more classes to take for my degree and a whole year of sports eligibility left. Coach Bert told me he was looking forward to having me back on the football team. We had some solid players, and he was pretty sure we had another shot at going to the Rose Bowl again.

Thoughts of my need for a career began to trouble me. My major was PE—I knew I could always get my teaching credential. But I had taken some education courses, and they were a real turnoff. Playing professional sports was already ruled out. I was a married man now. Children were sure to come right around the corner. I needed something for the long haul, something better than working at the studio. What did I want to do? What could I do? I could jump out of an airplane while getting shot at, I could help liberate a town in Holland, I could dig a foxhole while getting shelled in Bastogne, but none of these skills would get me a job.

I needed advice. Goodwin Knight, a high school classmate of my father's, seemed like a good place to start. Knight was a Superior Court judge (he later ran for office and became lieutenant governor and later governor of California) and received me warmly. He directed me to a former law partner, Sid Cherniss, who was a big sports fan and booster of USC, where he was an alumnus. Cherniss had often razzed me from the bench whenever USC played UCLA. To my surprise, Cherniss also received me warmly. He had a nice-looking office, wore a nice suit, and joked around as I asked him questions about potential careers.

"How do you get into this racket?" I asked.

"Well, you gotta go to law school," Cherniss said. "Would you be interested in going?"

Law school? It was the farthest thing from my mind. No one in my family had ever graduated from college, much less been a lawyer. None of us knew any lawyers. Sid Cherniss was the first lawyer I had ever met. My undergraduate record was something less than spectacular. PE majors weren't exactly known as academic heavyweights. With jobs and ROTC and practice and varsity games and fraternity life and girls—well, sometimes studying just had to take a backseat.

"It's not easy to get into law school," Cherniss continued. "With all these GIs returning from the war, there are twenty guys standing in line for every opening. And it's hard going when and if you get in— you really have to buckle down and hit the books. But if you want, I'll put in a good word for you with the dean at USC law school."

I nodded.

The dean at USC turned me down flat. No way would I even be considered, not even with Cherniss's recommendation. UCLA did not have a law school at the time, so that wasn't an option. But nearby Loyola University had a law school, and Cherniss knew Father Joseph Donovan, a Jesuit priest, who headed the law school there. Cherniss arranged a meeting for me. Loyola's undergraduate campus was located in Playa Del Rey, but their law school was located in downtown LA in those days. I drove over for the meeting. I knew it was a long shot to get in, but I figured it couldn't hurt to try.

"Buck Compton from UCLA," Father Donovan said. His face was grim. "So you're a football and a baseball player—what do you think of St. Louis?"

I shrugged. "The Cardinals are strong," I said. "Dizzy Dean, Leo Durocher, Ducky Medwick—they've got great players. They're one of my favorite teams." Father Donovan's face broke into a smile. As luck would have it, Father Donovan was a huge baseball fan and a devoted follower of St. Louis. We spent the rest of our meeting talking baseball. At the end of the meeting we eventually came back to the possibility of me applying for law school. His face grew grim again.

"Based on your academic record, I'm disinclined to even permit you to lodge an application for admission," Father Donovan said. "I just don't think you've got what it takes."

His response didn't surprise me.

We shook hands and left.

Something in me wasn't finished yet. I scheduled another meeting with Father Donovan. Again, we talked baseball. Again, I asked him about applying to law school. Again, he said no.

I scheduled another meeting. Same thing. "You won't make it," he repeated. "I won't permit you to apply. You don't have what it takes."

I scheduled a final meeting. I don't know exactly why. Maybe it was my competitive nature, but I simply wouldn't take no for an answer. I guess I had made up my mind that I was going to show him that I could make it. I knew I wasn't dumb. I knew I wasn't a great student—but a lot of the courses I had taken, I just didn't like. If given the chance, I knew I could do better. During our final meeting, Father Donovan shook his head, again. I got up to leave, extending my hand to shake hands with him. He kept his hands at his side. A moment of silence passed. He seemed to still be thinking.

"I admire your persistence," he said at last. "I'll tell you what I'll do. I've developed a legal aptitude test. The test is not easy, but there's no harm in you taking it. If you score well, I'll allow you to file an application for law school."

Father Donovan extended his hand.

I shook it.

The test was made up of a series of essays and factual analysis. I took the test and thought I did okay. Father Donovan allowed me to file an application anyway. So I did. Time passed and I heard nothing. I assumed I was rejected.

That was the final no I needed. I wouldn't try again.

WHEN FOOTBALL PRACTICE BEGAN AT UCLA AT THE END OF AU-gust, I turned out and was greeted by Coach La Brucherie. I held a starting spot at guard on the team. This was going to be our big year. All thoughts of law school were behind me. I still didn't know what I'd do for a career, but I knew something would fall into place. One week before classes and the 1946 football season began, a letter from Loyola University Law School arrived in the mail. I couldn't believe me eyes.

Accepted.

"Coach, what should I do?" I asked Coach Bert. I desperately wanted to go to law school, but I had already told him I'd play football at UCLA—hey, I *wanted* to play football. I also desperately did not want to let Coach Bert down; we had so much history together.

Coach Bert took a long look at me. "That's a hell of an opportunity you've got," he said. "But I don't think one season of football is worth passing up going to law school."

I respected him so much. I nodded.

In September 1946, I quit UCLA and enrolled at Loyola University's law school. The GI Bill paid my tuition as well as some living expenses. That was commonplace in the days before the ACLU woke up to the fact that the government was subsidizing Catholic schools with federal money. UCLA ended up going to the Rose Bowl again that season, this time without me. Illinois defeated us 45-14. UCLA had a powerhouse team that year, but J. C. Caroline and the great Buddy Young played for Illinois and ran UCLA ragged. Regardless of how the score turned out, I've always been a bit sorry that I can't say I played in two Rose Bowls.

In the long run, though, I knew I had made the better decision.

NOT ALL WAS SMOOTH WITH MY TRANSITION INTO LAW SCHOOL.

Jerry got a job that fall working for Farmers Insurance. We settled into a rather dull routine, her working and me going to school and studying. Our social life was zilch. Financially, we were just holding on. It didn't take long before the routine began to wear on my wife. She was a young girl who probably had the right to expect a little more excitement in life. I wasn't sharp enough to realize it. I was just so nuts about her—I thought that's all it took to make a successful marriage. If I were to do it all over again, I would have tried harder. I would have taken her out every chance I got. I would have made things work.

One evening a few weeks before Christmas, I came home from school to find our apartment looking like an isolation ward. It was stripped clean of everything. There wasn't a glass in the cupboard. There wasn't a spoon in the drawer. Lamps, clocks, food in the refrigerator—it was all gone.

I called her mother.

"Jerry's come home for a while," she said. "She wants some time to think things over."

The next thing I knew, Jerry was dating a Marine pilot.

The divorce was quick and simple. We had no property. She had all the wedding gifts. We went our separate ways. Surely it was more complicated than that. A divorce devastates you. But that's all I want to say about it.

The war was such an interruption in our lives. You leave and do your time and try to pick up as best you can afterward. Some pick up better than others. Do I blame my divorce on the war? No. Maybe Jerry and I got married too soon. Maybe we got married only because that's what all returning GIs and their sweethearts did. Sure, the war shook everything up—our timelines, our plans, our hopes—maybe it even colored our discernment. But it's far too easy to blame your mistakes on the tough times you've gone through in the past. Each mistake carries its own responsibility.

When Jerry and I split up, I did know this: Returning to normalcy wasn't going to be as easy as I first thought.

· 21 ·

Vice

WHEN JERRY MOVED OUT, I NEEDED SOMEONE TO HELP PAY THE
rent. My buddy from high school football days, Steve Williams, also
attended law school with me, and moved into the apartment. Steve
loved to eat. Right away he claimed control of the kitchen and insisted
on hearty, well-balanced meals. Steve was a fine cook, but money was
tight for both of us. We didn't even have money for dishes or cook-
ware, as Jerry had taken all the wedding presents. One day I suggested
to Steve that we could save some cash by cutting down on food.

"Absolutely not," Steve said flatly. "Cut down somewhere else,
but never on good food." I never asked him again. We ate like kings.

Steve and I were both attending law school on the GI Bill, which
covered tuition and provided a modest stipend. But money was always tight. We decided to start an attorney service business to make a
few extra bucks, operating it out of the apartment. Everything was on
a shoestring. Amazingly, we drummed up a few clients. We filed documents with the county clerk and served summonses and subpoenas.

It was all grunt work, but we didn't mind. We were working within our field of study and making some good connections along the way.

One day we got a job related to a lawsuit against actress Hedy Lamarr. A colorful woman, her first husband had been an arms manufacturer. She was a great beauty and known for playing love-hungry movie roles. She was also a woman of science and had invented technology that made radio-guided torpedoes harder for the enemy to detect or jam. Our job was to serve a summons and complaint against her. For some reason, Steve decided that I should be the one to go to her Beverly Hills mansion to serve the papers. Celebrities were not as well protected as they are today. I simply drove to her house and knocked on the front door. A maid answered.

"Is Miss Lamarr home?" I asked.

Suddenly I caught a glimpse of dark brown hair. The maid scrambled to get out of the way. Hedy Lamarr stood squarely in the doorway, wearing a bathrobe, and scowling darkly at me. I held out the papers. She grabbed them, wheeled around, and slammed the door. Neither one of us had uttered a word. That was my meeting Hedy Lamarr.

On another day in downtown LA, I ran across an old friend, Jack Colbern, a chance meeting that would prove to alter the course of my life. Jack had played some professional baseball and managed in the minor leagues. During my days at UCLA, Jack had umpired some of our games. As a catcher, I often developed a friendly rapport with umpires as they called the balls and strikes.

"Buck, nice to see you again," Jack said. "What are you doing these days anyway?"

"Going to law school just around the corner at Loyola," I said. "How about you?"

"I'm working central vice," he said. "You should join the force— LAPD's got a great baseball team."

"Become a cop?" I said.

"Yeah, so you can play baseball."

The idea was so crazy that I took Jack up on it. A few days later I applied to the city for a job with the Los Angeles Police Department. I took the written exam and went down to the Coliseum to take the physical exam. It was no problem to pass either. I got on the list and they soon called to offer me a job as a policeman. I joined the department in early 1947 and was sent to the Police Academy in Elysian Park. The training lasted for three months—eight hours a day, five days a week. This meant I had to shift all my law school classes to night courses and study on weekends. Steve assumed all responsibilities for the attorney service.

I went to the academy, passed, and was assigned to Central Vice, headquartered in the old central police station at First and Hill streets in downtown LA, about twelve blocks from the law school. I also joined the departmental baseball team right away. Central Vice was under the patrol division commanded by Deputy Chief Thad Brown. Chief Brown was well respected in police circles as well as by the press.

Chief Brown was also a big fan of baseball.

Some breaks in life are just handed to you. This was one of them. Chief Brown cherry-picked me for my first assignment. Plainclothes duty. Right out of the academy. It meant I didn't need to serve in uniform first. Pulling plainclothes duty immediately out of the academy is unheard-of today. In fact, it was unheard-of in those days. From my chance meeting with Jack Colbern on the streets of LA, in a few short months I had gone from grunt-work attorney courier to plainclothes policeman for the LAPD. It was a full-time career position with salary and benefits.

All thanks to baseball.

ALTHOUGH I NOW HAD A FULL-TIME CAREER, I DECIDED NOT TO drop out of law school. Getting into law school in the first place had proved such a challenge, I guess I didn't want to let that opportunity pass me by. With the academy finished, I continued taking sixteen units of law school classes each quarter, working 10:00 A.M. to

6:00 P.M. with the LAPD and carrying a full load of classes mornings and evenings. I was able to catch two classes each morning, one at eight, the other at nine (each class lasted fifty minutes), then sprint down to the Central Police station to do my shift as a policeman, then sprint back to do two more classes, one at six and the other at seven each night. The pace was tough, to say the least, but I wanted to get school over with. I decided to go year-round and not take summers off. Law school was a three-year program, but I stayed on pace to finish in two and a half years.

Baseball also hit with a fury. The LAPD team played in the various semipro leagues around the area, and also against the college teams at UCLA and USC. Besides that, we played spring training games against the LA Angels and the Hollywood Stars of the Pacific Coast League. We played a lot of our games at a field in Glendale, a suburb of LA. The Oakland Oaks of the Pacific Coast League trained there, and it was eventually named Casey Stengel Field. Stengel was manager of the Oaks, and Billy Martin (who went on to become one of the most colorful managers in the history of baseball) was just breaking in as a second baseman. I played ball against both. In 1948 our team went to Chicago to play three games against the Chicago PD team. We played two games at Wrigley Field and one at Comiskey Park and won all three.

While in the locker room at Comiskey Park, I found a bat used by Pat Seerey, who had set a record by hitting four home runs in one game at that park. The bat felt heavier than usual and had a very thin handle. It felt like a buggy whip when I swung it. It seemed as if the handle actually bent. I brought the bat back to LA with me and used it in our next game.

Whack! The first time I used it, I hit a ball so hard to the third baseman that it hit him in the chest before he could even get his hands up. I was onto something. The next time I was up to bat I eyed the same third baseman.

Crack! This time I caught the ball on the handle. The bat shattered. That was the end of that experiment.

I stayed active in the military reserves and joined an armored unit. A couple of my friends from the LAPD were in the same unit. In 1946 the United States Air Force was established as a separate branch of service. A high-ranking FBI agent, Joseph Carroll, was asked to form a unit within the Air Force comparable to the Army Criminal Investigation Division (historically referred to as CID). The unit was to be known as the Office of Special Investigations (OSI). It had both criminal and counterintelligence functions. Many of the personnel assigned were former FBI agents along with other military investigators.

A couple of my friends from the LAPD joined the OSI as reservists. I followed their lead. I was assigned to the unit at Maywood Air Force Base in LA County. One of my fellow reservists was a municipal court judge named Evelle Younger. A former FBI agent, Younger had served with the OSS (precursor to the CIA) during the war. Many years later Younger retired as a major general in the reserves. Younger would also play a key role in the development of my career.

I LOVED MY JOB WITH THE POLICE DEPARTMENT. I'VE ALWAYS been very fortunate that way. Not everybody gets to work at what they like to do. Except for some of the menial jobs I had in college or as a kid, I've always been able to say I enjoyed every career job I had. My first assignment was to crack down on illegal offtrack wagering on horse races. Remember how in junior high I organized offtrack betting among my friends at school? Well, this was the same thing, except at a grown-up level—and now I was on the other side of the law.

Bookmaking activity was widespread in LA, and, while not monolithic in scope, it was operated by several fairly well-organized groups of Mafia-type crime families. On-track betting was legal, but only one track operated at any one time in LA. One, called Santa Anita, was out in Arcadia. The other, Hollywood Park, was out in Inglewood. If you lived up in the San Fernando Valley, for instance, you couldn't afford the time or money to run out to the track every day, thus offtrack betting. And there were plenty of guys who played the horses every day.

Laws against offtrack betting always cause a big debate. As far as I know, laws against gambling were on the books long before the tracks opened, but a lot of horse players will tell you that the only reason offtrack betting is illegal is that the tracks with all their money behind them got the legislature to force everybody to go to the track. Whatever the reasons for the laws, they were there. The state took offtrack betting very seriously, and bookmaking was a felony. We seldom booked the bettor. We went after the people running the system. The bookmaking business was really a giant octopus of people. The guys at the center made all the money. That's who we wanted.

Being assigned to enforce laws against bookmaking sometimes felt like shoveling against the tide. You could control it, but never eradicate it. Gambling, like prostitution, is always going to go on, no matter what you do. We aimed to make arrests as public as possible. We knew we weren't going to stop every bookmaker in Los Angeles. But we wanted the public to know we were making effort to suppress it.

As a rookie plainclothesman, I was assigned to a partner, Al Boswell, a Texan who told stories as large as the state he was from. We called him Boz. He was a real character. Boz hated FDR so much that when the Roosevelt dime came out, he'd throw it on the floor and walk out of a store whenever he got one as change. He wasn't a redneck. He was simply opinionated. Boz had moved out from Texas to attend USC, where he graduated with a degree in marketing. Jobs were hard to find after the war, so he entered the LAPD. We had a lot of well-educated guys like him on the force. Every morning he'd stop the patrol car and buy a newspaper. We'd park in a lot and he'd read me Westbrook Pegler's syndicated column. Pegler was a Pulitzer-winning journalist whose conservative views frequently warned of the dangers of a dictatorship being created in America. Boz helped shape many of my political beliefs.

Boz was older than I, and his face more recognized in the neighborhoods we patrolled. No one recognized me yet. As a result, I often got sent to check things out by myself. When I went into bars, I never carried my gun. With the getups we wore, it was too hard to conceal a weapon. Mostly I felt safe. In those days you seldom ran into anybody who pulled a gun on you. Downtown LA was rough, but it wasn't the type of life-and-death climate it is today. Even the criminals had a certain respect for the law. They might spit on you. Or swear. But usually they'd go down without incident.

Sometimes, however, they'd back up their crime with their fists.

We had been tipped off that a bookie was working a certain bar in the area. I decided to check it out. I had acquired a cabdriver's cap somewhere that I wore as part of my plainclothes. With my cabdriver's getup on, I walked into the bar, ordered a beer, and glanced at the mirror over the back bar. In the reflection I could see it all going down. Sure enough, a guy walked over to another guy in a booth and handed him some cash and a marker, the piece of paper that recorded a bet.

I swung off the bar and walked toward the men. They seemed engrossed in their conversation and apparently didn't notice me. I doubt if anyone would've suspected a cabbie of anything. When I reached the booth, I didn't say a word; I just reached down to confiscate the marker and the money, which were both in the player's hand. I knew the bookmaker would go down easy—they never wanted any trouble. But the guy holding the money was a big lout who thought he knew better. He jerked his hand away. I caught his wrist and showed him my badge at the same time.

"I'm a policeman," I said. "Hand it over."

"You SOB," the player growled. Instantly he was off, running.

I took off after him.

He sprinted around tables and chairs, clattering across the bar's dance floor and toward a hallway. At the end of the hallway was a door. He flung it open only to discover it was nothing but a storage closet. Frustrated, he spun around and barreled by me in the hallway, headed back into the bar. I spun around and chased after him. He must have realized he couldn't go any farther—he stopped running and picked up a chair, ready to bash me. I was still running full steam and charged into him with my shoulder, knocking him down. The chair flew out of his hands and smashed across the floor. He didn't get up. I took a step over to where he lay and put my foot on his chest.

In downtown Los Angeles in the late 1940s, if you announced to an entire bar that you were a policeman, you'd never know exactly what to expect, or who might decide to join in. Respect for the law notwithstanding, I wasn't about to take any chances. With my foot still on the player's chest, I cleared my throat and glared at the rest of the men in the bar: "Any more tough guys in here who want to take me on?" I said loudly, so all could hear.

None stepped forward.

Did my years in combat give me a certain fearlessness in later years? Probably. If I could avoid a fight, I would. But sometimes you've got to fight. If needed, I had confidence I could do that, too.

Working for the LAPD wasn't all success.

Those were the days before some of the strict rules about police work were in effect. In those days you could just sort of show up at a door and bash it in. One day we got a tip that some bookies were operating a phone spot in a nearby apartment. We went to check it out. When we knocked, there was no answer, so I reared back and kicked in the door. Inside was nobody except a little old white-haired grandma, shaking like a leaf. I apologized profusely and paid to replace the door out of my own pocket. Whether the tip was a miscommunication or whether somebody set us up, we never knew. Those things happen.

My career with the LAPD was pretty well under way, but my social life was another matter. A divorce can really suck the wind out of your sails. I was never a big dater. I liked going out with friends whenever I had a free moment, but what I really wanted was someone to settle down with. Somebody to build a life with together. I had no idea where to start looking for her.

One day a phone call offered a glimmer of hope.

· 22 ·

Happy Again

MY UNCLE HAD WORKED HIS WAY UP IN THE PICTURE BUSINESS
and gotten a job as casting director at Republic Studios, where Roy
Rogers had started his movie career. One day out of the blue my
uncle called me up. "You know, Buck, there's a real cute gal working
down at the studio. Come on out and I'll introduce you to her."

"I don't know," I said. "The ink hasn't even dried on my divorce
yet."

"Just promise me you won't take advantage of her, okay?" he
said. The protectiveness in my uncle's voice surprised me. He didn't
say that because he was worried about me. I figured this girl really
must be something special. On a break from police work, Boz and I
went to the casting office to check things out.

Behind the desk sat a real sharp gal. Her name was Donna New-
man. She was only twenty, but she had worked at the studio right out
of high school. She wasn't what you'd call a *striking* beauty—not exactly a Marilyn Monroe type, but she had a nice face, cute short

brown hair, and a good figure—you'd call her a good-looking gal. We made small talk at the casting office. It was just an excuse to be introduced.

I got the nerve to ask her out.

She said yes.

Steve Williams and his girlfriend were set to double date with Donna and me. The plan was to go to the beach at Laguna, then out to dinner at Corona Del Mar. I knew dancing would be involved. My mother and my aunt had taught me how to dance a little, but I was never great at it. At the time, the samba was all the rage. I knew I would have to dance the samba with Donna.

"Steve," I said as we were getting ready, "what am I supposed to do?"

"Half an hour before a date?" He gave me a frown. "That's no time to learn."

"C'mon," I urged. "I really want to make a good impression on Donna."

You could see Steve wince. It felt like ten minutes went by while he thought about it. "Oh, all right," he snapped at last, grabbing my hand. "Come here. Your feet move lightly, three steps at a time. No—not like that. Bend your knee more. Good." And with that, Steve Williams taught me how to dance the samba. It must have been a hilarious sight—two hulky ex-football players bouncing around the room—but in the end I learned enough so I could get by.

Steve went on to marry the girl he went out with that night. They raised a family of seven children and had a long, happy life together. After law school, Steve became deputy DA of San Bernardino County, then went into private practice for a few years. Later he became a superior court judge. When he was in private practice, he volunteered as chairman of the Barry Goldwater campaign for his area. (Goldwater was the Republican nominee for the 1964 presidential race, which democratic incumbent Lyndon Johnson eventually won.) Once I asked Steve how he found time to volunteer when he had such a large family to raise. "If you aren't willing to get out and fight for what you believe in," Steve said, "you've got no right complaining about what's wrong with the country." Steve always did know how to put things plainly.

Donna and I got along swell. She was a great dancer and didn't seem to mind that I stepped on her feet a lot. She thought it was funny that I got so worked up on the dance floor that my celluloid shirt stays (tabs in the collar) got steamy and bent. I must have still been approaching the samba like a football player.

After that first date, Donna and I began seeing a lot of each other. She was gifted with an infectious sense of humor and a large reservoir of one-liners. Her work ethic impressed me immediately. She was raised in a family that had never been rich. I don't think there was a selfish bone in her body. To show you what kind of gal she was—she soon had a key to my apartment—she'd come over when Steve and I weren't there and clean the place 'cause we were such slobs. Donna also had a strong sense of morals. She loved children, and her major goal in life was to be a wife and mother. Everyone who knew Donna adored her.

We were married in October 1947. The marriage worked from moment one. We were always together from that day on.

Steve kept the apartment. Donna and I lived with her folks for the first couple of weeks after getting married. A fraternity friend of mine from UCLA had built some one-story apartments in Burbank, and we rented one soon after. I continued with law school and police work while Donna continued at Republic Studios, soon moving from casting to the publicity office. Not long after, she got a job with the Raymond Morgan advertising agency in Hollywood. Donna was assistant to the producer and writer of a TV show called "The Lucky U Ranch," which featured the western singing group Sons of the Pioneers. The show featured Arizona cowboy Rex Allen, a singer and actor, and Ken Curtis, best known as "Festus" on the TV series *Gunsmoke*. The company was a close-knit group, and we had a lot of fun at various house parties when they would all get together.

Sometimes Donna and I would jump in the car on a Friday night and head to Vegas for the weekend. We took a trip to New York City to see a friend who was getting married. Everything we did together worked out well. With both of us working and me still going to school as well as working for the LAPD, our schedules were crammed full all round. I still had to study and prepare for tests on weekends. There was usually a ballgame to play also. Donna hung in there and never complained once about the life we were leading. She always had a smile. If I lived another eighty lifetimes, I could never say enough good things about her.

I couldn't remember when I had ever been so happy.

IN JUNE 1949, I COMPLETED MY STUDIES AT LOYOLA AND PASSED the bar exam. I don't know why exactly, but I didn't seek work as an attorney right away. Maybe there was a part of police work that wasn't out of my system yet.

I was soon transferred to the Police Academy, where I taught legal subjects such as Criminal Law and Evidence. My supervisor at the academy was Lieutenant Tom Reddin, who later became chief of police. Daryl Gates, who also later became chief of police of LA, was a recruit in one of my classes. Gates's career came to an end following the 1992 riots in Los Angeles that transpired after the acquittal of police officers shown beating Rodney King, a taxi driver arrested for drunk driving.

Many policemen aspire to work in the Detective Bureau, and I was no exception. When Thad Brown became chief of detectives, he transferred me from the academy to the Detective Bureau. It proved to be some of the grimmest work I would ever encounter.

My first unit was known as the Business Office. In reality, it served as both the entry and exit point for detectives in their careers. The only guys in it were either young guys like myself, or older officers nearing retirement, often only interested in putting in their remaining time. The Business Office operated during graveyard hours, from midnight to 8:00 A.M., and that became my shift. The duty involved manning radio cars and patrolling the streets of a given area. We wore plainclothes and answered calls that required detectives. Frankly, I never thought the system worked in anybody's best interest. The old-timers, like the partner I worked with (not Boz, but another guy), were not particularly enthusiastic about working very hard. The young-timers such as myself were still green in many ways and tended to defer to the more senior officers.

Most of our calls were for dead bodies. They rarely turned out to be homicides. Mostly they were winos who'd died of malnutrition or druggies who overdosed in fleabag hotels. Our most important function seemed to be preventing overzealous hearse drivers from stealing cash off the bodies we found. The worst thing about the job was the hours. I never was able to flip-flop my schedule completely around. I'd sleep from the time I got home in the morning until it was time to get up and go back to work. How Donna ever put up with it, I don't know. Thankfully, the assignment lasted less than a year and I was transferred to the Central Burglary Division, headquartered in city hall.

Burglary is one of the most difficult crimes to solve. Suspects are seldom captured at the scene, and it takes a lot of tricks to figure out who committed the crime, then catch him. Our division was subdivided into specialties. One group of detectives kept watch over the pawnshops, searching for identifiable property that had been reported stolen. Another crew handled safe burglars. Another specialized in hotels. My partner and I handled residential and small business burglaries. This was the kind of police work I had hankered for.

One day the captain called me into his office.

"Know a guy named Danny Apple?" he asked.

I did. He was a kid I had known at LA High and a real character. We often ate lunch together; I'd say he was a pretty close friend. I hadn't seen him since high school.

"He's in Folsom," the captain said. "Held up a jewelry store in Beverly Hills. Why don't you go up there and talk to Danny about what else he knows." I nodded. Folsom State Prison had been built in the late 1800s and was known as one of the harshest around. I made the drive up to the Sacramento area to talk to Danny.

"Well, if it isn't good ole Buck Compton—how the hell are you?" Danny said as we sat down in the small conference room. His big grin surprised me. We talked about high school for some time, then got down to brass tacks. His friendly tone became hushed.

"There's this Greek shipping magnate," he whispered. "Gratzos is his name. Kept a full-time mistress at the Bel Air Hotel. She had jewels coming out her ears. Full-length mink coats. The real stuff. I knocked over his suite when they weren't there. Got off with a million cold. I was popping all those diamonds out of the settings—they were falling all over the floor like popcorn." He laughed his head off. I couldn't believe what Danny was admitting to me. This was one of the biggest burglaries in terms of value of property stolen in the history of the LAPD. Danny kept right on talking. He told me about job after job. He named all the people involved and to whom he had fenced the loot.

Danny was already doing hard time, so I guess that's why an additional prosecution was never pushed for. Keeping Danny's trust for the information he provided was too valuable. When Danny was paroled, he came back to Los Angeles and became a consistent informant for me. Through the information he provided, I was able to solve a wide number of burglary cases committed by other people and make the arrests.

I don't know how Danny ever pulled it off, but he ended up owning a fancy restaurant and bar over on Laurel Canyon and Sunset— quite a good place for food and drinks. He must have had some dough stashed somewhere. Every once in a while I'd take Donna to the restaurant, sometimes with friends or business associates. It never seemed to matter who was with us, Danny would pull up a chair at

our table and gab away about the various jobs he had pulled. Sometimes he caused some seriously raised eyebrows on behalf of our dinner guests. Donna and I just chuckled about it.

WHILE WORKING BURGLARY, I MADE CONTACT WITH AN FBI
agent who worked interstate jewel theft cases. We got to be close
friends and worked well together. I had applied to work at the FBI once
right after I passed the bar, but got turned down. I never heard the reason why, but my FBI friends suspected my divorce was a major factor.

Because of my law degree, I was asked by two other FBI agents who
organized training schools for smaller local police agencies to teach
some classes at these schools. Both of these agents also became close
friends. Conventional wisdom holds that police officers and FBI agents
often don't get along. The FBI has a habit of moving in on cases and el-
bowing the locals out. But I've always figured it was good policy to get
along with whomever I could. One of the agents with whom I became
very close friends, Bill McCloud, eventually became undersheriff for LA
County. The other, Bill South, became chief of security for Southern
California Edison. Knowing them helped advance my career later.

The longer you stay in police work, the more it becomes apparent
that you need to decide if you want to make a lifetime career out of it.
Frankly, I enjoyed the job and was pretty sure I wanted to make a go
of it for the next thirty years or so. I used to ride around in the police
car and see a guy breaking his back out on a jackhammer somewhere
and I'd think, *Man, I'd much rather be doing this than that.*

But it wasn't without its difficulties. While working Burglary, I
needed to work nights on several stakeout missions. I never could stay
awake nights worth beans. One incident was close to tragic. At the
time, a lot of Safeway stores in our area were getting broken into.
The crooks were hitting all the stores on Saturday nights. They'd
break in through the back of the store, locate the safe at the front of
the store, then drag it to the rear storage area, where they'd drill the

lock out and take the loot. They had the system down cold and could be in and out within thirty minutes.

Our captain devised a "rolling" stakeout. Teams of detectives from our division were assigned lists of stores that could be visited within a half hour. We kept moving from one store to another all Saturday night. After driving to a store, one detective would stay in the car. The other would get out, walk around, and listen at the store's back door for the sound of an electric drill.

One night my partner Bob Uribe and I had done the routine at several stores, with no results. It was nearing dawn and I was exhausted. One last store to go. Bob parked the car. I got out and dragged myself around to the back door. Nothing. I leaned against the store's backdoor and closed my eyes . . .

. . . just for a minute.

You know that jolt you get when you wake up suddenly and don't know where you are? Maybe you're in bed. Maybe it's the couch in your living room. Maybe you're standing upright with a loaded police shotgun in your hands.

"Compton! Wake up! What're you doing? It's me, for crying out loud!"

In the dim light of the back of the store, I jolted awake. I was pointing my shotgun at my partner's head. Because I had spent longer than usual at the backdoor, Bob thought I had heard the burglar's drill. He came running to check things out. His approach startled me out of a dead sleep. I had turned on Bob with the gun. Thankfully, I realized what was happening before I pulled the trigger. Later, we both had a nervous laugh about that one.

Fortunately the Safeway stakeouts eventually worked, and we captured the burglars.

I also got involved with phone taps. The idea of phone taps today tends to scare people, but you need to realize they're quite few and far between in reality. Basically, any time you tap a phone, you've got to have someone listening on the other end sorting out what's being said, so the whole operation is extremely time-intensive. The idea of cops sitting around listening to everybody's phone line just ain't going to happen.

The chief of detectives at the time had a squad of detectives whose specialty was planting listening devices and wiretaps. While working on a gang of burglars, I was able to use the squad's services. The chief controlled the squad closely and allowed detectives to use it only if they were working on a major case. Danny Apple had tipped me off to the name of one of the gang, so we stuck a microphone down the vent of the suspect's kitchen stove. For days we listened. Nothing good. All we heard was the sound of eggs frying and the burglar's wife hollering at her kid. The kid was a real terror and had to be ordered to eat each meal. "Johnny! Eat your breakfast! Johnny! Eat your lunch! Johnny! Eat your dinner! The little man in your stomach is hungry!" (That line I remember verbatim.)

The microphone proved useless. So we obtained permission to do a phone tap on the suspect. This was the jackpot we had been waiting for. A noted Hollywood stuntman called the burglar repeatedly. Through listening to the phone calls, we learned how the crime ring worked. Basically, the stuntman would scope out the residences of all the wealthy celebrities and power players he worked for, then tip off a group of burglars to the locations and contents of the homes as well as the whereabouts of the homeowners. For days the stuntman made calls about all the prime places to burglarize. We were able to bring the gang down.

IN 1949, DONNA AND I PURCHASED A SMALL HOUSE IN NORTH Hollywood. It was brand-new, built by the same fraternity brother who had rented us our apartment. The house was tiny, just two bedrooms and a bathroom, about 900 square feet, and cost us $9,000.

In 1951, I had been with the LAPD for five years. I was twenty-nine years old. Donna suggested that since we had invested a lot of

Me with my scooter. I'm about four years old here in front of our home on Lucerne Avenue.
Courtesy Compton family

Me, age eight, 1930. I don't know why I'm so dressed up.
Courtesy Compton family

My parents, Ethel and Roby Compton, who were married in 1918,
in San Diego during World War I.
Courtesy Compton family

Me with my dad, Roby Compton. I'm about sixteen. Note, we're at home
and he's got his tie on. It's not loosened.
Courtesy Compton family

Me with my maternal grandmother, Laura Cleveland.
I have my paratrooper boots on,
so I've just been through jump
school, but have not yet gone to
Europe. It's probably late 1943
here.
Courtesy Compton family

This picture was taken in
Aldbourne just before
Christmas 1943. Aunt Dot is
my mother's sister.
Courtesy Compton family

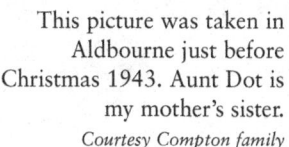

My wife Donna's high school
graduation photo.
Courtesy Compton family

Me in 1941. This picture
was taken for the UCLA
Athletics publicity office.
Note the leather helmet.
I played guard, both
offensive and defensive.
Courtesy Compton family

This is a group of ROTC guys at UCLA, probably 1942. We were heading out on a week-end campout. The campout must have been close to the campus, because we're hiking there. I'm in the front row, third from the right. Jack Singlaub is in the group too, though I couldn't tell you where. *Photo by Herb Dallinger, courtesy Compton family*

Members of the 2nd Battalion at the marriage of Ronald Speirs, to a girl he met in Aldbourne, where the wedding took place. Speirs is crouching, front row, on left. I'm in the back row, far right. Other members unidentified could be from companies other than E. *Courtesy Compton family*

Home alive, 1946. The war is over at this point, and I'm back in the States. My mother asked me to get a picture taken in my military uniform.
Courtesy Compton family

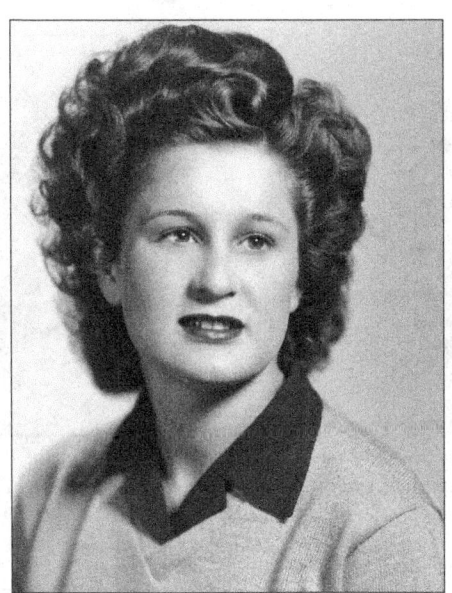

My wife, Donna, 1944.
Courtesy Compton family

Our daughters, Syndee and Tracy, ages three and four,
about 1960.
Courtesy Compton family

The Seine Clowns baseball team in France, 1945. I'm in the catcher's uniform in the front row. Chuck Eisenmann is next to me on the right.
Courtesy of Gary Bedingfield, www.baseballinwartime.co.uk

BASEBALL, TOO! Track won't be the ly event on the California docket tomor- w. The baseball team meets U. C. L. A.

right after the meet ends. Among the visit ing Bruins is Lynn "Buck" Compton, catcher Bears beat Stanford on Wednesday. 16-0.

Me in 1942. I think this was from the Cal Berkeley newspaper.
Courtesy Compton family

This picture was taken in 1946 for the UCLA Athletics publicity office.

Courtesy Compton family

ALL-COAST?

HARD-HITTING CATCHER—Buck Compton, who looks lik Art Reichle's leading hitter in the coming horsehide season will lead the Bruins against the Los Angeles Police nine her next Monday.

The UCLA paper, 1946, after I came home.

Courtesy Compton family

Two Good Appointments

TWO MEN in the prosecuting field we've long admired for capability, intelligence and fairness have just received key appointments from the new county District Attorney, Evelle Younger.

They are Ted Sten, who returns as head of the Long Beach office of the District Attorney, and Lynn D. Compton, appointed chief of the Branch and Offices Division.

It is gratifying that the new District Attorney has continued these good men on the staff of his office, capitalizing on their years of experience with his predecessor's administration.

Sten was chief prosecutor here for 18 years before moving to the main office in 1962, taking the job to which Compton now goes. He grew up in Long Beach and as a boy carried the old Long Beach Telegram. He is a law graduate of USC. We are glad to see him back with his old job here.

Compton, educated at Loyola and UCLA, is one of the state's outstanding prosecution officers. His appearances before legislative committees on matters pertaining to law enforcement have been most effective. He made an excellent record in the office here and in his new work will be District Attorney Younger's chief liaison officer.

The appointments of Sten and Compton help to give the new District Attorney's administration an auspicious start.

Editorial in the *Long Beach Independent*, December 24, 1964.

Courtesy Compton family

When I became Chief Deputy in 1964. My boss Evelle Younger (R) is handing me my badge, which I still have.

Photo by Lt. Walter Morgan, courtesy Compton family

Judge Compton. This picture was taken in the early 1970s for the Blue Book, a state directory of judicial and government officials.
Photo by Elson Alexandre, courtesy Compton family

My daughter Tracy and me in L.A., after a *Band of Brothers* screening.
Courtesy Compton family

My daughter Syndee and me.
Courtesy Compton family

Don Malarkey and me. This picture was taken for a school fund-raising event
in Washington.

Courtesy Compton family

Tom Hanks and me in L.A. at a screening of *Band of Brothers*, 2001.
Courtesy Compton family

Neal McDonough and me at a screening
of *Band of Brothers*, 2001.
Courtesy Compton family

time and effort in getting a law degree, it was time to make some use of it. She didn't make a big deal out of it, but her encouragement and the debt I felt I owed her for the struggle I had put her through when I was studying all that time made me sit up and take notice. Donna was right. We had both expended effort to get that law degree and it was time we made use of it. I could go farther in a law career than I could in the PD.

When you're a detective, you're in the district attorney's office quite a bit, showing him your evidence and what you've got. You're also in the DA's office for preliminary hearings, and if a case comes to trial. A detective tends to make a lot of connections in the DA's office. I had joined the Masonic Order, the Knights Templar, and the Peace Officers' Shrine Club as a policeman. I also went to the American Legion Luncheon Club a lot, which counted in its membership many public officials. In the course of those various connections I had met S. Ernest Roll, then chief deputy DA of Los Angeles County.

I went and talked to Ernie Roll about a job. Roll agreed to hire me as a deputy district attorney. As far as he knew, I was the first ex-policeman to make that move, he said. In making the move, I took a cut in pay. As a policeman I made $350 per month. As a deputy DA, I made $347.

· 23 ·

My First Trial

IN MY NEW JOB IN THE DA'S OFFICE, I WAS ONE COG IN A HUGE machine. It is amazing to me, as I look back on it, that this huge organization had no formalized training program for incoming lawyers. Everything was strictly on-the-job training.

In 1951, Los Angeles County was the largest and most populous county in California, with 7 million people, 55 incorporated cities, and covering 4,000 square miles. As the primary prosecuting official of all felonies and many misdemeanors committed in the county, the district attorney of LA County was (and still is) considered the third most important political job in the state, after governor and attorney general. At the time, there were some 700 lawyers, 100 investigators, and 300 clerical employees working for the DA's office of LA County. The office prosecuted some 35,000 felonies and 150,000 misdemeanors annually. It was and still is the largest prosecuting agency in the world.

If a crime was committed anywhere in LA County, and the case brought to trial, the DA's office usually would prosecute the alleged criminal in Superior Court. Some of the fifty-five incorporated communities within the county also had their own municipal courts and hired their own city attorneys to handle the prosecution of misdemeanors. The city of LA was one such city. In the unincorporated area were justice courts that had jurisdiction over misdemeanors.

When I began my service, the main office of the DA was in the Hall of Justice in downtown LA. There were also four major branch offices: Pomona, Santa Monica, Long Beach, and Pasadena. My first assignment was city preliminaries at the main office in downtown LA. Fortunately, in my previous work at the LAPD, I had witnessed and testified in many preliminary hearings, so I felt comfortable in that atmosphere. Preliminaries are sort of like checks and balances in the court system. A district attorney can't just order a full-blown trial against someone with the stroke of his pen. You have to show before a judge that there's reasonable cause to bring anybody to trial. That was my job.

After a few months on the job, one day I came back from lunch to my office in city preliminaries and was met with a surprise. My supervisor held out a case file in his hand. A case had been transferred and the supervisor didn't have any of his regular attorneys freed up to take it. "This just came down from the trial department," he said. "They don't have anybody there to handle it. You want to take it to trial?"

I had never tried a case in my life. I could've said no, but this was a pretty big break. Typically it took several years before a deputy DA got to do trial work. This was no small trial, either. The defendant had been charged with violating the Little Lindbergh Law, which prohibited kidnapping with injuries to the victim for the purpose of robbery or ransom. The punishment was death or life without parole.

The facts of the crime were straightforward: The defendant and an accomplice had held up a pharmacy at gunpoint, tying up the pharmacy owner in the process. They dragged the victim several feet into the back of the pharmacy to the storage room. That was enough movement to constitute a kidnapping charge. It was a tough statute. When the victim was lying on the floor, the defendant kicked the pharmacy owner in the mouth, knocking all his teeth out. That was an injury charge. This defendant could have gone to the gas chamber.

I picked up the file, walked into the courtroom, and tried my first case.

I pushed for the death penalty. The statutes called for capital punishment, and this crime was an awful nasty damn thing. The jury convicted the defendant but gave him life without parole.

Just like that, my career as a trial lawyer had begun.

I DON'T MEAN TO SOUND LIKE I HAD IT ALL TOGETHER RIGHT away. Learning how to become an effective trial lawyer doesn't happen overnight. Besides knowing the law cold, you've got to learn how to select a jury. Then you've got to learn how to act in front of a jury—you've got to be confident, but not brash or cocky. You've got to learn how to be persuasive and lay out facts clearly and logically. Every time I tried a case I learned something new.

Shortly after my first trial, I was transferred to county preliminaries. This meant I needed to travel all over the county handling preliminary hearings as well as misdemeanor trials. Mostly I tried drunk-driving charges and petty thefts, nothing major compared to the first case I tried, although I also handled preliminary hearings on felonies during that time. It was a flat transfer for me career-wise, neither up nor down, but it proved to be a good education, a training ground in just how varied the court system could look in the myriad of justice and municipal courts.

In this new role I was given a long leash. I might be in Pomona one day; Lancaster or Torrance or Redondo Beach the next. I conducted a variety of proceedings presided over by judges and justices of the peace. All the judges were full-time, but some JPs worked a variety of different professions in their off hours—some were lawyers, some real estate brokers. One was both justice of the peace as well as municipal lawyer in his small town. Scattered all over the county, courtrooms were as varied as the judges. Some courts held session in city council chambers. Others were held in the orchestra pit of the municipal auditorium. One court I appeared in held session in a vacant store building. The judge's bench consisted of some two-by-six planks laid across two barrels standing on end. The whole experience reminded me of the Old West.

Not long after I entered the DA's office, the chief deputy DA, who had hired me, Ernie Roll, became district attorney. He wasn't elected at first. The previous DA, Bill Simpson, had died, and the Board of Supervisors (the elected governing body of the county) elected Ernie Roll to serve out the remainder of Simpson's term. I liked Ernie. He was a friendly guy and in the same Masonic orders as me. He was a career guy in the office and had been there a long time, so he carried a lot of credibility with all the guys there.

His full name was S. Ernest Roll. I didn't know what the "S" stood for, but I learned a little too late that I probably shouldn't ask. One day when I was still new in the office, I came back from a preliminary hearing and was standing in front of the men's room urinals next to another attorney. The hearing I had just come back from had been presided over by a judge named F. Ray Bennet, a real pedantic type of guy.

"You know," I remarked casually, "I don't know what to make of these guys who use initials for their first names. Seems pretty highfalutin' to me." Just then, one of the bathroom stall doors opened and out walked S. Ernest Roll. He wasn't laughing. Neither was I at that point. Nobody said a word. We just all washed our hands and went back to work.

Everybody was pretty happy that Ernie got appointed to DA. Despite my blunder in the men's room, there was no animosity between us that I was ever aware of. But an incident soon happened that strained any goodwill I had ever felt in the office. I'm not sure Ernie truly knew what was going on. Looking back on it now, I think I made the mistake of trying to protect Ernie from himself. I was up against two guys who knew perfectly well what was going on.

It nearly cost me my career.

· 24 ·

Secrets of the DA's Office

IT HAPPENED LIKE THIS:

One day in late autumn after finishing my assignment early on the county run, I returned to the downtown office. I was sitting at my desk looking over papers when the receptionist buzzed me to say there were two plainclothes detectives from the LAPD West LA Division who wanted to file a legal complaint. All the complaint deputies were busy. Would I see them? I agreed. I knew a lot of detectives in the department, but had never met these two before. They came to my office with a young woman in tow. She was very attractive but looked like she had been roughed up recently. On her arms and legs were some very visible bruises and she had marks on her face. The woman claimed to be the victim of attempted forcible rape.

An aspiring actress, she had been invited by an agent to the home of a well-known television producer on the pretense of getting a part in one of his shows. While at the home the agent left, and the woman discovered she was in the house alone with the TV producer. He started chasing her around the place, eventually pinning her down by kneeling on her thighs, which is how she incurred the bruises. She managed to fight him off and fled to the bathroom, where she locked herself in. She escaped out a window and walked out of the LA hills in the dark, where she found a phone and called the cops.

I knew it was always difficult to prove sexual assault cases, but the woman's story sounded concrete. After further questioning, some quite strenuous, I was convinced her story was true. I'm sure the detectives did, too. Bringing a sexual assault charge against a Hollywood bigwig is never easy, and the case wouldn't have gotten as far as it had already if the detectives weren't convinced. My job was to decide whether the case warranted prosecution. Everything looked airtight to me, so I issued a complaint against the TV producer for attempted forcible rape.

When the story hit the press the following day, I received a call from a friend of mine who worked in the TV industry. "You've really nailed the right guy—that SOB has really got a reputation. He's long overdue," my friend said.

Having issued the complaint, I assumed I would have nothing more to do with the case. It would proceed through the system and be handled by other attorneys in the department who normally handled that sort of thing. I forgot about it and went about my business with county preliminaries. A few days later I was walking down the hall in the main office when S. Ernest Roll motioned me over. "That complaint you filed on the attempted rape is a lousy case," he said. "That girl is a tramp."

I shrugged. "That's too bad," I said. "It looked to me like she had been really roughed up."

Ernie drew back. "Yeah, we're going to have to take a long look at that one."

"Okay, if you say so," I said, and went on my way. I honestly didn't have an opinion about it. It surprised me that Ernie even mentioned the case to me. It was long out of my hands. All I had done was file the complaint and put it into the system. Ernie was the boss. I was a punk, grade-one deputy. He certainly didn't need my permission to do anything he wanted to do with the case. Not long after that I received a phone call from the same TV industry friend who had called me earlier.

"Buck, I saw that big-shot TV producer last night in a bar," he said. "It was a real packed house. Lots of TV insiders. Your boy was bragging that he paid someone in the DA's office fifteen thousand dollars to get the case dismissed. I just thought you ought to know."

This thing was really taking on a life of its own.

I didn't do anything with the new information. I just filed it away in the back of my head. I wasn't prosecuting the TV producer. All I had done was file the complaint. A few days later I was summoned to the private chambers of S. Ernest Roll. When I entered, I saw three men sitting there: Roll, the chief of the Bureau of Investigation, and an old-time deputy in the complaint division. Roll took charge right away.

"Have a seat, Buck," he said. "Here's the deal: We investigated the attempted rape case thoroughly and concluded that the victim was not credible and that the case should be dismissed." I was bewildered. Why had they called me in to tell me this? Roll continued. "Tomorrow you're scheduled to go to the Van Nuys Municipal Court. The case, along with several others, is set for a preliminary hearing. We want you to handle all the preliminary hearings . . ." (here he cleared his throat) . . . "except for this case."

I looked around at the three men. "Who's going to handle the prelim for that?" I asked. Roll motioned with his head toward the guy from the complaint department. He hadn't set foot out of the complaint division for the past ten years. I don't think he even knew what the inside of a courtroom looked like.

"Mr. Roll," I said. "For your own protection I want to tell you that the defendant has been heard out in the community bragging that he has a fix in with the DA's office. I personally don't give a damn one way or the other, but I want to warn you about that. It may be in your best interest to be careful in how you handle the case."

Roll nodded. "That'll be all," he said. He pointed to the door.

Sure, there were red lights going off in my brain. But Ernie was my boss. He was district attorney for Los Angeles County, for Pete's sake. I figured he was man enough to know what he was getting himself into. The next day I drove to Van Nuys. In the front of the courtroom sat the TV producer with his attorney. Across the courtroom sat the girl who had made the complaint, along with a couple I presumed were her parents. I handled my cases and stepped aside when the TV producer's case was called. The old-timer from complaints stood up and made a statement to the judge: "Your honor, we've investigated this case thoroughly and can't vouch for the credibility of the alleged victim. We move to dismiss the case."

The motion was granted.

The girl and her parents gasped audibly.

The TV producer stood smiling; he and his legal entourage filed out. The judge called for a recess. As he left the bench, he called me into his chambers. "What in the hell was that all about?" he asked.

"I have no idea."

He gave me a long, cold stare. "It sure smells fishy to me," he said. "What gives?"

"Don't ask me," I said. "I was just told to come out here and handle the rest of the stuff." The judge pointed me to the door. Others thought it smelled foul, too. When I got back to the Hall of Justice, the beat reporters from the all the major LA newspapers swarmed me, quizzing me about the case. All the reporters voiced their suspicions. I professed ignorance. I just wanted to be left out of it.

The following Saturday I was at home with Donna in the afternoon when a knock came at our front door. It was the chief of the Bureau of Investigation, one of the three who had been in the office when Roll told me to step aside for the case. When I opened the door, the chief was standing about halfway from the front door to the curb with his hands in his pockets. He wasn't smiling. I stepped outside and shut the door behind me.

"I don't trust you," he said. His voice hissed like a snake.

"What are you talking about?"

"You just better watch out, that's all!"

I shook my head. I had no idea where he was going with this. Right there on my front lawn, the chief launched into a long string of nonsense—some rambling accusation about me trying to shake down the TV producer and my organizing all the bookmaking in LA County. I was "trying to point the finger" at him, he announced, and he "would get" my job. It was completely ridiculous. How I could do all he was accusing me of from my position as a lowly deputy DA, I never knew.

"You be in my office at eight sharp Monday morning!" was the last thing he said. "We'll get to the bottom of this." He really didn't have power over me to give me orders like that. He wasn't my direct supervisor or anything. I figured what the hell. Monday morning I showed up at his office at the appointed time. His secretary told me to have a seat outside the chief's door. I sat. A few minutes later the chief stormed through the reception area, opened his office door, and slammed it behind him. He didn't say one word to me in passing. I sat there about an hour and he never came out, so I got up and left. That was the last I ever heard from him.

I spent a very miserable Christmas that year expecting to lose my job, maybe worse. I had no idea what to do except keep going forward. Right before the New Year, the assignments were posted for which division we would work at in the upcoming year. Usually everyone stayed in place. Deputy DA Nate Nathanson, a good guy and friend of mine, was standing beside the list when I got there. "What the hell did you do?" he asked. *"Long Beach?"*

Sure enough, I was transferred to the Long Beach office. That was about as far away from my home as any other assignment in the entire county. This was 1953, the days before many major freeways had been built. I'd have to take surface streets, coming over Laurel Canyon into Hollywood and Beverly Hills, down through Culver City, Inglewood, Hawthorne, Lawndale, Gardena, Carson, Signal Hill, and finally into Long Beach. The commute would take more than two hours each way. I knew my bosses knew that.

Clearly, I was expected to quit.

I DIDN'T.

I decided to tough it out. Ted Sten, the deputy in charge of the Long Beach office and my new supervisor, had a reputation for an acerbic personality and being difficult to work with. I reported for duty expecting the worst. To my surprise, Ted Sten greeted me warmly.

"Hmmm. Buck Compton," he said. "You live where?"

"North Hollywood."

He grinned. "Boy, someone sure must be mad at you." He shook my hand. "Welcome aboard."

Ted apparently felt some sympathy for me because he soon told me it'd be okay to come in a little late each morning and leave a little early in afternoons, so long as court appearances permitted it. He eventually became a good friend. Over time, my transfer to Long Beach worked out okay. I continued to make the long commute day after day, month after month. I feared that if I sold my house in North Hollywood and moved to Long Beach, they'd just transfer me somewhere else far away—to the San Fernando Valley or Pomona—and I'd be faced with the same problem. I didn't want to lose my job, problems with the DA's office or not.

The change I had been waiting for came a few years later. In October 1956, Ernie Roll died suddenly. He had only recently been re-elected. The Board of Supervisors appointed William McKesson to replace him as district attorney. McKesson had been a Superior Court judge. He was unknown to me, as he had spent most of his time handling juvenile court, but he had a reputation for being straight as an arrow. Judge McKesson promptly appointed a new chief of the Bureau of Investigation. He also appointed Manley Bowler as chief deputy, a man who also had record of high integrity.

The housecleaning of the DA's office was complete. My career was back on track.

EVERYTHING APPEARED THAT I WOULD WORK IN LONG BEACH for some time to come, so Donna and I felt secure in moving there. We purchased a lot in Palos Verdes Estates, a suburb a few miles from Long Beach. My fraternity brother who had sold us our first house sold us this lot as well. It was about twenty minutes from the office.

We paid $2,500 for the lot and built a two-bedroom, bath-and-a-half house for $15,000. People tended to live in smaller houses back then, but even this little house was a step up for us. The lot was ordinary, but located on an elevated corner with an unobstructed view of the Pacific Ocean. The surrounding area was largely undeveloped, with few houses around yet. Horses grazed the hills behind us, and on one side was a large expanse of garbanzo bean fields. Every once in a while we'd see a rattlesnake sunning itself on a rock. Anytime I saw one around the yard I'd shoot it with a pistol I kept.

Donna and I settled into life in Palos Verdes, expecting that I'd probably retire from the Long Beach branch after a smooth and satisfying career. I became secretary of the Long Beach Bar Association. Just for fun, and to make a few extra bucks, I got a real estate license and showed houses on weekends. I only showed houses in our neighborhood, which was growing like a weed, and I could walk to the showings, so it was pretty easy work. I coached a Babe Ruth League baseball team with Don Palmer, a good friend of mine from LAPD days. Neither one of us had any sons, but we figured it would be good to give back to the community. Don and I had both been catchers in university (he played baseball for USC), and Don played in the minors for a year after college. We jointly purchased a vacation cabin up at Lake Arrowhead. He had a second career as a teacher after his time with the LAPD. I always admired the guy.

I made good friends with Ted Shield, another deputy DA in the Long Beach branch. Ted went into private practice after a few years and did quite well for himself. His firm offered me a position, but I turned it down. I liked the security of a government job. If I went into private practice and failed financially, it wasn't like anyone was going to bail me out.

Activities and contacts have a way of weaving together to form a life pattern. I became active in the LA County Peace Officers Association and chaired the law and legislative committee. I also participated in the law and legislative committee for the State Peace Officers and DA's associations. This activity frequently took me to Sacramento, the state capital, when the legislature was in session. I testified before legislative committees on bills affecting the criminal justice system.

At the time, the chairman of the legislative committee for the state DA association was Frank Coakley, DA of Alameda County. Frank assigned one of his deputies to spend all his time in Sacramento during the sessions to ride herd on law enforcement legislation and coordinate the testimony before the committees. That deputy was Ed Meese, who later became legal affairs secretary to Governor Ronald Reagan. Following that, Ed became White House counsel and ultimately attorney general of the United States, when Reagan became president. Ed had an assistant named Herb Ellingwood, who later followed Ed as legal affairs secretary to Governor Reagan and was also deputy White House counsel when Reagan became president. Both Ed Meese and Herb Ellingwood were outstanding prosecutors and fine men. We enjoyed a close friendship and worked hard together to improve the effectiveness of the criminal justice system in California.

Life moved on. After eight years of marriage and no children, Donna decided to quit her job and work on having a family. We had struggled for some time without becoming pregnant and went through all sorts of tests. Turns out, Donna had some problems with her fallopian tubes. It was a big decision to adopt. I wasn't all that crazy about the idea at first, but Donna really wanted children. I did, too. Still, adoption is no small matter. I contacted some attorney friends who specialized in adoptions.

First crack out of the box, a child came up for adoption who we were sure we were going to get. The lawyer phoned a few days later saying the adoption process fell through. I told Donna. She broke down in tears. It felt like nothing else we had ever experienced.

We decided to keep our names in the running.

On April 6, 1955, our first daughter, Cindy Ann, was born. Three days later she was ours. (Several years later Cindy began spelling her name Syndee, and uses that spelling today.)

On December 26, 1956, our second daughter, Tracy, joined us by way of the same private adoption process. Again, we got her at three days old.

Both children were baptized in the Episcopal Church in Palos Verdes Estates. In many ways we were the typical American family. Our children have blessed our lives immensely. They are the greatest thing that ever happened to us.

OUR LIVES WERE PRETTY WELL ESTABLISHED IN PALOS VERDES and Long Beach, and for the next several years I was engaged in trying cases in the Long Beach courts. I was able to obtain the first death penalty verdict in the history of that branch. Other death penalties followed, and death penalty cases, some of which were commuted to life in prison. Some of the cases were quite grisly.

One involved a defendant who had crawled through the bedroom window of the home of an eighty-year-old widow and raped and suffocated her. The liberal Democrat Edmund G. "Pat" Brown, a fervent opponent of capital punishment, had come to office as governor of California. It seemed like Governor Brown was constantly finding some reason to commute the death sentence. In a capital case, after all appeals have been exhausted, the governor generally holds a hearing to determine whether he should exercise his power of executive clemency. In the case of the raped and suffocated widow, the governor read a psychiatrist's report that noted (only in passing) that the defendant "suffered" from voyeurism. Brown grabbed hold of the psychiatrist's declaration and granted clemency. I was in the governor's office for the hearing when it happened. *So, I thought, basically if you're a Peeping Tom, you're allowed to rape and kill elderly widows. Good grief!*

In another case a well-known elderly lawyer had been doing some barhopping. The lawyer had a few drinks too many and ended up back in his office with two men he had met in bars, one of whom was seventeen. The two men tried to get the lawyer to open his safe and beat him to death in the process. I prosecuted the older defendant, a brash, cocky, and totally unrepentant individual. A jury sentenced him to death and he applied for clemency from Governor Brown. (I prosecuted the seventeen-year-old, too, but he was ineligible for the death penalty because of his age.) Brown called me to discuss the case. I told him I couldn't really see any mitigating circumstances that would justify clemency.

"Well, Buck," said the governor. "Don't you think that Milo [the victim's first name] kind of asked for it?"

"With all due respect," I said, "I don't see how anyone could ask to be beaten to death." Apparently the governor disagreed with me because he commuted the sentence to life.

The Long Beach office grew. I received a couple of promotions. The county let it be known that management skills were valued in county employees, so I went to night school at a local junior college and took courses in business management. I also began teaching Criminal Law, Evidence, and Constitutional Law at a night law school in Long Beach. Ted Sten, my boss in Long Beach, was promoted to chief of branch and area offices. I was promoted to head deputy of the Long Beach office. That was a big break.

In 1964, Bill McKesson decided to retire and not run again for re-election as district attorney. His chief deputy, Manley Bowler, filed to run for the office. My old friend from reservist days, Evelle Younger, now a Superior Court judge, decided to run against him.

I liked and respected both Bowler and Younger and was torn between who to support. My first loyalty needed to be Bowler, because I worked for him. But I was closer to Younger on a personal basis. Soon after the campaign began, Bill McKesson (who was still the DA until his successor took over) stood up at a meeting of the Shrine Club, where we were members, and announced that I was being appointed executive assistant to the DA. This was a complete surprise to me. It was a newly created position that McKesson had just made specifically for me. It meant that I was to function as pro tem district attorney, in order to remove any political influence on the operation of the office during the campaign. It meant that, for a while, I basically ran the whole show as the DA of LA County.

In the end, Evelle Younger won the election and became the new DA. One of his first acts was to promote me to chief of branch and area offices. Within a few months I was promoted again, to assistant district attorney, the third-highest spot in the office. In 1968, when I was forty-six, I was promoted again, this time to chief deputy, the second-highest spot in the DA's office—the same position that S. Ernest Roll had held when he first hired me.

It was from this position that I believe I did some of my most effective work. One endeavor in which I take some personal pride was a major reorganization of the Office of District Attorney. Younger gave me full freedom of action, and with the cooperation of the budget analysts from the county administrator's office, we accomplished something that had never really been tried before.

Lawyers pride themselves on their legal skills, but most of them eschew anything that smacks of business management. Over the years, the DA's office had grown and expanded without much thought to establishing written policies or processes or effective chains of command. Before the reorganization, at least nine different elements or sections had direct access to either the chief deputy or the DA himself. I created three top-level supervisory positions. I believe it was well worth the money as it reduced the DA and chief deputy's span of direct control to three managers. We also created a training division to supervise the development of incoming attorneys, something I always wished I'd had when I started in the office. We also generated a written policy manual that contained everything from forms for written communications to dispositions of cases. We achieved the effective management of seven hundred attorneys and uniformity in how cases were handled. Some insiders consider it the single greatest reorganization of that office in history. That organizational system is still in place today.

We had some fun, too. At one point during my tenure as chief deputy, Jack Webb of *Dragnet* fame was producing a TV series called *Adam 12*, which dealt with the adventures of two LAPD policemen who worked in a patrol car whose call number was "Adam 12." He was a stickler for authenticity and approached us in the DA's office about doing a similar series about us.

Webb produced a two-hour TV pilot about us called *Murder One*. I was portrayed in my job by Howard Duff, a TV and film actor who later appeared as Dustin Hoffman's attorney in *Kramer Vs. Kramer* and became a familiar face on *Flamingo Road, Knots Landing,* and *Dallas*. The main character was a fictional deputy DA played by actor Robert Conrad. The pilot was well received and aired several times in subsequent years, but the series never got off the ground. Donna used to kid me about it, saying she hoped they'd get Doris Day to play her.

In our personal life, the early years with our girls were almost all fun. But Donna and I, like many parents, did not escape the antiestablishment and antiauthority trends that plagued the country in the 1960s. Once when Syndee was a teenager, she told me she did not want her friends to know what I did for a living because I was "too close to the fuzz." But both our daughters turned out well in the end. As adults, Syndee had Samantha, our first granddaughter, then Shannon, our first grandson. Tracy delivered Lyndsie, our second granddaughter, then finally Hayley, our youngest grandchild.

My boss, Evelle Younger, went on to do some pretty amazing things himself. He worked on the Richard Nixon campaign of 1968 and headed up a task force on law and justice, helping to prepare position papers on matters affecting national law and order. Younger was close to Nixon, having been involved in California Republican affairs for several years. The rumor began to circulate locally that Younger was in line to become attorney general of the United States if Nixon got elected president. The story really got legs when Nixon, in his acceptance speech, promised that he would appoint as AG a true professional prosecutor, and not just some political operator, as had been the case with some AGs in the past. Younger himself put enough credence on the possibility that he asked me if I would be willing to move to Washington, D.C., to serve as his chief deputy if the thing became a reality.

For some reason, Nixon chose John Mitchell as AG, as seasoned a political operator as you could find. Clearly Mitchell was not a professional prosecutor, and history has shown that to be the case. It's my opinion that Nixon's appointment of Mitchell and not Younger changed the course of history. Younger was a straight arrow, and with his background in the OSS, the military, and the FBI, he would have prevented Watergate from ever happening. I'm sure of it.

I stayed with the district attorney's office from 1951 until 1970. All in all, it was a good run. I mentioned that I prosecuted a number of death penalty cases during those years. Several cases would prove exceptionally challenging, and the results of four of those cases remain of interest today.

· 25 ·

Key Cases

ANITA O'DAY WAS A BIG-TIME RECORDING ARTIST, ONE OF THE great American jazz singers of the first half of the twentieth century, on par with Billie Holiday, Ella Fitzgerald, and Rosemary Clooney. In those days all the big bands had singers, like Sinatra sang with Dorsey. Anita was one of the best.

In the early 1950s, when I prosecuted her on drug charges, Anita was arguably on a downward slide and singing in Long Beach bars. The police got a tip that she was using heroin and selling it to sailors. She had been busted for marijuana once in Los Angeles several years earlier. When Anita was arrested before, she had been represented by an identifiable Communist lawyer. When she got busted in Long beach, she hired a similar left-wing attorney. He practiced what I call "courtroom terrorism"—where attorneys disrupt judicial proceedings with all kinds of shenanigans, objections, and yelling. They're not there to win a case by logic, truth, or justice. They just want to create confusion and win that way.

This was a simple case: one-count possession of heroin against Anita. The preliminary hearing under ordinary circumstances should have taken half a day at the most. But Anita's lawyer dragged the preliminary hearing over two weeks. It was all over nothing. For example, when the police chemist was on the stand to testify that what was found was indeed heroin—a very routine type of testimony in narcotic cases—the lawyer asked question after meaningless question of the chemist such as, "When you were in high school what subjects did you take? Did you take history? Did you take English? When was the last time you washed the dishes?" And on and on.

The situation of the case was this: When Anita was busted, three policemen from the narcotics squad had received a tip and gone to a bar where Anita was entertaining. She used the women's restroom as a dressing room. So the policemen stood outside at the restroom window where they could see her reach up to a shelf, take a packet, snort a substance, and put it back on the ledge. They moved in, confiscated the packet, and discovered heroin. A simple case in many ways.

When the officers saw her reach up to the shelf, they saw a big, flashy ring on her hand. They booked the ring as evidence. I didn't pay much attention to the ring initially. The case seemed open and shut all the way along. But as the trial began, Anita's lawyer really dug into the policemen who busted his client. I thought the lawyer was all over the place, indiscriminately asking questions. One of the lawyer's line of questions was if one of the policemen had noticed anything unusual about Anita's hands.

"What do you mean?" asked the cop.

"Did she have any scars or unusual markings or jewelry?" the lawyer asked. He was being very vague.

"Yeah, as a matter a fact, she had this big ring on."

"Nothing further, Your Honor," said the lawyer.

Anita O'Day was called to the stand. She held to complete innocence. Never used drugs, was never in the bathroom—just denied everything. "By the way, Miss O'Day," asked her lawyer, "did you have a ring on the night you were arrested?"

She held up her hands to the courtroom. "I don't have feminine hands," she said. "I don't wear jewelry."

Both the question about the ring and Anita's answer threw me. I walked to the witness stand and asked the clerk to bring the ring over. I held it out to Anita. "Isn't this your ring?" I said.

"No," she said. "I've never seen the thing before in my life."

"You're sure about that?" I asked again. Lying on the stand is perjury, but it happens all the time. That's why so many defendants don't even take the stand these days. They can't stand cross-examination. I assumed the ring must be a rhinestone and she must not have cared about it.

Again, Anita said she had never seen the ring.

We broke for the day.

Next morning, Anita's lawyer showed up with a jeweler's loop, one of those cone devices that rings are sized with. The lawyer sat at his council table, plainly so the jury could watch what he was doing, and sized the ring again and again. He put Anita back on the stand.

"Miss O'Day, you say this is not your ring?" the lawyer asked.

"No I've never seen it."

"See if you can put it on your hand."

She took the ring and tried to put it on, just like O. J. Simpson with the bloody glove. "No, it doesn't fit me," she said. The lawyer went on and on for a while, then quit. Despite the ring question, there was still enough other evidence for the jury to come back with a guilty verdict.

When the verdict was announced, the lawyer exploded. He stood up and screamed: "I demand that this jury be polled!" He reacted so violently, I wondered if he had an insider on the jury. But jury polling is fairly routine. So the clerk went through the jury: "Juror number one, is this your verdict?"

"Yes."

"Juror number two, is this your verdict?"

"Yes."

And so on. The clerk came to one woman, a hairdresser and union member, and asked the same question.

"Well, I went along with it," was her answer.

The lawyer jumped up: "I demand that her answer be no!" he screamed.

The judge, a very savvy man I had known back when he was one of my ROTC instructors at UCLA, ordered the lawyer to shut up and sit down. Then the judge queried the hairdresser himself. "Is your verdict guilty?" he asked.

"No," she said.

The jury was sent back to deliberate some more. I guess they never brought the hairdresser around, because they came back eleven to one. A hung jury.

So the case against Anita O'Day was set for retrial. A few months later, it came to trial again. We picked a new jury and went through the same rigmarole, only this time the lawyer brought up the ring question right away. In the meantime, Fred Schott, a beat reporter working for the *Long Beach Press Telegram*, pulled me aside one day. "You know," he said, "when she was arrested that night, one of our photographers got a picture of her. Let me see if I can find it. We might find something." I don't know what the relationship between the press and the DA's office is like today, but back then it was friendly. They were all savvy people.

Sure enough, Fred came back with a picture taken by one of their photographers that showed Anita O'Day in the police station. Her hands are by her side. You can see the same ring on her finger. In those days, there was not what is now called "discovery." With discovery, the prosecution has to turn over to the defense all the evidence to let them examine it before a trial is held. We didn't need to do that. So, the next time the lawyer mentioned the ring, I was ready. We had blown up the picture so that everybody could clearly see the ring on Anita's finger. When the whole charade began again, I pulled out the picture, walked up to her on the witness stand, and held it up to her: "You recognize this photograph?" I asked.

Her jaw dropped about a foot. She looked at her lawyer. He called for a recess. They huddled and whispered. She got back on the stand. Her lawyer began the examination: "Miss O'Day, have you refreshed your memory about this ring?"

"Yes, now I remember the ring," she said.

"How did this photograph come about?" the lawyer asked.

"Well, after I got arrested, I was sitting in custody, and this cop walked up, pulled the ring from his pocket, and shoved it on my finger. Then they called for a photographer, who took my picture."

I walked to the stand. "Do you remember the last trial of this case, Miss O'Day?" I asked.

"Yes."

"Do you remember that your lawyer had you try to put this same ring on your hand?"

She gulped. "Yes?"

"And you couldn't do it then. You couldn't get this ring on your own finger. And yet you tell me that this policeman was able to get this ring on your finger even when you couldn't?"

This time, it didn't take the jury more than a few minutes to find her guilty.

THE SECOND CASE WAS MUCH MORE SEVERE. IT WENT LIKE THIS:

When a man named Frank Caventer showed up one day with a small, homemade coffin at a Maryland farm, no one, particularly the owner of the farm, suspected Caventer was telling anything but the truth. The farm owner was a dog breeder who maintained a pet cemetery on the farm. Inside the coffin, Caventer said, was the body of a dog that had saved Caventer's life during the Korean War. Caventer, who had showed up in a full Navy captain uniform, asked to bury his faithful dog. The farm owner agreed.

Unknown to the farm owner, Frank Caventer was also known as Larry Lord Motherwell, a man whose life was filled with so many dips and turns, it could be turned into a made-for-TV movie.

The story went like this: In 1948, years before he ever walked onto the Maryland farm, Caventer served a six-month jail sentence for impersonating a military officer. When he got out, he moved to Washington, D.C., after his wife divorced him. In Washington he became friends with his apartment neighbor, the gregarious sixty-two-year-old Pearl Putney, widow of a prominent attorney and former U.S. State Department official. Pearl was known for keeping large sums of cash on hand, and was not afraid to carry as much as twenty thousand dollars on her person, a huge amount of cash in the late 1940s. Caventer convinced Pearl he was a retired Navy officer and doctor, a frequent guest at the White House, an adviser to the U.S. space program, and a world traveler who had been on numerous "secret missions." He snowed her pretty good, and the two were known to fraternize for years.

In 1949, Caventer moved away from the apartment building he shared with Pearl Putney and married librarian Sarah McLurken, a frail girl from Alabama. Four years later, Sarah gave birth to a daughter named Heather Robin, who had Down syndrome. As was common for the era, they placed the child in a home for "retarded" children. A few months after Heather was born, Sarah mysteriously drowned in a bathtub. Caventer found his wife's body. The death was ruled an accident. A short time later, Caventer showed up at the institution where young Heather was staying and told officials he was moving to Florida and wanted to take his daughter with him. As he was the legal father, they consented.

Caventer and Putney apparently kept up their fraternization on the side during these years, because in 1957 she wrote in her diary that she had seen him on the streets of Washington, D.C., after he had broken a dinner date with her. Sometime in the 1950s, Caventer switched his name to Larry Lord Motherwell. Also in the mid-1950s, he married for a third time, a woman named Josephine Smiraldo, who accepted Motherwell's explanation for his frequent long-term disappearances: He was involved with government operatives on secret missions.

In 1958, Pearl Putney's elderly mother died. Motherwell was on hand to help her manage the sizable estate. After the belongings were sold, Putney and Motherwell headed out on a road trip together. In the car were $20,000 cash and $30,000 in securities. At various motels, the couple registered under different names, including Dr. and Mrs. Motherwell and Dr. and Mrs. Putney. Putney sent frequent postcards to friends and family members, keeping them abreast of their whereabouts. A telegram sent to a brother announced that the two would soon be flying to Mexico to be married. After that telegram, friends and family members of Putney's heard nothing from her except silence.

With Putney's disappearance, police became suspicious of Motherwell. He could not be found. His wife, Josephine, only knew that he was away on government business. Police discovered that the Florida institution where Motherwell had claimed to take his daughter, Heather, did not exist. That led them to the pet cemetery on the Maryland farm. The farm owner said that Motherwell had come back several times over the years to pay homage to his faithful dog. Police dug the coffin up. Inside was the badly decomposed body of a baby girl.

A nationwide manhunt was launched. Motherwell was nabbed in Las Vegas (where he was now going by the name Art Rivers) and extradited back to Maryland. But prosecutors there were unable to pin the murder of baby Heather on him because they couldn't determine a cause of death. Motherwell admitted Heather had died when in his care, but said she had choked on a bottle and he had buried her in a panic. Without a body, police were also powerless to arrest Motherwell for Putney's murder, so he was let go. Motherwell told police that he and Putney had separated during the road trip when Putney decided to marry a South American diplomat she referred to only as "Mr. D'Avious."

About a year after Motherwell was questioned and let go, a woman hunting pinecones in the high Sierras stumbled across the remains of a human skull. Pearl Putney's identity was confirmed through dental records. The FBI captured Motherwell while trying to board a plane in Atlanta headed toward Cleveland. He had only recently given another lady friend some jewelry that police traced back to Putney's ownership. Motherwell claimed Putney had given the jewelry as a gift.

That's where I entered the story. Because the body had been found in Sierra County (population about 3,000), it was under their jurisdiction to prosecute the case. But small counties rarely prosecute high-profile murder cases such as this. Sierra County had a three-man sheriff's department; I think the most serious thing they had come across before was nabbing someone for not having a fishing license. So, wisely, the California AG decided that his office would exercise the power it has under the California constitution to take over the case, and went casting about for another prosecutor. Our office was used to prosecuting large-scale cases. The state chose Miller Leavy, our best-known trial lawyer, but he didn't want it. So Leavy asked me. At the time I was deputy DA. I agreed. Prosecuting Larry Lord Motherwell fell to me.

The case began in February 1960 and was held in Downieville, the Sierra County county seat, about two hours from Reno. I took a leave of absence from LA County and went on the payroll of the State of California. Donna and I loaded up our kids in the station wagon and prepared to spend an indefinite amount of time there. We rented a cabin in a fishing resort along the Yuba River.

Right away there was a logistics problem, as we had witnesses flying in from all over the country. There was only one motel in Downieville, and it was immediately filled with press from the Bay Area. So we flew witnesses to Sacramento, then sent out vans to pick them up to testify. From a financial standpoint, the case quickly broke Sierra County. The state legislature provided reimbursements for them in the end.

We were up in Downieville for several months. The trial itself took three weeks. Motherwell took the stand and told one unbelievable story after another. At one point we were in the position of doing something quite difficult—of proving a negative—that Mr. D'Avious, the Latin American diplomat whom Motherwell claimed Putney had dumped him to marry, did not exist. One of the reporters covering the case for the *Oakland Tribune* connected me with a professor at Cal-Berkeley, the foremost authority in the country in the subject of onomatology, the study on the derivation of names. I contacted the professor, who researched the last name, D'Avious. The professor researched reams of material and concluded that the last name D'Avious does not even exist anywhere throughout the world. As part of his research, the professor examined every telephone book from every major city in Europe, Central, North, and South America. That's a lot of phone books. The professor found one name that was remotely close—D'Avios. The FBI was sent to check out D'Avios, who lived in New York City. He didn't know anything. Our conclusion was that Putney had never married D'Avious, as Motherwell claimed. The man simply did not exist.

In the end, a jury convicted Larry Lord Motherwell of the first-degree murder of Pearl Putney and sentenced him to life in prison. He died of a heart attack in San Quentin in 1966. Although the crimes could not be proved, Maryland police have stated that Motherwell confessed to them that he had killed seven women altogether, including his infant daughter, Heather. Motherwell was particularly remorseful about his daughter because he had buried her alive.

I found a grim satisfaction in helping to put this type of sociopath away.

THE THIRD CASE HAS TO DO WITH THE MACHINATIONS OF THE very liberal California Supreme Court.

When I began to try death penalty cases, each jury would render a single verdict that included both the determination of guilt and a sentence of life or death. In subsequent years the procedure changed to a two-step process. Guilt was determined and special circumstances warranting death were described in step one, then another proceeding was held, generally before the same jury, that determined a sentence of life or death.

I often argued to juries that the death penalty, besides being a just punishment for severe crimes, was an effective deterrent to future crimes. If executing a defendant would save the life of one innocent person, it was worth it. I would often bring in representatives from the parole board who would testify to the average release time for a person sentenced to life. That came out to about thirteen years, with eligibility after only seven years. In my mind, the only way to make sure a criminal didn't get out and repeat the offense was to impose the death penalty.

One case really threw a wrench into things.

A gang of criminals had committed a series of armed robberies up and down the state. One day two of the gang were disposing of a stolen car on Terminal Island in LA Harbor when they were stopped by two policemen from the Long Beach PD. The officers thought the two were simply having car trouble and stopped to offer assistance. As the first officer got out of his patrol car, he was shot between the eyes with a .44 Magnum, killing him instantly. The other officer was shot in the leg and wounded. Quick response by the Long Beach PD resulted in closing escape routes off the island. The shooter and his cohort were captured.

I prosecuted the defendant who had done the shooting. A jury gave him the death penalty. This cop killer had previously been convicted of armed robbery in Oklahoma. He had also been convicted in California of sexually molesting two little boys. He had appealed that conviction and was at liberty on an appeal bond when he shot and killed the Long Beach policeman. The conviction on the California case had just been affirmed and his bond revoked, but he was not yet in custody.

The defendant appealed three times. Three times he was resentenced to death. But his appeals set two precedents: First, they made it impossible for a prosecutor to argue to a jury that the death penalty was a deterrent to crime; second, a prosecutor cannot use parole statistics anymore to argue that the death penalty helps reduce repeat offenses.

Finally, in 1972, the California Supreme Court declared the death penalty itself to be cruel and unusual punishment, therefore unconstitutional; 107 inmates were taken off death row and resentenced. In 1977, the legislature reenacted the death penalty for some types of first-degree murder.

One of the primary beneficiaries of that 1972 holding was the person you'll meet in the next chapter.

· 26 ·

RFK Assassination

ALL WAS QUIET WHEN I OPENED THE FRONT DOOR TO OUR HOME in Palos Verdes Estates, a small bedroom community in the southwest corner of LA County. My watch read a few minutes after 10:00 P.M., June 4, 1968. Donna greeted our neighbor Genevieve Kruthers, who had been watching the girls while we were out, and headed upstairs to check on our two daughters, now in bed. I wandered into the family room and flipped on the TV for a little background noise. Nothing seemed unusual about the evening. Nothing spectacular.

Donna and I had returned from a victory party at the Biltmore Hotel in downtown Los Angeles. My boss, Evelle Younger, had just been reelected district attorney of LA County. After the polls closed at 8:00 P.M., we gathered to watch the returns, followed by lots of hearty congratulations, eating, drinking, and shaking hands.

Across town at the Ambassador Hotel, Senator Robert Kennedy, from New York, was also celebrating that night. He had taken the California presidential primary, a win that boosted his chances for the Democratic nomination in the November presidential election. A younger brother of John F. Kennedy, Bobby had always been well liked by the American public. His popularity seemed only to be rising.

As U.S. attorney general from 1961 to 1964, Bobby became one of President Kennedy's most trusted advisers. He helped develop the strategy to blockade Cuba instead of initiating a military air strike that might have led to nuclear war. He was a hard-hitting prosecutor and had gone after organized crime. Now as he campaigned across America, Bobby had strongly identified with the poor and disenfranchised. He made a strong stand against segregation. He stood on a ticket of nonaggression in foreign policy, decentralization of power, and social improvement. A crucial element to his campaign was his ease in developing rapport with young people, whom he named as being the future of a new American society based on partnership and equality.

People everywhere seemed to love Bobby. Winning the California primary put icing on the cake. Four years earlier, at the 1964 Democratic National Convention in Atlantic City, Bobby came onstage to introduce a showing of a memorial film dedicated to his brother. When Bobby entered, thousands of delegates broke into thunderous applause that lasted a full twenty-two minutes. That was the type of response Bobby could produce. I knew RFK had a good chance of defeating Richard Nixon and becoming the next president of the United States.

When Bobby left the stage at the Ambassador Hotel that night in LA, no one knew his next few steps would change the world irreparably. We would only find out the full details of the night of June 5, 1968, in the days to come.

The horror-filled details.

Chants of "We want Bobby! We want Bobby!" could still be heard after he was ushered offstage, out a side door, and through a food preparation area, a shortcut to the press, waiting in another

room. The commercial kitchen was tiny, stuffed with steam trays and
metal counters. Well-wishers plugged the route, plus kitchen staff and
Kennedy supporters. One report suggested that as many as seventy-
five people had crammed the room, sardine-style.

When a swarthy, short-statured young man approached the senator, Bobby's first reaction would undoubtedly have been true to character. RFK would reach out to shake his hand, just as with anybody
else in the room. Reports showed later that although the swarthy man
was standing in front of Kennedy, the senator actually turned first to
shake the hand of someone behind himself. Dozens of people saw the
young man act. He stepped in front of Kennedy, called him a dirty
SOB, and opened fire. The crowd flinched. Some thought a metal pan
had clanged to the floor in the kitchen. Others recognized the sound
immediately and ducked. In reaction time, the gun exploded again
and again and again.

Surrounding Kennedy were hotel maître d' Karl Uecker, writer
George Plimpton, Olympic gold medal decathlete Rafer Johnson, and
professional football player Rosey Grier. As shots rang out, they
jumped on the attacker. Grier jammed his thumb behind the revolver's trigger to prevent further shots being fired. In the confusion,
it took a total of forty seconds to detain the gunman. By then his revolver was emptied.

When the dust settled, it became clear that ABC news reporter
William Weisel had been shot in the stomach, radio reporter Ira
Goldstein was hit in the hip, Democratic Party activist Elizabeth
Evans was unconscious from a head wound, and United Autoworkers
official Paul Schrade was hit in the left leg, as was teenage volunteer
Irwin Stroll. Senator Kennedy lay on the floor, bleeding heavily. Hotel
busboy Juan Romero placed a rosary in Kennedy's upward palm. As
Romero bent down, he heard Kennedy whisper in a barely audible
voice, "Is everybody all right?"

The news report interrupted my TV set's drone—one of those
flash statements that displaces regular programming. Details came

sketchily at first—terse, abrupt. The shooting itself was not broadcast live, but a reporter with audiotape had caught the shooter being subdued. Bobby Kennedy clung to life. His condition, critical. A suspect was already in custody. That's all that was known. I threw on my coat and headed for the door. "I don't know when I'll be back," I said to Donna, who had come downstairs and stood beside me, watching the report.

Donna's brow furrowed. "Be careful," she said. Always sensible and down-to-earth, she never worried about me or me doing my job. In my driveway sat an LA County car, a Pontiac sedan with a two-way radio. I had to get to Parker Center (the police headquarters where the suspect was being held) as quickly as possible. I jumped behind the wheel and made the drive in record time. I knew this event would be huge.

Parker Center's gray-bricked, multistory face was lit up. A crowd of detectives already jammed the center's central homicide quarters. Present in the room were investigators from the DA's office as well as detectives from the LAPD. As I entered through the front doors, I glanced at John Howard, deputy district attorney, and nodded at Tom Reddin, chief of police for Los Angeles. Younger had come directly from the Biltmore and approached me.

"Where is this guy?" I asked.

"They've got him in one of the interrogation rooms off the main," Younger said, his face grim. "Nobody knows who the hell he is."

"Not talking?"

"No. A couple of LAPD investigators have already tried to talk to him. He won't answer. Doesn't have any ID on him, either. [LAPD detective William] Jordan just came from interviewing him. Funny. All the suspect said was, 'Well that's a good name.'"

I shook my head. "Jordan. What would that have to do with anything?" Younger shrugged.

"How's your back, by the way?" I asked. Younger shot me a dirty look, a slight grin on the corners of his face. Younger and I played a lot of handball together at the LA Athletic Club. A short time earlier he had collapsed with a back spasm on the court, and an ambulance took him to the hospital, much to his chagrin. He prided himself on being in good shape and considered it poor policy for elected officials to show any sign of poor health.

"Never been better," he said.

Reddin walked over, a cup of black coffee in his hand. He and Younger had already compared notes. Throughout the room, detectives were scratching on legal pads and making phone calls. "We've got to figure out who this guy is," Reddin said. He took a sip of coffee. I agreed.

"Look, Compton," Younger said. "How many murders have you prosecuted by now, anyway—a ton?" I knew what he was getting at. In this type of case, the public would expect the DA, an elected official, to step in. It would mean a lot of publicity. Prior to becoming DA, Younger had been a lawyer and a judge, but he didn't have extensive trial experience. I doubt if he had ever prosecuted a murder case—and although Kennedy was still alive, the situation could well enough end up much grimmer.

Younger looked me in the eye. Clearly, he had made up his mind. "Buck, I think you need to handle this," he said.

I nodded. Younger's specialty was administration, not running a murder trial. He ran a good office and I respected him, but it made sense for me to handle the investigation. I didn't look at it like he was placing a wreath around my neck. I had prosecuted seven or eight death penalty cases plus a lot of garden-variety murders around Los Angeles. With an office of more than seven hundred deputy DAs, I was Younger's number two man. Me running things would communicate to the public that we weren't handling this case like any old run-of-the-mill investigation.

I poured coffee for both Younger and me and we began to compare notes. Reddin topped up his cup. A blue tinge of cigarette smoke hung heavy in the air. We stayed at Parker Center most of the rest of the night, making plans for our next steps. Already we had gained a sense of the magnitude of the case. When one of the most popular men in America is shot—the man who will probably become the next president—where do you begin? I didn't make an attempt to talk to the suspect, nor did I see him that night. I figured that if he wasn't talking to anybody else, why me? There would be plenty of time to do that later. I wanted this investigation to go off poker straight. Absolutely flawless.

I don't remember what time I got home. I grabbed an hour or two of sleep before getting up again. Donna met me with a cup of coffee at the breakfast table. She nodded and kissed my cheek as I headed out the door again, back to the DA's office.

The real work was just beginning.

Because the crime happened in their jurisdiction, the LAPD was the primary investigative bureau responsible for the case. Reddin directed Bob Houghton, chief of police, to draw together 40 to 50 detectives from all parts of Los Angeles to work the case, mostly to work the angle to see if other people were involved. They called their unit Special Unit Senator (SUS). But both Reddin and Younger knew the scope and size of the investigation required a separate, independent task force that could closely coordinate the LAPD with the DA's office, as well as all the other investigative agencies that would become involved in the case, such as the FBI, the U.S. Attorney General's Office, the LA County Sheriff's Office, and the U.S. Secret Service.

So Reddin and Younger created an overarching task force, a mechanism for coordinating the investigative efforts of the various investigative agencies. It drew together the heads of each agency, including chief of DA investigators George Stoner, U.S. Attorney Matt Byrne, and FBI representative Frenchie LaJeunesse. I was put in charge of this task force. Even though the LAPD wasn't normally responsible to me, Reddin agreed to have the SUS work directly with me for this case.

If you wanted to investigate someone—the power represented be-hind the task force was a dream team. It was a combined effort with federal and state agencies to cooperate and share information. It meant anybody who had anything to do with the case was working together, and each man on the task force was backed by the full power of each bureau. The task force proved to be significant for an-other reason. Years later, conspiracy theory proponents would accuse the LAPD of dropping the ball on the investigation. That was com-pletely unfounded. The LAPD *couldn't* drop the ball. We had all the other bureaus involved—the task force stood as a built-in system of checks and balances.

And word came. This was murder—it was official now. News of the senator's death landed hard, but it didn't come as a surprise: Bobby Kennedy had been shot in the head. Few survive that. Al-though we had expected it, expressions around the room were stunned when we heard; we exchanged few words. The senator lived until the early morning hours of June 6, 1968, then passed away at Good Samaritan Hospital in Los Angeles. Ironic for me—June 6 would always be D-Day in my mind. Twenty-four years earlier, June 6, 1944, I had parachuted into Normandy, headed toward Brecourt Manor.

The senator's body was flown back to New York City, where he lay in state at St. Patrick's Cathedral for several days, events that cul-minated in a funeral Mass. Immediately after the Mass, Kennedy's body was transported by special train to Washington, D.C. Thou-sands of mourners lined the tracks and crammed the stations, paying respects as the train passed by. Bobby was buried next to his brother John in Arlington National Cemetery. RFK was forty-two years old.

In coffee shops, walking down the street, broadcasting the news on TV—people everywhere had a strange sense of somberness, almost defiance. The nation fell into mourning. And the nation rose in anger. RFK felt like the last straw. This decade had seen far too many assas-sinations of well-loved public figures. This wasn't the America we knew. Or maybe it was—and we were all just coming to grips with what that meant.

We were still smarting from JFK's death in November 1963. Martin Luther King Jr. was assassinated March 28, 1968. Now, just two months later, it was Bobby's turn. Who would be next? The country stood poised, waiting to see justice be done. That was our job—justice. We had a suspect. Getting a positive read on his identity was job number one. We found help from two unlikely sources.

Sometime during that first day after the shooting, two brothers walked into a police station in Pasadena. They had seen a television report on the previous evening's events at the Ambassador Hotel, including pictures of the unidentified suspect. The brothers, Adel and Munir Sirhan, knew who the suspect was beyond a shadow of a doubt—their younger brother, twenty-four-year-old Sirhan Sirhan.

Pasadena alerted the LAPD. Detectives from all involved law offices were soon knocking at the door of a small house at 696 East Howard, Pasadena. Adel, who co-owned the house with his mother, Mary, readily allowed police to enter and search. In Sirhan Sirhan's room, detectives found an odd assortment of Sirhan's writings. He had studied the works of Karl Marx and written rambled regurgitations of Marx's books in his notebooks, including, "Workers of the world unite. You have nothing to lose but your chains." In another Sirhan diary, found on his desk, were the words "RFK must die," written over and over again. Detectives packaged the notebooks and other effects and took the evidence to the center.

Now we knew our suspect's name: Sirhan Bishara Sirhan. Our investigation would follow two main tracks: 1) prepare the trial against him; and 2) find out if anybody else out there was connected to him. If there was a conspiracy, we'd find it.

We soon learned that Sirhan was born in Jerusalem to Palestinian parents, but he wasn't a Muslim. He was raised a Maronite Christian, a sect of Eastern Rite Catholicism. At age twelve, he and his family emigrated to the United States and lived in New York City, eventually

moving to California. As an adult, Sirhan frequently changed reli-
gions, from Baptist to Seventh-Day Adventist to the cult of Rosicru-
cianism. His father, troubled with American customs, eventually
returned to his homeland, leaving Mary to fend for herself.

Sirhan, considered a polite and quiet young man, worked as a
salesman for a health food store, sometimes as a groomsman at the
Santa Ana horse racetrack. He had dreamed of being a jockey, but a
fall from a horse ended that career path. His largest possession was
his car, an unassuming 1956 DeSoto.

The date of the murder proved significant for another reason. A year
earlier, on June 5, 1967, Israel had launched a preemptive air strike attack on the Egyptian Air Force, marking the beginning of the Six-Day
War against the Arab states of Egypt, Jordan, Iraq, and Syria. There was
a lot of speculation in the media around how Sirhan felt betrayed by
Kennedy's support for Israel in the war. In addition to the "RFK must
die" entries in his diary, we found many other entries, some incoherent
and repetitive, including: "Robert F. Kennedy must be assassinated before June 5, 1968," and "My determination to eliminate RFK is becoming more [and] more of an unshakable obsession. . . . [He] must be
sacrificed for the cause of the poor exploited people."

At the beginning, possibilities that Sirhan could have been helped
seemed endless. If this marked an organized terrorist attack on the
USA, the list of potential aggressors was innumerable. Besides chasing down every conspiracy theory possible, we decided to organize
the specific case against Sirhan into three components: 1) investigat-
ing the crime itself; 2) marshaling the evidence against Sirhan; and 3)
determining his mental state at the time of the crime. The mental state
of a slayer is critical in any homicide prosecution. For us, in order to
prove a first-degree murder and seek the death penalty, it required
proof that Sirhan was the one who did the shooting, that he did so
knowingly and intentionally, and that he premeditated the crime. If
he had any help from other people, we were prepared to prove who
they were and what their motive was.

I assigned two deputy DAs, John Howard and David Fitts, veteran trial lawyers, to organize and prepare the specific case against Sirhan. Among the three of us, we had at least fifty years' experience prosecuting murder cases. The Ambassador Hotel offered us a conference room, which we turned into an office. Fitts and Howard, plus a law clerk and a secretary, set up shop in the room at the Ambassador. It meant we could interview witnesses directly at the crime scene.

I assigned John Miner, our deputy DA in charge of the medical legal section, to stand beside the coroner, Thomas Noguchi, when he performed the autopsy on Kennedy. Noguchi was an experienced coroner. The procedure was also witnessed by three forensic pathologists from the Armed Forces Institute of Pathology in Washington, and two of Noguchi's associates.

One immediate problem: the number of bullets fired and how they corresponded to the number of people wounded. Sirhan had used a .22-caliber Iver Johnson eight-shot revolver. He had fired all eight bullets, emptying his gun. Four bullets slammed into Kennedy. Five other people were wounded. That added up to nine. Almost immediately, a second-gunman theory was birthed.

Meetings melted into meetings. Endless briefings. Every morning, five days a week. Documents, notes, files, and transcriptions poured in. We had committed to investigate every lead we got. Sirhan sat on our number-one burner. The tips received were almost innumerable. Anybody who knew (or thought he knew) anything at all about Sirhan contacted us. Postcards, phone calls, letters, and notes poured in. Some tips were crazy, vague, far-fetched, implausible, but we investigated them all anyway. We didn't leave any stone unturned no matter how nutty it sounded.

An example of a briefing among task force members:

Houghton: "Here's a good one, Buck. Somebody sent us a postcard this morning. Claims that the day before RFK was assassinated, he saw Sirhan sitting on a park bench talking to a person with a dark complexion."

Me: "A dark complexion, huh? Well, that narrows it down. Any other description?"

Houghton. "Nope. Just a dark complexion."

Me: "Where was Sirhan supposed to be when this alleged conversation took place?"

Houghton: "Postcard was convinced Sirhan was up in Lompoc."

Me: "Lompoc? The small town up in Ventura County?"

Houghton: "Yep—just down from Vandenberg Air Force Base."

Me: "Okay, that's not much. Why don't you send a couple of your boys up to check it out."

LaJeunesse: "You won't believe this one, Buck. We got another letter this morning. Someone says he knows Sirhan's brother has a thing for belly dancers. Says we should go check out these belly dancers."

Me: "Belly dancers, huh? Does he name which belly dancers and the club they perform at?"

LaJeunesse: "Yep."

Me: "All right. Have someone go talk to people at the club to see if they know anything more about the brother. Our guys are going to have a field day with that."

To this day, I'm infuriated when people suggest that we closed the book because we already had Sirhan and never bothered to look for anybody else. Over the months of the investigation, I estimate that nearly 75 percent of the effort went into tracking down conspiracy theories.

When the California State Archives received the records from the RFK assassination investigation in 1987, they received some 50,000 pages created by SUS, including a card index of more than 8,200 entries, 4,800 interviews, 2,900 photographs, 155 items of physical evidence, and a large number and variety of audio- and videotapes. In all, the investigation consumed more than 6,400 personnel hours during a thirteen-month period.

One conspiracy theory insisted a radical right-wing plot was be-hind the assassination—all the assassinations of that decade, actually. At times it seemed that the far left would never be satisfied until they could lay the slayings of MLK, JFK, and RFK on the right. Some-where toward the end of the investigation, I phoned Fred Vinson Jr. in Washington, D.C. We had done a lot of prior homework related to this theory, but as a latter check, I wanted to hear from someone well connected with the left. I figured Vinson Jr. might be in a position to know things we didn't.

Vinson Jr.'s father, Fred Vinson Sr., had been chief justice of the United States, appointed by Democratic president Harry Truman. Vinson Jr. was chief of the criminal side of the U.S. Justice Depart-ment at the time. He had been selected by Ramsey Clark, attorney general of the United States, a strong liberal. Vinson Jr. had been a key player in the trial of James Earl Ray, the killer of Martin Luther King Jr. Vinson Jr.'s politics fell left of center, just like his father's. Clearly the Democratic officeholders had no motive to cover up, con-ceal, or minimize a so-called right-wing conspiracy. In fact, quite the opposite would be true.

Vinson Jr.'s secretary patched me through. I introduced myself and my job, stating that we were running down every possible lead regard-ing the Sirhan prosecution.

"I wanted to find out from you if you think we're missing any-thing," I said. "In your opinion, is Sirhan connected to anyone? Are there any theories we might not have overturned yet?"

Vinson Jr. paused for a minute. "They're all three loners," he said. "Oswald, James Earl Ray, and Sirhan. Loners. You haven't overlooked a thing."

He hung up.

I was satisfied. We were going to trial.

· 27 ·

Sirhan Sirhan's Trial

WE TOOK OUR TIME WITH PRETRIAL PROCEEDINGS. NOTHING could be rushed through. Fitts and Howard questioned the jurors and were satisfied with who was picked. A juror's stance on the death penalty could be key. Regardless of anyone's personal beliefs, the possibility of the death penalty was allowed by law and had to be a factor in this case. If a juror couldn't stomach the thought of Sirhan possibly receiving what the law called for, he or she had to be rejected.

The official trial began January 7, 1969. Sirhan pleaded not guilty. Television cameras were banned from the courtroom, only court artists allowed. Every day, reporters lined up outside the court's front doors. Every night another collection of news reports aired. Every night I saw another artistic rendition of Fitts, Howard, and me on TV. Fitts and Howard conducted the main flow of the prosecution, with me supervising. I cross-examined Sirhan. We lined our witnesses up and proceeded like any regular trial, sequentially, from the beginning. We started with the coroner's establishment of death. Then eyewitnesses were called one by one: Grier, Plimpton—anybody near Kennedy when the shooting took place—which included a lot of people.

One evening, Paul Schrade, head of the United Autoworkers, called one of our guys on the phone and let fly. His statements didn't deal with the case, merely his own irritation. He had taken the stand near the end of the day and his testimony needed to spill over to the next. He groused about not finding a parking spot near the courtroom. "I'm not going to be here tomorrow unless someone can find me a better place to park," Schrade announced. He was dead serious. To my knowledge, nobody in our office jumped to find him a better spot. And he showed up the next day to finish his testimony.

The number of bullet holes (nine) compared with the number of bullets in Sirhan's gun (eight) proved not nearly as problematic as thought earlier, and certainly not as knotty as has been made out in subsequent years. Technicians from the LAPD crime lab accounted for where all the bullets went. They showed bullets spattered all over the room—the ceiling, through the shoulder pad of RFK's suit, doorposts, everywhere. Bullets bounce. Bullets ricochet. And all the bullets were accounted for. People in subsequent years contested the shooting based on the number of holes found in nearby walls. We investigated every hole in that old kitchen down to the detail. What some thought to be holes turned out to be imbedded nail heads, nothing more.

Others found problems with Sirhan's placement in front of Kennedy. One of the main bullet holes was found near the back of Kennedy's right ear. Also, bullet numbers three and four entered Kennedy's back, the fourth bullet exiting the senator's body through the right front chest. The question emerged: How could Sirhan stand in front of RFK yet shoot him in the back? Testimony showed that Sirhan was indeed standing in front of Kennedy, but immediately before Sirhan fired, Kennedy turned to the side to shake hands with a well-wisher, easily exposing his back.

Still others suggested that the bullets appeared to come from an upward angle, so maybe another shooter lay on the floor. Sirhan was on the same level as the senator. Again, easy—Sirhan wanted to be a jockey. He stood a full seven inches shorter than RFK. Any bullet he shot at RFK was bound to fly at an upward angle. This was nothing like JFK's murder—with shots coming a long way from an office building, making a single shooter harder to establish. People were packed shoulder to shoulder in the kitchen area. No balcony. No upstairs. No broken windows. Nothing like that.

Another problem arose because of the distance of RFK from the gun. Testimony varied—some witnesses said it went off point-blank, others said it went off up to fourteen inches away from RFK. That happens—different people can easily see different distances from different angles. The coroner said the shots were virtually point-blank, as there was a powder burn found behind RFK's ear. Years later some guy wrote a book and used only one testimony—whoever had said the gun was fourteen inches away—to promote a conspiracy theory: If Sirhan's gun was that far away, there had to be some other shooter firing point-blank between Sirhan and RFK. The other shooter must have popped up in the fourteen-inch space. Easily debunked when you look at all the evidence.

Sirhan had three lawyers, none slouches. Abraham Lincoln Wirim, chief counsel for the local branch of the ACLU, helped secure a team known for championing high-profile cases. These were top-drawer attorneys, definitely not greenhorns or has-beens appointed by the court. Attorney Grant Cooper led the defense team. A former chief deputy district attorney before he went into private practice, Cooper did a lot of criminal defense work and had been president of the Los Angeles Bar Association. He had also represented several high-profile cases, including actress Shirley Temple in her 1950 divorce from John Agar. Russ Parsons assisted Cooper. Parsons had years of experience as a criminal defense attorney and an outstanding reputation in Los Angeles.

Fearing the trial would turn into an Arab versus Israel situation, the team also hired Emile Zola Berman, a Jewish criminal defense attorney from New York, Kennedy's home state. Berman was well known for taking cases of underdog clients and unpopular causes.

Early on, defense lawyers approached us with a plea bargain: Sirhan would plead guilty in exchange for no death penalty and the promise of life imprisonment. We supported the proposal, but Judge Herbert Walker shook his head. He believed that the public was already skeptical of the American judicial system because Jack Ruby had shot Lee Harvey Oswald, JFK's assassin, before Oswald could be tried. Sirhan's trial continued.

Fairly early into the trial, with things leaning in our direction, Fitts, Howard, and I met with Sirhan's three attorneys at the back of the courtroom to propose another deal. Younger was never a strong proponent of the death penalty and wanted to absolutely exhaust every possible method of seeing if a conspiracy was out there. All of us, including Younger, were sure there wasn't, but even if there was one-tenth of a percent of a chance, we wanted to know.

"Here's the offer," I said. "If you can show that anybody helped Sirhan, we won't push for the death penalty. We'll let him go for life."

The lawyers all nodded. "We'll talk to him," Grant said.

A day or two later, we met again.

"Did he understand the deal?" I asked.

Grant nodded.

"What did he say?" I asked.

Grant shook his head. "He can't come up with anybody."

Their defense began on February 28. Central to their argument was that Sirhan allegedly didn't know what he was doing at the time of the assassination. They discussed Sirhan's troubled upbringing as a child in war-torn Palestine. They scrutinized his bad father, and the fall off the horse as a stable hand. They claimed Sirhan landed on his head. One psychiatrist led us through a long string of Freudian gobbledygook, claiming that Sirhan had no free will. None of us did, for that matter. In discussing Sirhan's journals, the psychiatrist claimed that when Sirhan wrote statements such as "RFK must die," he had absolutely no idea what he was doing, and probably continued writing into the air with his hand off the page.

Another established that Sirhan had looked into a mirror when he had gone into the bar at the Ambassador Hotel shortly before the assassination. When he did so, Sirhan supposedly hypnotized himself in the mirror and was acting in a trance when he shot the senator. Another psychologist, up for his fifteen minutes of fame, had run Sirhan through the ink blots and diagnosed him in a very elaborate report as a paranoid-schizophrenic, incapable of understanding his actions. A newspaper reporter got a copy of the report and determined the psychologist had lifted large sections of it, verbatim, from another book that had nothing to do with Sirhan, and hadn't bothered to credit the source. We walked into court with twelve copies of the original book, handed a copy to each juror, then read sections from it in cross-examination. I think the guy lost his license.

Sirhan remained fairly expressionless throughout the trial, but he squirmed when the subject of his mental stability came up. At one point, in an uncharacteristic outburst, he asked to change his plea to guilty. At that point his own defense said he was raving, because he was truly unstable. They continued.

After fifteen weeks, the trial ended on April 14, 1969. Testimonies from eighty-nine witnesses had been heard.

The jury deliberated for three days.

On April 17, the jury reached a verdict: Sirhan Sirhan was guilty of the first-degree murder of Senator Robert Kennedy, as well as five counts of assault with a deadly weapon. Sentencing took place May 21. Judge Walker imposed the sentence recommended by the jury: the death penalty by gas chamber.

Sirhan sat stoically through both the verdict and sentencing.

We had won, but I felt anything but triumphant. Justice was done. That was it. Sirhan Sirhan killed Senator Kennedy. Under the laws established by a civilized society, a killer received the justice he deserved. I had always assumed that Sirhan would get the death penalty if found guilty. If there is any case in the United States that calls for the death penalty, it's the assassination of a high-ranking public official. This country does not change its government with guns.

Sirhan's conviction was automatically reviewed by the State Supreme Court of California, as required by law. The appeal took about a year, and the conviction was affirmed. Carrying out any death penalty never happens overnight, and in 1972, Sirhan, still awaiting execution, was spared when California changed its law and abolished capital punishment. Sirhan Sirhan remains in California's Corcoran State Prison to this day. As of 2006, he has been denied parole thirteen times. His next possible chance for parole is set for 2011.

To the best of my knowledge, the offer we once made to Sirhan is still on the table. If Sirhan can produce any credible evidence that suggests he did not act alone in the assassination, I'm convinced he could buy his freedom with it today. Personally, I don't think Sirhan has kept his silence all these years because he's being heroic, or loyal to anybody. The fact is, there wasn't anybody else. Given the size of the room and the number of people jammed in that room, it would have been physically impossible for someone else to have been firing a gun in the room and escape undetected.

In my experience over years of law enforcement, I have seen example after example where it is very difficult to keep any kind of a conspiracy secret. There is always a weak spot. For example, the Italian Mafia, one of the most secretive and highly despicable criminal organizations out there, ultimately cracked with the Valachi papers, and some of the mobsters ratted out each other. It's awfully hard to keep a crime a secret when there's more than one person involved.

A few years back, the History Channel produced a show that featured some guy who had written an off-the-mark book about a second-gun conspiracy. The guy suggested the LAPD was lazy, sloppy, and had Sirhan nailed to the cross from moment one. The

History Channel approached me for comments, saying they would
lay all the information out there and put this matter to rest. I agreed
to the interview, thinking there would be no bias to the report. Representatives from the History Channel interviewed me for several
hours about bullets, trajectories, testimony—anything anybody could
come up with. I answered all their questions.

In the end, the theme of the show leaned heavily toward supporting
a conspiracy theory. They used only one quote from me: "If anybody's
out there who feels there's something we missed, they've got to believe
that I was incompetent or part of a conspiracy." They absolutely did
not use any of the detailed counterinformation that I provided.

A few years later the History Channel decided to issue a remake
of the documentary. They called me to authorize the use of my quotes
from the previous interview. I agreed, again taking them at their word
that they wished to dispel rumors around this case. I had high hopes
for the second show. I gathered my daughters to watch it with me.
But the same thing happened all over again. The show leaned heavily
toward accusing the LAPD and DA's office of being sloppy. By the
end of the show my own daughters were giving me suspicious looks.
One of the new pieces of "suspicious" evidence that the show claimed
to unearth was that I had okayed the destruction of evidence.

I did. Here's what happened:

Some years after the case was closed and all appeals exhausted,
the chief of police in LA phoned me and said, "We've got these two
big wooden doors in storage, left over from the Sirhan trial. They're
taking up room. How much longer do we have to keep the stuff?"

"Ah hell," I said. There was no chance the case was going to be
retried. "It's long over. They have absolutely no value."

So the doors were trashed. Good grief.

When we finished the case, Younger told me to take every file,
every report, every shred of evidence we had and file it with the
county clerk so nobody could ever accuse us of stealing anything.
Which we did. Every stack. If anybody wants to pore over the reams

of information available, be my guest. I am resigned to the fact that conspiracy theories will always be around, no matter how much clear evidence is presented. People have tried to tie RFK's assassination everywhere except to Sirhan—the CIA, General Motors, the mob, corporate America. It's almost forty years since Sirhan's conviction, and we're still dealing with people like Oliver Stone who see a conspiracy behind every rock.

Today when I think of the Sirhan case, I'm reminded of one incident. This is the stuff I'd rather people thought about when it comes to Sirhan: After the jury had rendered its verdict, the press assembled as they did every day to ask questions of Fitts and Howard and me. The questions were wide-ranging and generally supportive of the verdict. One reporter asked me: "What can we learn from this experience?"

I answered that in the United States we do not accomplish political goals by violence, but by the ballot. An assassination is the most repugnant political action of all and cannot be tolerated.

He asked me to clarify my answer.

I discussed how we had experienced the excesses of the sixties, brought about, I believed, by the radical left and the so-called peace movement. As a result of this movement, we had seen state legislators imprisoned in their offices by mobs, access to public buildings blocked by people lying in doorways, people lying on the tracks to stop the movement of troop trains, vandalism against businesses, streets plugged by mobs, and the ROTC building at Stanford University burned down. All this had euphemistically been referred to in the press as "protest," or "an expression of free speech," allowable, worthy of encouragement as expressing our right to freedom of speech.

I told the reporter that these so-called "peace protesters" were all incipient assassins. Free speech does not embrace any form of physical force, whether passive or active. A mob blocking streets is using physical force and is not the same thing as protected free speech. People who are willing to resort to any form of physical force (because they are frustrated by the failure of their words to be effective) have progressed up the rungs of the ladder of violence. As each level of this ladder is climbed, history has shown that progressive degrees of physical violence fail to produce a desired political result, and it becomes easier to take the next step. At the top of this ladder is assassination. Cases in point: JFK, MLK, and RFK.

Some of the press did not appreciate my remarks that day and called me a "John Bircher," among other things (the John Birch Society was an active and vocal anti-Communist organization of the era). I still believe what I said then is true today. The ballot is the mechanism for changing things in America, not violence in any form. Our representative democracy, as established by our Constitution, contains within it all the mechanisms required for peaceful change. You don't have to take up a gun in this country, all you have to do is persuade.

Somehow, Sirhan Sirhan forgot that.

· 28 ·

Finishing on the Bench

IN MANY WAYS, PROSECUTING SIRHAN SIRHAN WAS THE PEAK of my career in the DA's office. At least, it's been the most widely known thing I've done. But it wasn't the only thing I did while an attorney. My war for justice continued. The political and social climate of the late 1960s presented problems never before faced by a prosecutor's office. The typical attitude of a vocal segment of the public was that all law enforcement was the Gestapo. That included the DA's office. We were all in the same bag.

In the Watts riots of August 1965, police made hundreds of arrests each day of the six-day melee. Arrests ran the gamut of crimes, from arson and vandalism to assault and murder. Processing these arrests required the courts and our offices to go on an emergency footing and reallocate personnel away from various regular duties. From Watts, we were able to codify an emergency procedure in the DA's office that has lasted to this day.

One day, when I was chief deputy, I was asked to come to what was described as a "seminar" at the UCLA School of Law to discuss the function of the grand jury. I often visited major law schools around the country for recruiting trips and always enjoyed being back on college campuses. This seminar, however, proved to be not one of those enjoyable times. When I drove up to the UCLA Law School, I was met with TV cameras and a hostile crowd of students handing out leaflets. I took one of the leaflets. It invited other students to attend the seminar and *Off the Pig*—1960s slang for *kill the policeman*—in this case, *me*.

To explain: A recent case had received considerable press attention. I hadn't prosecuted the case, but it had been presented by our office to the grand jury. A group of deputy sheriffs had made a raid on some drug dealers in an apartment building. The deputies entered the third-floor apartment with their pistols drawn. One deputy was carrying his weapon at his side when the gun accidentally discharged. The bullet went through the floor into the apartment below, killing an infant. It was a horribly tragic accident.

The grand jury, after hearing all the witnesses, did not indict the deputy. Their conclusion was that no crime had occurred, even though the deputy had been negligent and tragic consequences had resulted. Nevertheless, it was not a case calling for criminal prosecution. The victim's family had adequate redress in civil court. The climate in parts of Los Angeles definitely leaned toward the family.

For a moment after arriving on campus, I saw the mob and contemplated walking straight back to my car, but I decided to tough it out rather than back down. I was here to do a job, and I'd uphold my end of the commitment. I entered a large amphitheater classroom, already jammed with students and faculty. I was the only guy onstage. The professor acting as a moderator began the seminar by asking a few questions, but each time I opened my mouth to answer I was shouted down with boos and bedlam. Some of the faculty members popped off just as much as the students. I was neither the policeman nor the prosecutor in the matter of the accidental shooting, merely a representative of the DA's office. That didn't seem to matter. I was Authority—and all Authority in their minds needed to be *offed*.

Again, I contemplated walking out. But then I thought, *No, I'm not going to cave in and let the bastards get the better of me. I'll just stay here and sit them out.* I was on the stage for a good half hour. The crowd just went nuts. Finally, one of the professors came up and asked me to leave.

I left. Sometimes there's just nothing more you can do.

RIGHT AFTER THE SIRHAN SIRHAN TRIAL, MY CAREER WAS SET to change again, in late 1969. Most lawyers, whether they admit it or not, aspire to be judges. I was no exception. I would come to my new position by a circuitous route.

That same year President Nixon appointed John Mitchell as attorney general of the United States and bypassed my boss Evelle Younger. After Younger shook off the disappointment, he began to set his sights on the California state attorney general position. That meant I was in prime position to become the next district attorney of LA County. Ronald Reagan was California governor at the time and had the power to appoint judges. My friend Ed Meese was Reagan's executive secretary, and my other friend Herb Ellingwood was Reagan's legal affairs secretary. One day the call I had been waiting for came. It was from Governor Reagan's appointment secretary telling me the governor was appointing me to the bench as a Superior Court judge. I was flattered and thrilled, but I told the secretary that I wanted to discuss the appointment with Ev Younger before I accepted.

"Superior Court?" Younger asked when I told him. "Those jobs are a dime a dozen. Stay here and be the next DA when I become AG."

Younger's plan sounded good, so I called the governor's office back and declined the judgeship because I wanted to stay in my current position and work with Younger. "Okay," said the governor's appointment secretary. "We'll put you on the back burner." Later that year the chief justice of California, Roger Traynor, announced his intent to retire. This meant that Governor Reagan had the opportunity to appoint Traynor's successor. Herb Ellingwood called me. He had a list of three people being considered for the position and wanted my opinion on the names.

"What do their qualifications need to be?" I asked Herb.

"Really, there are only two," Herb replied. "The appointee has to be under age fifty and a strict constructionist of the Constitution."

"I fit that description," I said, half jokingly. "Where do I apply?"

"I thought you wanted to be DA," Herb said. "Are you really interested?"

"Hell, I'd walk on my hands to Sacramento to be chief justice," I said.

"I'll throw your name in the hat," said Herb.

As it turned out, I didn't get the job as chief justice, but everything worked out better for me in the end. The job of chief justice went to Don Wright, a former associate justice of the Courts of Appeal who had a good reputation as a conservative judge, both on the trial court where he previously served and on the appellate court. The twist was this: Judge Wright's new appointment left his old seat open on the Courts of Appeal. Herb phoned me back to ask me if I was interested in Wright's old job. I was ecstatic. I never dreamed I would ever be offered such a position. It was very rare to go directly to the Courts of Appeal for someone who hadn't served at a lower level such as Superior Court.

Younger agreed that it was the best job for me. "By all means," he said when I asked. "Take it! Those appointments are few and far between."

Donna was equally enthusiastic about my new position. She had not relished the prospect of my becoming DA because of the necessary political campaigning that would have been involved. "You do realize," I said to Donna, "that being a judge means a very quiet life compared to being DA. No chauffer-driven limousines. No invitations to a lot of big fancy affairs."

"I couldn't possibly care less for those things," Donna said. "I don't want ever to sit at a head table again. I want a quiet family life."

I took the job.

As far as I've ever known, I've been the only ex-policeman to sit on the Appellate Court in California, if not in the whole country. To explain my new position: The California court system, like all other jurisdictions in the U.S., is a three-tiered system. The basic trial court is the Superior Court, which sits in each county. Depending on the population of a county there may be one or a hundred Superior Court judges. Highest on the ladder is the Supreme Court of California, the position that Don Wright received. The Supreme Court is a court of "discretionary" jurisdiction, meaning they only take a select number of cases as they see fit.

The middle rung is the Courts of Appeal, which is the position I got.

The state is divided into appellate districts, each of which handles the appeals from the superior courts of several counties. I sat on the Courts of Appeal for the 2d Appellate District. At the time, the district embraced Los Angeles, Santa Barbara, Ventura, and San Luis Obispo counties. It was the most populous district in the state and handled the greatest volume of cases, both civil and criminal.

The Courts of Appeal issues written opinions, which are published in law books and serve as precedents in future cases. Because the Supreme Court only takes a limited number of cases, the Courts of Appeal has the last word in 90 percent of all cases.

In hindsight, I am quite glad that I never became DA of LA County. When I departed from the DA's office, I was replaced as chief deputy by a friend named Joe Busch. He was a career prosecutor and one of our top trial lawyers. He, like me, was not a politician at heart. Evelle Younger ran and won the position of California attorney general. Joe Busch was appointed as the new DA of LA County by the county supervisors. He campaigned two years later for the same position and won. Midway through his second term, Joe Busch died in his sleep from a heart attack. His death came as a complete surprise. He was a vigorous individual, only in his midfifties and in good health. Most of us who knew him attributed his early death to the pressures of the DA's office. As I look back, I believe that had I taken the job, I would have suffered a similar fate. I never had the stomach for politics. I thank my wife for her good influence in helping to keep me out of that role.

Work in the DA's office had proved to be pretty intense over the years. I always had butterflies in my stomach when I went to work in the morning. Trial work is a contest, like playing a football game. I had never consumed liquor as a young man because of my father's situation, but I started drinking a bit during my years in the DA's office to help relax at nights. I picked up cigarettes, too, and worked my way up to probably three packs a day. I couldn't wait for a recess in court so I could go have a smoke. When my kids were little they bugged me about smoking, so one day I completely quit cigarettes cold turkey. But I liked smoking so much that I picked up a pipe a while later. It's kind of a comforting thing, puffing away on a pipe. Still do it today. At eighty-five, I'm not about to quit.

In 1978 my good friend Ev Younger ran for governor of California but lost to Jerry Brown, son of former governor Pat Brown. Ev went into private practice. He died unexpectedly of a heart attack in 1989 at age seventy. I miss him dearly.

Throughout my time in the DA's office I continued my activity in the Air Force Reserve. During my last three years there I served with the JAG (Judge Advocate General) Corps, the legal component of the various military branches. During my required active duty periods, I was attached to the headquarters of the Space and Missile Systems Organization (SAMSO) in El Segundo, California. I eventually retired from the military as a lieutenant colonel. The JAG at SAMSO, who was my superior officer when I was on active duty, was a full colonel.

After I was on the court, he retired from the Air Force and came to work for me as my research assistant.

I BEGAN AS A JUDGE IN 1970, WHEN I WAS FORTY-EIGHT YEARS old. I retired from the same position twenty years later, in 1990, at age sixty-eight. I loved the work. The majority of our work consisted of reading and researching cases and writing opinions. Our court convened one day a month to hear oral arguments from lawyers. I did the bulk of my preparation and research from my library at home. Four years before I retired, Donna and I moved to the San Juan Islands and built a house. I worked from my home office in the San Juans and flew back to LA once a month to deliver opinions.

To explain my position as a judge a bit more: Since the volume of cases in the 2d District was so large, we were divided into five divisions of four judges each. Each appeal was handled by three judges, with one of the three being designated to write the proposed opinion (decision) for the court. At least one of the other two judges needed to sign off on the opinion. Dissenting judges could also write dissenting opinions. The assignment of cases and participants in each decision was done on a random basis by the clerk of the court. On average, any one judge would write the majority opinion in about 125 cases annually and participate in the decision on perhaps twice as many.

Appellate work and cases in Appellate Court are decided primarily on the basis of written briefs submitted by the opposing sides, which set forth the facts in legal issues. Appellate Courts do not decide facts. They take the facts as decided by trial court and deal only with legal issues. A day or two before we went on the bench, we had a meeting of all the judges in a division. In that conference we'd go over every case and discuss them in depth. After we heard oral arguments on the bench, we'd come off, get together as a division, and ask if anybody's minds had changed. Ninety-nine percent of the time, the answer was no. Then we'd sign off on the opinion and the case would be filed.

For the most part, the job itself was free of controversy. Many of the opinions we wrote became precedent and were cited in other cases. To a certain degree, we made the law of California.

It wasn't all smooth. We dealt with the appeal of many high-profile cases, including a very controversial rape case where we believed the evidence weighed in favor of the accused man. A waitress was hitchhiking along an LA freeway when a guy in a camper stopped. He drove her up to nearby hills and had his way with her. A friend of the waitress had been hitchhiking earlier in the same location and raped and murdered also in the same area, so when this guy proposed having sex with the waitress, she claimed she was so afraid that she didn't say a word and made no verbal or physical effort to decline the advances. At the end of the session, the guy drove her home and asked her for her phone number and another "date." She gave him her phone number and agreed. When the guy showed up for the date, the cops were waiting for him. He was convicted for forcible rape.

Forcible rape is a very vicious crime, and anyone convicted of rape bears a stigma unlike a conviction for any other crime. I like to think of myself as pro-woman. After all, I had a wife and have daughters, and today I even have granddaughters. Over the years I successfully prosecuted a number of forcible rape cases that were nothing like this. In this case we decided that some gesture needed to have been made to indicate a lack of consent. Somewhere along the line, the woman needed to communicate "no."

We overturned the case. Our decision incurred the hostility of prominent women's movement representatives, including famed attorney and feminist Gloria Allred. Picketers surrounded the courthouse the morning after the decision came out. For some reason I seemed to take the lion's share of the heat, though two judges signed off on the decision in addition to myself. I received hate mail from all over the States and Canada for some time. Even Richard Dawson, then the host of the TV game show *Family Feud*, made a crack about me on the air. In time, it all blew over.

In another controversial case, we wrote an opinion regarding life support. Two doctors were accused of murder for causing the death of a person in a coma. The patient's condition was terminal; the neurologist said he would never regain consciousness and would be on some form of life support forever. With the consent of the patient's wife, the doctors removed the patient's hydration and nutrition systems. These were the days before living wills.

In deciding the doctors' appeal, there were two issues: the first, regarding whether the withholding of artificially administered nutrition and hydration constituted medical treatment or not. We held that both were medical treatment, and if the man was conscious, he would be able to decide for himself whether he wanted this medical treatment. The second issue was, if the patient was not able to make the choice, who then could? We held that, absent any evidence or indication of conflict of interest or ulterior motive, the wife was able to act as a surrogate for her husband, and that the doctors had a right to rely on her statement. So we found that the doctors were not guilty of criminal conduct. The case (*Barber v. Superior Court*, 1983) is a seminal case in California on this issue.

THE SAN JUAN ISLANDS, FOR THOSE WHO HAVE NEVER SEEN them, make up a pine- and fir tree–dotted archipelago off the coast of the Washington State mainland. Whales swim by on their way to Alaska. Tourists rent bicycles and pedal all over the islands. Everything is slow-paced and friendly, a real paradise. I had never been to the islands before, but we had a judge friend with a house on Lopez Island. One summer Donna and I drove up the coast in our motor home and stopped at Anacortes. We took the ferry over to Lopez to visit our friend. The beauty of the land amazed us. Donna and I sat in his living room, right on the water, and watched the ferryboats go by in the evening.

He introduced us to a friend of his on the island who was a real estate broker. She had a nine-acre waterfront lot for sale. We didn't want the whole thing, but she found another buyer and we split the property. Donna and I built our house on Lopez in 1986. Originally we planned for just a vacation cottage, but the thing grew into our dream home. In the end it was about three thousand square feet, an open pattern, with one great room on the first floor. We sold our house in Los Angeles and moved north for good.

It was a very happy time. Through the main windows of our new home we could see Decatur Island and up the coastland to the north Puget Sound. We walked on the beach and went clamming in the mornings. I set crab pots on Fisherman's Bay on the other side of the island. Donna's best friend from high school, Betty, moved to the island, and Donna and Betty worked with various volunteer groups in the area. They played bridge and every year made Christmas wreaths. After I retired, I still traveled down to various Superior Courts to fill in for judges on vacation. Our daughter Syndee moved to the island for a time and opened a beauty salon. Our other daughter, Tracy, moved to the mainland near the island and we often saw her.

A few wonderful years passed.

IN 1994, DONNA TURNED SIXTY-SEVEN.

As a kid, she had contracted scarlet fever and had experienced problems with her heart over the years, but never anything major. Now she began experiencing some setbacks, so a doctor suggested she have bypass surgery to replace a vein in her neck that was causing her problems. It involved open-heart surgery, quite major, and we took the ferry over to a hospital in Everett, Washington, for the procedure.

The surgery went fine. Donna was released from the hospital and came home. I got a hospital bed for her and put it in our living room downstairs. A nurse came every day to check on her. One night Donna was sitting on the davenport watching television with her arm near her head. I was in the living room with her, piled on the hospital bed because she never liked it much. I fell asleep. In the morning I got up. Donna needed some medications each morning, and I went to the table where the meds were. She was still sitting watching television. Her eyes were closed. I figured she was asleep.

"Donna, time for your medication," I said. She didn't respond. I walked over and touched her eyes.

She was gone.

Donna died in her sleep. Doctors couldn't figure it out. The autopsy showed her death had had nothing to do with her surgery. She had gone into a cardiac arrhythmia, which can strike an otherwise perfectly healthy twenty-five-year-old—it's an electrical impulse where your heart goes out of whack and just quits.

We held a memorial service for her at the golf club. One of the ministers from the area came out and said a few words. All of our friends came, and we had a catered meal. Everybody took turns talking about her. There were a lot of tears. We had her body cremated. We placed her ashes in an urn and brought them home. We thought about scattering them somewhere, but home was the place Donna always loved best.

Donna was absolutely one of a kind. I talk to people today who can't close a conversation without mentioning how loving and unselfish she was. Everybody liked her. She never had any enemies. She was the absolute love of my life.

I told you before I only cry at three things. The death of my father and the love I have for America are two.

When I remember Donna is the third.

After Donna died, I was just rattling around out there on Lopez Island, and I didn't like being alone. I sold the house. Syndee had moved to the mainland by then, so I moved to the mainland to be near both my daughters. I bought another motor home and lived in a campground for a while. Then I sold the motor home and lived in an apartment. A few years later I moved in with Tracy and her family, which is where I live today.

· 29 ·

Band of Brothers

IN THE EARLY 1990S, AUTHOR STEPHEN AMBROSE WROTE A
book that would irrevocably change my life, as well as that of countless other World War II veterans.

At first, we just heard rumors that someone was interested in writing a book about Easy Company, which kind of surprised me. I wasn't
sure why anyone would want to write about us. I had never heard of
Ambrose before. A professor at the University of New Orleans, he had
written several bestselling books about the war and about other facets
of American history, but I hadn't read any of his books.

Really, I didn't think much about it. Ambrose phoned me at one
point during his writing. We talked for about half an hour, primarily
about Brecourt Manor. If it hadn't been for Bill Guarnere, I don't
think there ever would have been a book. Bill kept track of everybody
from Easy Company and had made detailed lists of everybody's ad-
dresses, phone numbers, and birthdays. Bill still regularly phones me
on my birthday to wish me well.

As I mentioned, Ambrose was a neighbor with E Company member Walter Gordon. One night, apparently, they were sitting around talking, and Ambrose asked Gordon if it would be okay if he came to one of our reunions. In the interim, Bill had been the catalyst behind organizing our own company reunions. We had started out having division reunions, but the 101st is a big outfit with a lot of people. Anytime you went to one of the reunions, you'd end up talking to the guys who were closest to you anyway. So it was Bill's idea to meet just as Easy Company. That's when Ambrose came in. Apparently, after talking to some of the guys, the idea about writing a book about this one company was born. I've always thought that without Bill Guarnere and his records, Ambrose would have been hard put to track everybody down. So I give Bill a lot of the credit for the book's inception.

After my phone conversation with Ambrose, I didn't hear about the project for some time. Finally we heard that the book had been published and that there was going to be a party in New Orleans to celebrate its release. Ambrose hosted the party, which took place in 1992. Donna was still alive then, and we went to it together.

Several years later, I heard that Steven Spielberg and Tom Hanks were making a ten-part miniseries based on the book, set to be shown on HBO. Cameras were set up at our reunions, and they had us talk about different experiences during the war.

An actor named Neal McDonough was set to play me in the series. One day soon after the announcement of roles was made, Neal called me up, then flew over to Washington to meet me. We had lunch together. I found out he was a baseball player and had gone to Syracuse University on a baseball scholarship. We got along great and have kept in touch over the years. He's always very friendly and deferential. He says I made his career. I think that's bunk. He's highly capable in his own right. The funny thing is that if you follow Neal's career, he went on to act in *Minority Report,* where he played a policeman, then to *Boomtown,* where he played a deputy DA in LA

County. It's become a joke between us—he calls me up and says he's tracking my career. I say, what are you going to do next, play a judge?

They shot most of the *Band of Brothers* series in England. While the shooting was going on, sometimes the actors called us to talk about stuff. The actors told us how they became a unified group, more so than on previous shoots. Sometimes they'd conference-call us, mostly just to talk. It wasn't to question us about scenes; it was mostly just about friendship with us.

Eventually, the producers had the series put together. A screening was held in LA. About half a dozen of us from Easy Company went to the screening. We watched the whole series straight through in a day or two. They asked us if we had any suggestions. I told them a couple things, little stuff, that they accommodated. One voice-over didn't seem right to me. They changed it. I don't even remember what it was. All in all, the series took some literary license, but that was okay by me.

The next thing was the big event in Normandy, where they had us come over first-class. We stopped in New York first and stayed at the Waldorf Hotel. Then we flew an American charter over to Paris, then up to Normandy. They had created a movie theater inside a tent, with theater seating and a big screen. Very nice and plush. A great big banquet was held with French dignitaries and flyovers from the French Air Force. Then they showed certain segments of the miniseries—not the whole thing. The foreign press was there as well as a lot of civilians. It was really a big, first-rate operation.

The series first showed on HBO in 2001. It was nominated for nineteen Emmys and won six. It won a Golden Globe for Best Mini-Series, an American Film Institute Award, a Peabody Award, and the 2003 Writers' Guild Award. It was a real hit. We went to the Hollywood Bowl for a day or two for another screening. I took my two daughters with me to that. We didn't go to the Emmy ceremonies, but were staying at another hotel when the Emmys were announced. Then we did a USO (United Service Organizations) tour. It was Don

Malarkey, Earl "One Lung" McClung, Darrell "Shifty" Powers, and me. We went to various military bases around Hawaii, Tokyo, and Seoul, Korea. The idea was to boost the morale of U.S. troops stationed overseas. It was a lot of fun.

Other invitations came. We went down to Fort Campbell, Kentucky, to visit with some of the 101st, and to Paso Robles, California, where they dedicated a bridge to Robert Rader, a sergeant in the 1st Platoon. Bob had taught school in Paso Robles. A lot of us have spoken at various functions all around the country. People lined up to meet us and shake hands. I get letters to this day from people who have read the book or seen the series asking for autographs on pictures, books, postcards, stamp-collecting books—you name it. The widespread variety of people who have been affected by the series continues to astound me—schoolteachers, young kids, adults, veterans, people from all over the world—they write with comments or to ask me what I think about various things. I try to answer every letter.

The notoriety of the book and miniseries brought all of us from Easy Company a fame and international recognition none of us had ever expected. As a whole, *Band of Brothers* afforded me a lot of opportunities to go to many far-flung places and meet a lot of interesting people. To me, it's been quite an amazing thing to see the popularity of the series and book.

The only downside to the recognition is that not everybody who deserved it got it. The starting point of Easy Company was about 150 guys, maybe 200, while we were in combat in Europe. A lot of them did some pretty brave things and suffered a lot of hardships. Many were wounded and killed. All kinds of guys did as much as or more than I did, whose names were never heard of or mentioned. That's not anybody's fault. It would be simply impossible, if you were in Ambrose's spot, to write a book that mentioned everybody. The book and the series had to be limited in scope. But I can understand that there are guys who feel left out. Like, *Why is Compton mentioned and not me?*

I don't know the answer to that. But I hope people will take it that we were representatives of combat soldiers everywhere. There's no question in my mind that there are guys who aren't known who should be. Sergeants, privates, lieutenants—every guy who went through difficult times—they're the ones who should all be known. Both guys from our company and from other units. From our war and other wars. Paratroopers capture the attention of people due to the fact that we jumped out of planes. But we didn't have it as hard, for instance, as the guys in the 1st or 4th or 29th divisions, who were grinding it out day after day in Europe, many of whom were not pulled back from the line to England after thirty days like we were. Or beyond that, the poor guys who served in the Pacific. I wouldn't have traded with the guys in the Pacific for anything. None of them got the recognition we did.

In spite of the drawbacks, I think the widespread success and recognition of *Band of Brothers* has been good for the country. It has helped elevate patriotism, pointed out duty to country, and resonated with young people. I've had soldiers on active duty in Iraq tell me that they enlisted because they read or watched *Band of Brothers* and were inspired. That's good, and we need more of that. People sometimes criticize us for exploiting *Band of Brothers* like that, but I'll exploit the hell out of *Band of Brothers* if it helps our troops in any way.

I've traveled back to Europe several times to see various sights from the war, including Normandy, Bastogne, Eindhoven, Germany, and more. Seeing Brecourt Manor and Bastogne, my main fighting spots, affects me the most. The one thing that comes to my mind when I look at the countryside is that it's hard for people who haven't been through it to know what it was really like. You have a tendency to think of wars as being fought in arenas set aside for fighting. But when you go through these farms and little towns, you realize wars are fought in people's backyards, stores, streets, and cities. It was all so very real then. It's real to me today.

· 30 ·

Last Rants and Reflections

ANY BOOK WITH MY NAME ON IT WOULDN'T BE COMPLETE IF I
didn't give one or two of my political views at the end.

As a result of the popularity of *Band of Brothers*, I have had a lot
of opportunities to talk to many varied groups and attend a number
of Veterans Day events. I've also received a great amount of corre-
spondence from people from all over the country. It's flattering and
amazing to me how many people say things like "Thank you for pro-
tecting our freedom" and "Thanks for fighting for our freedom."

My response generally comes in two parts. First, I point out that
while I spent three years on active duty, saw some combat in Europe,
and suffered a minor wound, I got back in one piece and had the luxury of having a great family life and a rewarding career. My service
really cost me only three years of my time. I consider that a small
price to pay for the privilege of being born in America. The people to
whom we all must pay our respects and honor for their service are
those who gave life and limb in performing their duty.

I feel strongly that every able-bodied male citizen has an absolute duty to serve in the military when called upon. In fact, I support universal military training in this country. Every male, after reaching eighteen, would be required to spend a short period of time in military training. Perhaps a year. After training, he would be assigned to some discreet unit so that if we ever needed rapid mobilization, we wouldn't have to go through a draft. Women would be welcome to train as well, but not by compulsion. I also believe that when the president and commander in chief makes a decision to call upon us, we do not have the discretion to select where we will fight or to select which enemy we will fight.

As to fighting for our freedom, I try to focus people's attention on what that really means, and that in honoring our dead and wounded we should ourselves continue the fight to preserve it.

The word "freedom" is rather generic today, and in my mind, sadly, an ill-defined term. Many people think it simply means nothing more than saying whatever you want and doing whatever you want whenever you want. But true freedom is easy to overlook today. Too many of our fellow citizens are willing to go to the polls and vote away the freedoms of themselves and others simply because they have been convinced of the supposed worthiness of some social goal.

I find it easier to define true freedom—what we fought for in World War II and what we still fight for today—by pointing out what we fought *against* in the war. The Nazis of Hitler's Germany were officially known as the National Socialist Workers' Party. It was a euphemism for a collectivist form of government, a government that wanted to erode personal freedoms. Following WWII, we have fought a series of wars, both hot and cold, against a similar type of collectivism. Sometimes it's called communism, sometimes socialism, sometimes terrorism. These are all terms for the same thing—collectivism—the idea that government can control the production, distribution, and economic systems of a country better than individuals can. That struggle continues today in the Middle East and around the world. The current enemy is even more dangerous in that it is a collectivist ideology driven by a fanatical religious zeal.

Our true freedom, for which we have paid a high price in life and blood, is freedom from a collectivist society and government. I wish there could be a bumper sticker on every car in this country and a sign on every corner reminding people that collectivism, aka socialism, is the enemy of all freedom-loving people. Freedom and socialism cannot coexist.

Our Constitution stands as a bulwark against collectivism and guarantees us a free-enterprise capitalist economy, where we are free to contract for and enjoy the fruits of our labor. Freedoms that we fought for are being unthinkingly and frivolously squandered today in many places. Every time our fellow citizens fall prey to class envy arguments and the siren song of socialism, we dishonor those who have fought and died in previous wars. Collectivism as an ideology promises to redistribute wealth through the graduated income tax and estate tax. Collectivism sees nothing wrong with seizing private property without paying for it, all in the name of environmental protection. Collectivism ignores the precious blood that has been spilled in freedom's defense. The America I fought for was based on individual freedom, never collectivism.

Think of it this way: The Nazis were socialists. The Communists in Korea and Vietnam were socialists. The terrorists of today are ideological socialists—they're certainly not proponents of individual freedoms. Terrorists want to knock out our form of government, which allows freedom of thought, travel, religion, and speech. They want to do away with our social climate, which allows us the room for dissenting and controversial opinions and practices. They want to destroy our economy, which allows for individual successes based on initiative and hard work.

As I write this book in 2007, the war against terror in Iraq and Afghanistan is now in its fifth year. Anytime a war stretches this long, it is bound to become unpopular. Yet I must strongly state my beliefs that the war against terror needs to be fought and won. As horrible as any war is, the war against terror is not an unjust war. World War II is often seen as the classic justifiable war because of Japan's attack on us at Pearl Harbor. But people forget that Germany never attacked us, and was never even close to invading or occupying the United States homeland. It was a threat to Europe, obviously, and a threat to international stability. But it didn't come close to anything like 9/11.

To try to distinguish between our objectives in World War II and the war we are fighting today—that one war was justified and one isn't—is a complete fallacy. All wars are wars of choice. The Revolutionary War was a war of choice—we could have stayed British subjects if we had wanted. Equally so, we could have chosen not to fight World War II if we had wanted. But there were compelling reasons to fight both the Revolutionary War and World War II, as there are compelling reasons to fight the war against terror today.

International terrorism is not confined to Iraq and Afghanistan, yet terrorists including Osama bin Laden have chosen to make those two countries the grounds for launching their operations. Let's not forget who the real enemy is. When Saddam Hussein attacked Kuwait more than a decade ago and the United Nations drove him back, Saddam signed a cease-fire agreement that he never kept. Saddam was a defeated foe, and he didn't live up to his end of the bargain. Lest any liberals forget who the real human rights opponent is, Saddam was the one who had slaughtered literally hundreds of thousands of his own countrymen, not to mention killing thousands of people he didn't agree with. Saddam was the one who lit his oil refineries on fire as he fled the country, creating environmental havoc for years to come. Saddam and his regime crushed his country's educational systems, economic opportunities, cultural activities, and women. He's the real enemy. In many senses, we are still fighting the first Gulf War today. It's not finished yet.

Terrorist regimes such as these have vowed to destroy the United States, whom they refer to as "the Great Satan." That's as much of a threat as Hitler's Germany ever was. People argue for "peace at any price." Well, peace is cheap. You can get peace with anybody as long as you're willing to surrender to their terms. We could have had peace with Hitler if we wanted.

It's obvious to me that the left wing in this country, which is behind the so-called antiwar movement, is moving to coalesce with the Communists such as Chavez and Castro, even with the terrorists themselves. Our greatest domestic threat at this moment is this collectivist left-wing movement, which is homegrown.

One last thought:

The United States Constitution is based on the idea that the federal government shall exercise only certain specified powers. Basically, the federal government needs to provide a common currency, provide a national defense, conduct foreign affairs, and ensure a free flow of interstate commerce. There are some who think that our Constitution is obsolete. Some suggest it's an amorphous document that should be applied according to the whims of the particular judges involved at the time. In short, I believe strongly in the so-called original intent to constitutional law—that judges should try to discern in every case what the framers of the Constitution intended, not what the judges happen to think will suit their fancy. I was shocked when Al Gore, while running for president in 2000, made a statement that he would appoint judges who did not feel bound by obsolete language written two hundred years ago. To him, the Constitution is an obsolete document. That is the thinking of many in this country. And it's a disgrace.

Of the three branches of government, the federal judiciary is the greatest offender of the desire of the framers of the Constitution to limit federal power.

That's it for my political rants. Agree or disagree with me, you can find lots more if you do an Internet search for my radio show. Right now it's at www.buckcompton.blogspot.com. It's not hard to track down.

HOW DOES MY LIFE SHAPE UP IN THE PRESENT DAY?

As fiery as I am in my political beliefs, for the most part I lead a fairly quiet life. Every morning except Tuesdays and weekends, I go hang out with a group of friends called the "Koffee Klatch." Eleven guys, all of whom were in World War II, get together at a coffee shop. We meet around a table in front of a fireplace and shoot the breeze and swap stories, mostly about the old days. That's how this book got started. One of my buddies suggested I write down my stories. So I did.

The second big event of my day is to go home and wait for the mail, which is a joke among the Koffee Klatch guys because I don't have a wife to go home to anymore—that is, my life is so dull that's all I have to do all day. Plus, Every Tuesday I man the office at the Republican headquarters of Skagit Valley. Each month I write an article for their newsletter.

The radio thing started several years ago. Tracy, unbeknownst to me, wrote an area radio station telling them about me. I think she described me as a "poor man's Rush Limbaugh." The station was just switching to a talk format. So they called me. I had never done radio before, but I figured I'd give it a try. It started out as a one-hour talk show once a week where I invited people like judges and county commissioners in to interview them. After a while the station was sold and went all-syndicate, so I was out of a job. But then the station was sold again, and I was brought back. This time the format for my show called for short commentaries, mostly on political and legal issues, sometimes military issues. I tape the shows beforehand and they're played twice a day. It keeps me thinking. I've got to watch the news and read papers so I can find things I want to talk about. So that's the radio show.

I keep active in my grandchildren's lives. Right now, they range from fifth grade to college age. I see them for family dinners and of course at home. Sometimes we go to the driving range. I don't play much golf anymore because my back hurts too much. I started my grandson in Little League baseball a while back. He's a computer whiz; he's quite good at fixing them and will probably make a living at it someday soon. I encourage him in that direction.

I love the TV show *Jeopardy!* and watch it almost every night. I work a lot of crossword puzzles. I also read a lot. That's about it. I can see how it's easy in old age to want to sit and do nothing. But I don't want to do that. I feel mentally alert. I think I'm still on top of things.

Although my parents were never churchgoers, I believe I was raised with Christian values. I experienced a bit of religion as a kid with the YMCA. When I was in the DA's office, a friend was quite active in the Episcopal Church and I got involved a bit. We took our kids to Sunday school at the Episcopal Church where they were baptized, but we didn't go so much when they got older. When I went through the Masonic Order, you had to declare a belief in God, and in the Knights Templar you had to say you were a Christian, which I did. But as far as being much of a practicing Christian, I never was.

In later years I met an Oregon attorney named Vance Day, a very astute guy who handles some estate and financial matters for me. He's a strong Christian and we talk off and on about religious subjects. There are a lot of questions I have still, but I wanted the same type of inner tranquility I saw in Vance Day's life, so I guess you could say I made a decision in that direction. I go to church every Sunday now. The pastor there, Bruce Wersen, is very informative and I enjoy hearing him. I've talked to some of the other pastors there. I'm not one of these people who say they have become born again suddenly, but when it comes to following Jesus Christ and what he taught, I guess you could say I'm getting there. I believe in God. I know there's a God who created all of this—it's all too complicated and complex to come from nowhere. I start there in my faith. I don't ever pray for personal reward. I pray for my kids, my family, and my country.

ON CLOSING THIS BOOK, IF I WAS TO LEAVE YOU WITH ONLY one thought, it would be this: My life story could only happen in America.

Look at my life: Here was a guy with very little observable potential—nothing much behind him except a couple loving parents. But because of the way this country functions I was able to make my way through and have a very good life. I don't think I had any special talent or ability. Anybody could do what I did if he wanted to. I've never resented anybody who has something I didn't have, because I knew that in this country if I worked hard enough I could have it, too. The system in America allows for and welcomes success. That's worth fighting for if someone threatens to take it away.

You can have anything or be anything you want in this country if you put your mind to it. Don't let anybody take that away from you.

Epilogue

by *Band of Brothers* actor Neal McDonough

I WOULD DO ANYTHING IN THE WORLD FOR BUCK COMPTON.
It was an absolute honor to portray him in *Band of Brothers,* and that's an understatement. Buck never likes being called a hero, but that's what he is to me. Not only did he serve his country well in the war, but he went on to do exemplary things in life. When you consider the scope of what he's done—college sports star, paratrooper, detective, attorney, judge—if a person does just one of those things, you'd say it's an accomplishment. Buck has done them all.

Personally, I owe a lot to Buck. Portraying him marked my big break as an actor. Also, I would never have met my wife, Ruvé Robertson, with whom I have two wonderful children, Morgan and Catherine, if it hadn't been for Buck. My life is exceedingly blessed today, and Buck has played a large role in that.

To explain: before I did *Band of Brothers,* I had been acting in professional roles for about a decade but hadn't done anything major, just independent films and smaller roles on TV. In early 2000, I decided to move from Hollywood back to Cape Cod, Massachusetts, where I grew up. It was a time of reevaluating my career. Maybe it was time to give up my dream. My parents were motel operators. Maybe I should take up that.

A friend of mine called me to audition for *Band of Brothers*. Initially, I auditioned for a much smaller part than the role of Buck Compton—I don't even remember what it was. Tom Hanks read with me and immediately diffused any nervousness I was feeling. Tom asked me to come back the next day and read for the role of Buck. Two months later I received the call of a lifetime. The first thing I did was phone my dad to tell him the good news: "I got *Band of Brothers*."

I wanted to meet Buck in person, so I flew up to Washington State where he lives. I arrived in the morning and called Buck. He offered to meet me in a restaurant for beakfast. He had already eaten, he said, but he'd have another. I had never seen a picture of him, yet when he walked into the restaurant, instantly I knew it was him. He shook hands with me with these huge hands of his, just the size of canned hams, and ordered a five-egg omelet, his appetite for breakfast reflective of his appetite for life.

We talked for some time. Buck's a real straight shooter. Over and over again, he said he just did his job. Nowadays, my goodness, people celebrate mediocrity to death—any little accomplishment is met with huge self-applause. People always want to be noticed for any above-average act. Yet Buck excelled in every way and shrugged off his accomplishments like they were no big deal. Buck never says, hey look at me. If you do something great, that doesn't mean you're great—that's one thing I take from Buck. Any time I start tooting my own horn, I can feel Buck at my shoulder saying: "What are you doing?"

A few months after I met Buck I flew over to London to start filming *Band of Brothers*. Two friends came with me. The first day we were out at a pub and I noticed an incredibly beautiful South African woman. She stood six foot three and wore this black leather coat from head to heels. I couldn't even speak. She was doing PR for various clubs and just happened to be working the door for guest lists. All I could say was, "You're so tall." All she said was, "And you're American." We talked for a while, but the next day I was off to boot camp. Two weeks later an administrative assistant tracked her down for me. Ruvé and I have been together even since.

About three days into our training, which was quite arduous, Tom Hanks and Steven Spielberg arrived. Tom gave this amazing speech about why we owe it to these guys to give it our all. We didn't want to let Steven and Tom down, but we certainly didn't want to let down the veterans we were portraying. We owed it to those guys to do it right.

During the filming, I phoned Buck a bunch of times. I probably drove him nuts with all my questions: How did you wear your hat, to the left or right? Which gun did you favor? What guys would you hang out with? Buck was so helpful on lots of stuff.

When I was in boot camp, one of the guys had a machine gun and slapped me by mistake in the face, chipping three of my teeth. Blood was gushing down my chin, but, still in character, I didn't want to let on how much pain I was in. So I finished the exercise. Doc Roe, the actor, came over, took a thread and needle, and sewed me up. He wasn't a real medic, mind you, but we all wanted to stay true to our roles. After two or three days the cut was festering, not looking so good, so I went to the hospital still dressed in my fatigues. "What's your name?" the doctor asked.

"Lieutenant Lynn Buck Compton," I answered. It was the first thing that came to mind.

Here's an example of Buck's humility. After *Band of Brothers* came out, we were featured in *People* magazine, so Ruvé and I flew up to Washington to get some pictures taken with Buck. The journalists asked Buck if they could see his medals. Buck's daughter was with him when they asked this, and she was like, "What medals are they talking about, Dad?" Buck sort of hemmed and hawed and rummaged around in his attic for them. He had never showed his daughter his medals. With Buck, it's never about the awards you get in life; it's about doing the right thing. That's the prize in itself.

I'm thankful to Buck for the career advancement his portrayal brought me. Being in *Band of Brothers* brought me in close contact with Steven Spielberg for the first time. All of us got along great with him. When *Band of Brothers* was nominated for the Golden Globes, all of us "soldiers" were downstairs in the theater. We made a pact that if *Band of Brothers* won, we'd rush the stage when Tom and Steven were on it. The bouncers let us in just as the announcement was being made that *Band of Brothers* had won. So we all ran onto the stage. Tom and Steven laughed right along with us. Shortly after that, Steven called me to do *Minority Report*, then *Boomtown*, then I got *Flags of Our Fathers*. I've never stopped working since *Band of Brothers*. I've been blessed beyond measure. Buck and I have a running joke that our careers are parallel, his in real life, mine on film. After I portrayed him as a soldier in *Band of Brothers*, I played a detective in *Minority Report*, then a district attorney in *Boomtown*. The joke is that I'm going to play a judge next.

I've been asked to speak in public about Buck on several occasions. I do so willingly, but I always find it a bit emotional. It's hard to speak about Buck without getting tears in my eyes; he's such an amazing person. There's been some talk about opening a justice hall with Buck's name on it. I think that's a great idea, and hope it happens. For all he's done for our country, the least we can do is put his name on a building. A few months ago I presented a lifetime achievement award to Buck on behalf of the Adventurers Club in LA. I was happy to do so. My only thought was that they could never make a big enough lifetime achievement award for Buck.

He's an amazing man, although he'd never say it himself. So I'll say it here for him. Buck Compton—you're an admirable person. I'm honored to know you. And to say you're my friend, that's the best part of all.

Neal McDonough
France, 2007

ACKNOWLEDGMENTS

My heartfelt thanks go to the numerous people who have encouraged me throughout life, as well as in the writing of this book. (My apologies in advance if I leave anyone out.)

Thanks to Neal McDonough, Merav Brooks at HBO, Tom Hanks, Steven Spielberg, and Stephen Ambrose. To my editor, Natalee Rosenstein, assistant editor Michelle Vega, and all the team at Penguin. To attorney Vance Day, literary agent Greg Johnson, and writer Marcus Brotherton.

Thank you to Don Malarkey, Bill Guarnere, Dick Winters, and all the men of Easy Company and to General Jack Singlaub. Thanks to the Koffee Klatch of Skagit County: Stan Bruhn, Bill Collins, Doug Erspamer, Harry Follman, Chuck Higgins, Elliot Johnson, Vern Johnson, Frank O'Brien, Doug Olson, and Ed Pierce.

Thanks to my many friends, relatives, and colleagues: Herb Weiner, Fred Donnelly and his parents, George and Eleanor Donnelly, who provided me with hospice in the aftermath of my father's death. To Francine and John Maroney, Vadis and Jack Curran, Chuck and Carol Drexel, Genevieve Kruthers, Reverend Bob Tourigney, Conna and John Marin, Bob Thomas, Tom Gilroy, Rondi Edwards, Jackie and Paul Morgenstern, Kate and Don Palmer, Bob "Peanuts" Walcott, Don Paisley, Kenny Washington, the Sons of the Pioneers, and Rex Allen, Harry and Sybil Brand, the Makos family and *Ghost Wings* (now *Valor*) magazine. Thanks to our friend in Holland, Peter van de Wal. To Pastor Bruce Wersen at His Place Community Church and to my son-in-law Jerry Miller.

Thanks to my friends over the years from the press: Ron Einstoss, Tom Cameron, Pat and Olive Foley, Peggy Cook, Lloyd Emerson, Bill Thomas, Paul Zimmerman, and Bob Hunter. Thank you to Bill Berry and Glen Harris at station KLKI in Anacortes.

Thanks to influential teachers and coaches: Dan Sprague, Babe Horrell, Lowell MacGuiness, Art Reichle, Walter Cook, Tom Cunningham, "Tillie" Parisi, Norm Duncan, and Cece Hollingsworth.

Thanks to Bill Ackerman, A. J. Sturzenegger, Wilbur Johns, and Frank Kroener of the UCLA athletic department.

To justices Lester Roth, Macklin Fleming, Roy Herndon, Ed Beach, Don Gates, Morio Fukuto, John Allport, and John Aiso—thank you for making my life on the bench a wonderful experience.

Thank you to my faithful secretaries, Lily Ring (Balian), Kayko Sonoda, Ethelyn Firkey, Lenore Walsh, Esther Mott, and Helen Piroutek.

Thank you to LAPD chiefs of police Bill Parker, Tom Reddin, Ed Davis, and Daryl Gates, Assistant Chief Mert Howe, deputy chiefs Thad Brown and Lynn White, Inspector Hugh Farnham, Captain Jack Donahoe, Lieutenants John Gregoire and Ed Blair, and my fellow officers A. T. Boswell, Jack Colbern, Ken Scarce, Bob Uribe, and O. J. Lockliear.

Thank you to Bill South, Bill McCloud, Bill Burke, Jack Canny, and "Frenchie" Lajeunesse of the FBI—federal and state cooperation can work.

Thank you to career shapers Sid Cherniss, Goodwin Knight, Ronald Reagan, Ed Meese, and Herb Ellingwood.

Thank you to my fellow prosecutor and dear friend Ted Shield and to preeminent defense attorneys Albert Ramsey and Paul Caruso, both dear friends.

To my invaluable research attorneys, Colonel Carroll Kelly and now judge Ray Hart, thank you.

Thank you to my friends and attorneys Betty Hix and Joe Madden, who arranged for Donna and me to adopt our two precious daughters.

Thank you to my colleagues in the DA's office, Ted Sten, Manley Bowler, Harold Ackerman, Gordon Jacobson, George Stoner, Bill Ritzi, and J. Miller Leavy.

Thank you to judges Maurice Sparling, Gordon Howden, and of course my great benefactor, Judge and DA Bill McKesson.

My vocabulary is simply inadequate to express my gratitude to Evelle and Mildred Younger for what they meant to me and my family.

And finally, a special thanks always to coaches Bert La Brucherie and Carl Brown and to Father Joe Donovan.

INDEX

A6M2 Zero (Japanese fighter plane), 81
Academy of Motion Picture Arts and
    Sciences, 27
accidental killing of infant, 232
"actives," 57, 59
Adam 12 (TV show), 197
ad-lib fighting vs. model small-arms assault,
    Brecourt, 105
adoption, 194
Afghanistan war, 249–250
Agar, John, 224
airborne unit (1944), organization of, 14
aircraft identification classes, 77, 79, 81, 82
Air Force Reserve, 154, 168, 236
Aldbourne, England, 89, 90, 91, 92, 96, 112,
    113, 115, 117
Allen, Rex, 174
Allred, Gloria, 238
Ambassador Hotel, 210, 211–212, 219
Ambrose, Stephen, 73, 93, 94, 118, 242, 243
America, love of, 44, 54, 241, 254. *See also*
    United States of America
American Express, 149
American Legion Luncheon Club, 181
American soldiers with German equipment,
    killed, 107–108
ammunition, Bastogne, 134–135, 138
Angels Flight "The World's Shortest
    Railway," 20
Anne of Green Gables (film), 24
anticipation of war, 62–64, 65
appeal, Sirhan Sirhan's trial, 227
Appellate Court, 234, 237
Apple, Danny, 176–178, 180
appointment to judge, 233–234
Arch of Triumph (film), 157
Ardennes Forest, 133
Arlington National Cemetery, 216
armed forces recruiters on campus, 63
Army Parachutist Badge "jump wings," 87
Arnhem, 121, 122
asking vs. ordering men around, 98
assassination as most repugnant political
    action, 229–230
athletic program (Paris) run by Buck,
    150–151

attitudes and character formed by childhood,
    20
attorney service business, 164–165, 166
autopsy on RFK, 219
awards, *Band of Brothers*, 244

Babe Ruth League baseball coach, 192
back of RFK, bullets entering, 212, 223
Baldwin Hills, CA, 34
Band of Brothers (Ambrose), 73, 93, 94,
    118–119, 243
Band of Brothers (miniseries), 73, 93, 94,
    99, 112, 118–119, 242–246. *See also*
    Compton, Buck
    inaccuracies in, 117–119, 122, 132,
    141–142, 143, 147, 151
Barber v. Superior Court, 239
bar exam, passing, 175
baseball, xv
    college (UCLA), 60–62, 154
    high school, 39, 43
    LA Angels professional career, 155–156
    Los Angeles Police Department (LAPD),
    165, 166, 167
    major league players in military, 79, 80
    morale tool for military, 80, 81, 83
    Neal McDonough (actor played Buck in
    Band of Brothers) and, 243
    176th Infantry Regiment, 79–80, 81–82
    paratroopers and, 4–5
    Paris and, 150–151
Bastogne (last battle), 133, 134–150, 246
Bastogne battle site tour, 53
battalion, defined, 14
Battle of the Bulge, 67, 133, 149. *See also*
    Bastogne (last battle)
Bel Air Beach Club, 59
Bennet, F. Ray, 185
Bergman, Ingrid, 157
Berkeley recruiting trip, 43–44
Berman, Emile Zola (Sirhan lawyer), 225
Beyond Band of Brothers (Winters), 19n
bin Laden, Osama, 250
Blackwell, Ewell "The Whip," 5, 80
bladder control lesson, 25
Bloser, Robert, 120

Index

Simpson, Bill, 185
Simpson, O. J., 201
Singlaub, Jack, 88–89
Sink, Robert (Colonel), 89, 147–148
Sirhan, Adel and Munir, 217
Sirhan, Mary, 217, 218
Sirhan, Sirhan Bishara, 217–218, 225–226.
    See also RFK assassination
Sirhan Sirhan's trial, 222–230
Six-Day War (Israel vs. Egypt, Jordan, Iraq,
    Syria), 218
6th Parachute Infantry Regiment (German),
    109
Skagit County Republican Party, 53
slaughter at Bastogne, 142–143,
    144, 146
Smiraldo, Josephine, 205
"smokers," 30
smoking by Buck, 119, 236
Sobel, Herbert (Captain), 94–96
Sobel, Michael, 95
softball in living room scene, 25
soldiers not mentioned in Band of Brothers,
    245–246
somehow you continue, 53–55, 64
Sons of the Pioneers, 174
South, Bill, 178
Soviet Union, casualties from World War II,
    152
Space and Missile Systems Organization
    (SAMSO), 236
speaking engagements, 53
Special Unit Senator (SUS), RFK
    assassination, 215–216
Speirs, Ronald (Lieutenant), 148–149
Spielberg, Steven, 243
sports. See baseball; football
sports career, ruled out, 155–156, 158
squad, defined, 14
St. Patrick's Cathedral, 216
stage crew, 34
Star, Jerry (Buck's girlfriend), 45, 48, 54, 59,
    74–75, 76. See also Compton, Jerry
    (Buck's first wife)
Star, Lorrie, 44
"star" football and baseball player
    reputation, 99
Stars and Stripes, 151
State Peace Officers Association, 193
static lines, 2
Statue of Liberty, new meaning, 153–154
staying awake at night (difficulty with)
    incident, 178, 179
Ste.-Marie-du-Mont (France), 9
steering parachute, 8
Stella Dallas (film), 24
Sten, Ted, 191, 195
Stengel, Casey, 167
Stone, Oliver, 229

Stoner, George, 215
Strayer, Colonel, 110
streetcar accident, 22–23
Stroll, Irwin, 212
Studio Electricians Union, 157
success, Band of Brothers, 244–246, 247
suicide of Buck's father, 49–51, 54, 64
Sunset Fields, 31
Superior Court, Barber v., 239
Superior Court of California, 233, 235
supply drop, Bastogne, 139
Supreme Court vs. Court of Appeals, 235
Supreme Headquarters, Allied Expeditionary
    Forces, 131
surrender
    demanded by Germans, Bastogne, 139,
        140–141
    Germany, Bastogne, 137–138
    Germany, Brecourt, 15
    Germany, World War II, 151
    Japan, World War II, 151–152
survival of WWII, implausibility of, 152
suspect (identity of), RFK assassination, 213,
    214, 217
Sweeney, Pat (Second Lieutenant), 92, 96
Sword Beach, 101
Syracuse University, 243

tattoo (Jerry Star), 74–75
Tatum, Frank, Jr. "Sandy," 42
Taylor, Maxwell (General), 145–146, 148
teaching by Buck, 175, 195
technological advancements in parachuting,
    2–3
Temple, Shirley, 224
terrorism, international, 249–251
Thirlkeld, Charles (Lieutenant), 131–132,
    142
Thomas, Bob, 40
Thompson submachine gun (borrowed), 16,
    18, 103, 105
Three Men on a Horse (stage show), 37
Tibbetts, Lawrence, 30
Time, 62
tips received (investigation of), RFK
    assassination, 219–220
Toonerville Trolley (comic strip), 26
Toye, Joe (Sergeant), 10, 17, 97, 124, 139,
    143
training
    first training jump, 1–2, 6–8, 13, 87
    Jump School, 86–87
    Officer Candidate School (OCS), 73–74,
        75
    paratroopers, 1, 5–6, 87–88
Traynor, Roger (chief justice), 234
trench foot, 139
Trucks, Virgil "Fire," 80
true freedom, 248–249

ABOUT THE AUTHOR

Collegiate sports star. Esteemed war veteran. Detective. Attorney. Judge. Lieutenant Lynn "Buck" Compton, eighty-five, serves as an example of a true American hero. As a college athlete, Compton competed alongside legends such as Jackie Robinson. Among combat veterans, Lieutenant Lynn "Buck" Compton's name and autograph are recognized internationally along with Dick Winters, "Wild Bill" Guarnere, and Don Malarkey. As a public servant, Compton's name will forever be associated with high-profile cases.

Born December 31, 1921, Compton grew up in the Great Depression. He graduated from public high school in Los Angeles and attended UCLA in the fall of 1939, where he majored in Physical Education with a minor in Education. He lettered two years in football and three years in baseball and was captain of the baseball team, where he played catcher. Compton played guard on the Rose Bowl team in 1943. He was a member of the advanced ROTC program and served as cadet executive officer to Cadet Commander John Singlaub (today major general, U.S. Army, retired).

World War II disrupted his studies at UCLA. Compton graduated from the school's ROTC program and was commissioned as a second lieutenant. He commanded the 2d Platoon of Easy Company in the 506th Parachute Infantry Regiment, part of the 101st Airborne Division. He parachuted into Normandy during the early hours of D-Day, was part of the assault group that destroyed German artillery during the battle at Brecourt Manor, fought on the line at Carentan, helped liberate Holland during Operation Market Garden, and fought in the freezing cold of the Battle of Bastogne.

As a combat veteran, Lieutenant Compton received the Silver Star, for valor in the face of the enemy, the Purple Heart, for being wounded while in the U.S. military, the World War II Victory Medal, for active duty during World War II, the Orange Lanyard of the Royal Netherlands Army, for bravery, leadership, and loyalty in the defense of the Netherlands, the Combat Infantry Badge, the American Campaign Citation, the American Defense Medal, and the European, African, Mid-Eastern Campaign Medal. Compton, along with his unit, was awarded the Presidential Unit Citation for extraordinary heroism against an armed enemy when holding the main line of resistance during the Battle of the Bulge.

Following the war, Compton worked his way through Loyola Law School as a policeman for the LAPD, and later as a detective in the Central Burglary Division. He was admitted to the California Bar in 1949.

He served as deputy district attorney for LA County, 1951–70, and had extensive trial experience involving the prosecution of major felony cases of all types. As chief deputy district attorney, he served as second in command of LA County, the largest prosecuting agency in the world. Compton handled a number of high-profile cases, including the prosecution of Sirhan Sirhan for the murder of Robert F. Kennedy.

In 1970, Compton was appointed by Governor Ronald Reagan to the California Courts of Appeal as an associate justice. During his term on the bench, Judge Compton authored more than two thousand written opinions in all areas of law.

Compton was portrayed by actor Neal McDonough in the acclaimed HBO miniseries *Band of Brothers,* produced by Steven Spielberg and Tom Hanks.

A widower since 1994, Compton lives in the Pacific Northwest today, where he stays in close contact with his two children and four grandchildren. Compton is a sought-after speaker, and in his spare time provides policy and political commentary on an e-mail blog based in Anacortes.

About the Collaborative Author
Marcus Brotherton

Marcus Brotherton is a professional writer, the author or coauthor of sixteen books. A former newspaper reporter, Marcus holds a master's degree with an emphasis in writing from Biola University. He has collaborated on memoirs with Dr. Nancy Heche (mother of actress Anne Heche), former *Playboy* playmate turned international humanitarian Susan Scott Krabacher, and most recently with Sparrow Clubs USA executive director Jeff Leeland on a tribute book about children in medical crises.

Printed in the United States
by Baker & Taylor Publisher Services